Philosophy Illustrated

Forty-Two Thought Experiments to Broaden Your Mind

EDITED AND ILLUSTRATED BY

Helen De Cruz

NEW YORK OXFORD

OXFORD UNIVERSITY PRESS

Oxford University Press is a department of the University of Oxford.
It furthers the University's objective of excellence in research, scholarship,
and education by publishing worldwide. Oxford is a registered trademark of
Oxford University Press in the UK and certain other countries.

Published in the United States of America by Oxford University Press
198 Madison Avenue, New York, NY 10016, United States of America.

For titles covered by Section 112 of the US Higher Education
Opportunity Act, please visit www.oup.com/us/he for the latest
information about pricing and alternate formats.

Library of Congress Cataloging-in-Publication Data

CIP data is on file at the Library of Congress

978-0-19-008053-2

9 8 7 6 5 4 3 2 1
Printed by Sheridan Books, Inc., United States of America

For my parents, Mike and Greet, for encouraging both a love of drawing and a love of philosophy

Contents

Preface : Pictures as Philosophy

Helen De Cruz

Pablo Picasso's *Guernica* (1937) depicts a war atrocity. The painting shows the bombing of the Basque Spanish town of Guernica by German Nazis who were helping the Franco regime. For his monumental, landscape-wide monochromatic painting, Picasso deliberately mixed a paint that would have the least possible gloss. The work conveys that war is not glamorous, both in the choice of medium and in the depiction of confusion and suffering of humans and animals. In the 1930s, photographs were black and white, so the painting evoked at the time a raw, documentary feeling. Its power persists today. In 2003, when then US Secretary of State Colin Powell was making the case to wage war on Iraq,[1] a copy of the painting in the UN Council was covered up: it would not be fitting to have an anti-war image hanging in the background when you make the case to bomb people. Is *Guernica* philosophy? If so, how can pictures be philosophy?

Philosophy comes in many different forms. Take the aphorisms by Nietzsche and Wittgenstein, the sayings by Confucius, or the short, evocative parables by Zhuangzi, two of which are illustrated in this volume. Autobiography can be philosophy, too. Examples include Simone de Beauvoir's *A Very Easy Death* on the death of her mother (de Beauvoir 1964/1985) and Augustine's *Confessions*, which recounts his tumultuous conversion from Manichaeism to Christianity (Augustine fourth century/1992). We can also think of the philosophical novel, for example, Camus's *The Plague* (1948), which explores existentialist themes such as the tension between an individual and a larger-scale situation that the individual is unable to influence.

All these different forms of expression are philosophical, because they challenge us to see the world differently. They shake our preconceptions and help us think about weighty questions such as what a good life is or what a morally relevant action consists of. In academic philosophy, there has been a tendency to narrow the range of acceptable forms of expression (almost always

[1]https://www.nytimes.com/2003/02/05/opinion/powell-without-picasso.html

papers and monographs) and even the topics that are deemed philosophical. "How is this paper philosophy?" (see Dotson 2013) remains a common charge for philosophical works that don't fall within the mainstream. But if we broaden our scope to philosophies of the past and present, also outside of the academy, we see a much wider diversity in topic and in medium. In this broad conception of philosophy, a painting such as *Guernica* can be philosophical, because it invites its viewers to look at war in a different light.

Philosophical visual imagery often plays with the audience's background knowledge, including their knowledge of other imagery. For example, René Magritte's *Perspective II: Manet's Balcony* (1950) is clearly inspired by Édouard Manet's *Balcony* (1868–1869), with the young, wealthy people in Manet's original replaced by coffins. Those coffins make us reflect on the brevity of life. But the work is more than a simple memento mori (reminder of death); as Magritte remarked to Michel Foucault, "my painting reveals where the decor of the 'Balcony' is suitable for placing coffins. The 'mechanism' at work here could serve as the object of a scholarly explanation of which I am incapable. The explanation would be valuable, even irrefutable, but the mystery would remain undiminished" (Magritte, letter to Foucault, 1966, cited in Foucault 1983, p. 58). In Magritte's view, the imagery conveys a richer range of philosophical meanings than he (or anyone else) could express in words.

The drawings presented in this book are nonverbal visual reflections and interpretations of the thought experiments they depict. Philosophical thought experiments tend to be terse, without much sensory detail or descriptions of the people or scenes involved. Drawing them, however, requires fleshing them out. You cannot draw a generic person, except perhaps as a stick figure; you can't draw a generic room or a generic garden. The fact that I needed to make choices also opened possibilities for what to draw—for example, how wild should the garden look in John Wisdom's *Invisible gardener* [39]? The thought experiment is ambiguous. For my design of the garden, I was inspired by the Dutch garden architect Piet Oudolf, with his emphasis on a natural look and plants that move along with the seasons, but mine is one possible interpretation among many.

The aim of these drawings is not merely to provide visual illustrations as anchors or learning aids. These drawings are themselves nonverbal interpretations of the thought experiments, including the emotions and moods these evoke. Emotions, such as anger and happiness, are of shorter duration and more directed than moods, such as nostalgia and irritability; moods are important in how we evaluate information, and moods dispose us to certain emotions. Many philosophical works bring with them a specific mood—think of Nietzsche's mature works, Fanon, Augustine, and many others, and those moods are an integral part of the philosophical work. Illustrations can help to set and enhance the mood already inherent in some thought experiments.

For example, to me Jackson's *Mary in the black-and-white room* [19] seems a melancholy story of a lonely young woman growing up in a black-and-white room. What would happen to Mary once she is released? Perhaps Mary would not immediately run away from her black-and-white prison. She might linger near the wall of the cell, gazing in wonder at the poppies just outside of it. My illustration aims to evoke both Mary's newfound freedom and her wonderment at the color red. For Plato's *Allegory of the cave* [28], I drew on American comics and on Greek vases for the visuals, the comic format to emphasize the drama of the story, the vases to evoke red-figure pottery of Plato's time. My protagonist is a teenage girl, drawing on the fact that Plato thought women were equally capable as philosophers, and because the thought experiment has a young adult fiction feel, with its dramatic twists and turns, and its emphasis on personal transformation.

The use of visual representation can both bring to light elements implicit in a thought experiment and be a source to further think about possible ways to interpret it. Here is an example. Judith Jarvis Thomson's *People seeds* [5] is a wonderful weird tale, a little horror miniature:

> [S]uppose it were like this: people-seeds drift about in the air like pollen, and if you open your windows, one may drift in and take root in your carpets or upholstery. You don't want children, so you fix up your windows with fine mesh screens, the very best you can buy. As can happen, however, and on very, very rare occasions does happen, one of the screens is defective; and a seed drifts in and takes root. (Thomson 1971, 59)

From the perspective of a reproductive-age woman who has access to contraception, the prospect of contraceptive failure is a horror, aptly captured in Thomson's thought experiment. It obviously does not capture all the intricacies of pregnancy, nor is it meant to. Having a child grow on your carpet is not the same as having it grow inside yourself. Given the genre of horror, I decided to go with a protracted, uneasy perspective, unnatural colors, and a creepy doll. The drawing takes inspiration from a wide range of visual sources, such as the three *Bedroom in Arles* paintings by Vincent Van Gogh, and the Annunciation, an enduringly popular image in Western religious art, where the Virgin Mary learns she is pregnant. This not only echoes the religious influence in the abortion debate but also helps us think of some aspects of unplanned pregnancies. In many Annunciation paintings (e.g., *Ecce Ancilla Domini* [1849–1850] by the Pre-Raphaelite artist Dante Gabriel Rossetti) Mary looks vulnerable and confused. I wanted to show a protagonist who is in a similar situation of insecurity and worry.

This book is structured as follows. Each entry presents the thought experiment itself, in a reworded version (for harmony throughout the book, and also, the original wording is not always clear), alongside a reference to the original source. The picture reflects on the thought experiment; often it is close to the original text, but in other cases, I have taken liberty to change the setting. For example, Jean-Paul Sartre's *Pierre's absence from the café* [20] is no longer set in a Parisian café but in a dojo and sports bar, so as to convey that the situation Sartre describes can occur in many everyday settings. I also had to introduce Pierre somehow so that the viewer could notice his absence.

Each thought experiment is accompanied by a reflection, written by an expert in the field. In some cases, such as Ruth Millikan's *Accidental you* [22], Tamar Gendler's *Skywalk* [21], and Andy Clark and David Chalmers' *Extended mind* [16], the original authors offer their reflections on their own thought experiments. The reflections provide context and background for each thought experiment and guide the reader to think through its key features as well as situating it in a broader philosophical discussion. Each entry has a list of further reading as well as questions to help you think along with the thought experiment. Whether in a group setting or on your own, I hope that these pictures and reflections can give you the experience to philosophize along with them. A good thought experiment doesn't provide a definite answer; it opens up new philosophical questions and possibilities.

I would like to express my gratitude to all the people who have encouraged me in this project, and with whom I shared early sketches and drawings, during the past three and a half years. In particular, David Chalmers encouraged me to propose this volume to Oxford University Press; Meena Krishnamurthy and Johan De Smedt saw the possibilities of this project for educational purposes and helped me to think seriously about this as more than a hobby project but see its philosophical relevance. My children, Aliénor and Gabriel, were enthusiastic and encouraging. Bryan Van Norden, Ethan Mills, and Julianne Chung have offered their valuable expertise about the thought experiments outside the Western tradition. Richard Pettigrew was on board with this project in its very early stages and has provided much encouragement. A particular word of thanks for the Oxford University Press editors Robert Miller and Andy Blitzer for their thoughtful input throughout this project. Thank you to Yiling Zhou, my research assistant, for help with the formatting and proofreading of the manuscript. I am grateful to the authors of the reflections, particularly given the difficult circumstances of a pandemic under which they wrote these valuable pieces. I dedicate this to my parents, Michael and Greet, who have always encouraged both my artistic and academic work. In a metaphysical as well as a *Bildung* sense, this project would not have come about without them.

I would also like to thank the following reviewers for their helpful suggestions: Robert Arp, Johnson County Community College; Paul Blaschko, University of Notre Dame; Ellen B. Stansell, Texas State University and Austin Community College; Christy Mag Uidhir, University of Houston.

References

Augustine. (Fourth century) 1992. *Confessions*. Translated by James Joseph O'Donnell. Oxford: Clarendon Press.

Camus, Albert. 1948. *The plague*. Translated by Stewart Gilbert. London: Hamish Hamilton.

De Beauvoir, Simone. (1964) 1985. *A very easy death*. Translated by Patrick O'Brian. New York: Pantheon Books.

Foucault, Michel. 1983. This is not a pipe, with illustrations and letters by René Magritte (trans. and ed. by James Harkness). Berkeley: University of California Press.

Dotson, Kristie. 2013. "How is this paper philosophy?" *Comparative Philosophy* 3, no. 1: 3–29.

Thomson, Judith Jarvis. 1971. "A defense of abortion." *Philosophy & Public Affairs* 1, no. 1: 47–66.

· INTRODUCTION ·

How to Use a Philosophical Thought Experiment, by Helen De Cruz and Johan De Smedt

This book is a collection of forty-two philosophical thought experiments from around the world. They range from very mundane, everyday situations, such as a teacher who tells her students something she does not believe herself [13, *Creationist teacher*] to a bunch of molecules that coincidentally arrange themselves to form your exact copy [22, *Accidental you*].

What are thought experiments for? Philosophers could just lay out their arguments rather than come up with fanciful stories. For example, why would John Rawls, when discussing liberty in democratic societies, ask his readers about a hypothetical person who counts blades of grass for fun [7, *The happy grass-counter*]? Why does Rawls ask his readers whether it's permissible to count blades of grass, rather than asking the more direct and abstract question of whether it's permissible for people to engage in useless, perhaps frivolous pursuits? Let's look at some ways in which philosophical thought experiments can be used.

When philosophers conceive of thought experiments, we can see this as instances of a much broader category of mental activities, namely building scenarios. We build scenarios in our daily lives in order to guide our actions. For example, if you see a large glass jar at the edge of a table, you might imagine that the jar will tip over and that the contents will spill. Perhaps there will be many glass shards on the floor that will keep on appearing from under furniture for weeks to come, no matter how diligently you sweep them away. Running scenarios like these leads to useful actions, in this case, moving the glass jar to a safer location. We devise such scenarios all the time, both about the physical and the social world. For instance, how will your colleague react when she finds out you got promoted, while she didn't? What should I buy for my spouse's birthday? Will he be happy with the Dutch oven I saw online? Will it improve his bread-making? We also frequently imagine more fanciful scenarios, for example, what if the world went carbon-neutral tomorrow? How would I get to work?

Imaginings like these are *epistemic actions*. We undertake pragmatic actions to change the world, for example, opening a door to get into a room, or driving from home to the supermarket.

By contrast, epistemic actions are activities we undertake to change what we know about the world, for example, opening a door to find out what is behind it, or driving around a new neighborhood to get to know it better. Such actions help us gain insight, understanding, and knowledge. Imagining hypothetical scenarios helps us discount some possibilities, or to consider possibilities we might not have taken into consideration before. They give us a better sense of what is possible, particularly given that our imagination is constrained by the actual state of the world.

Thought experiments are hypothetical scenarios we build to gain insight (see Miščević 1992; Gendler 2004; Cooper 2005). Take Robert Nozick's experience machine [4]. In this thought experiment, you are invited to step into a machine where you will experience your every dream come true and perfect happiness. Meanwhile, in reality, you would be suspended in a nutrient-rich tank with electrodes attached to your scalp, while a computer simulates all your experiences. Do you want to step into the experience machine? Nozick's thought experiment helps us think about the value of pleasure, particularly if that value is divorced from things it is normally part of, such as living in a real community with other people and fulfilling one's life projects. Maybe pleasure is not the main thing that makes our lives worthwhile. By focusing on some aspects of reality, we get a better sense of our intuitions and reactions in given situations.

According to Daniel Dennett (2013), the main job of thought experiments is to furnish us with such intuitions: thought experiments are *intuition pumps*, handy devices that provide us with intuitions, which we can use as evidence for philosophical claims we make. This view is plausible for many philosophical thought experiments. Take David Christensen's restaurant case [10, *Splitting the bill at a restaurant*]. Christensen considers the question of whether you should accord any weight to an opinion of an epistemic peer, that is, someone you consider to be equally intelligent, diligent, and well-informed as you are, but who in this case disagrees with you. This scenario plays out in a variety of messy real-life contexts, for example, people might disagree about the best policies for healthcare, whether God exists, or whether abortion is permissible. Should such frequent disagreements lead you to revise your beliefs, or can you just stand firm in your earlier convictions? To approach this question, Christensen provides a clear case you have probably encountered in some form: suppose you and a friend are at a restaurant, split the bill, and calculate how much each of you owes plus tip. Suppose your sum diverges from that of your friend, and you're both equally good at calculating. It seems that you should lower your confidence that your answer is correct. Christensen uses this uncomplicated case to argue that we should do the same for the messy cases of politics, religion, and other situations where we disagree with epistemic peers. Yet, in spite of Christensen's arguments, and this famous thought experiment, plenty of philosophers think it is fine to be steadfast in your beliefs. Perhaps not all cases of disagreement are equal. Perhaps we are justified in keeping to our original idea in religion or politics, but not in mental mathematics. After all, in the mental mathematics case one doesn't usually check thoroughly for the possibility of error, but a person with well-founded religious or political beliefs has usually already considered potential objections.

If thought experiments provide us with evidence—through intuitions—they are just one line of evidence among many. For one thing, significant variation among people from different cultures indicates that we need to treat our intuitions with caution. One well-attested example is the Gödel/Schmidt case [25]. Saul Kripke uses this thought experiment to argue against descriptivism about proper names. He holds that, in our everyday language, we don't see names as a shorthand for descriptions. If descriptivism were true, then "Gödel" is, for many people, just shorthand for "the man who proved the incompleteness of arithmetic." However, imagine that the incompleteness of arithmetic was really proved by another mathematician, called Schmidt, and that Gödel somehow got hold of Schmidt's manuscript and passed the proof off as his own? Would we then say that "Gödel" refers to the true author, who mysteriously died in Vienna? Kripke's intuition is that "Gödel" refers to the man whose last name was "Gödel," no matter who proved the incompleteness theorem. This intuition would count as evidence against descriptivism. But Edouard Machery and colleagues (see Machery 2017 for an overview) found that East Asian participants are more likely to endorse a descriptivist view than Europeans and Euro-Americans. This finding has been replicated several times. Moreover, even within a small and homogeneous subset of people—professional philosophers—participants differ considerably in their intuitions about epistemology and ethics (Schwitzgebel and Cushman 2014; De Cruz 2017), so what do we conclude from that about the evidential value of intuitions in philosophy? Is the majority opinion correct? Could the dissenting minority be right?

Moreover, many thought experiments can't really be categorized as evidence by any stretch of the imagination. Take *Plato's allegory of the cave* [28], an imaginative, poetic scenario where humans are prisoners in a cave from childhood, shackled at a wall by their neck and legs, gazing at the cave wall where images are projected. Plato likens the effects of education and philosophy to breaking free of the shackles, and being released out of the cave. This thought experiment is rich, evocative, and emotionally compelling, but given its outlandish scenario, it doesn't give us evidence, at least not in the usual sense of the word.

According to John Norton (2004), thought experiments are really just repackaged arguments. They don't give us anything beyond the argument. For one thing, they don't provide us with new empirical data. The only thing they do is to make explicit what we already know. For instance, we already know our first impressions can be mistaken, but it may be helpful to remind us of this fact with a vivid example of someone who mistakes a rope for a snake at night as in Asaṅga's *rope/snake analogy* [41]. Norton's claim that philosophical thought experiments are really arguments is plausible if we consider that many thought experiments are evaluated as arguments. William Paley [38] makes an analogy between watches and biological organisms and is explicitly argumentative. Focusing on parts of a watch is a helpful way to steer our attention toward complexity and goal directness, characteristics of living things Paley is interested in.

However, thought experiments cannot be reduced to arguments. For one thing, sometimes it is unclear what the argument is supposed to be. Take the charming dialogue between the Daoist philosopher Zhuangzi and the logician Huizi on a bridge on the River Hao [12]. Zhuangzi claims that the fish swimming underneath are happy. Huizi denies that Zhuangzi knows this; after all, he is not a fish. Zhuangzi agrees he's not a fish, but retorts that Huizi cannot know his state of mind, since Huizi is not him, and so forth. This thought experiment is not clearly geared to a single conclusion. It is also about other things, such as the goods we can gain from having philosophical conversations between friends. If thought experiments were only, or mainly, arguments, then it would seem that thought experiments that end discussions by their sheer argumentative force would be more compelling than thought experiments that continue to be debated throughout the centuries. But this does not seem to be the case. Among the most compelling thought experiments are those that continue to stimulate our thinking, that are conversation-starters rather than conversation-enders. For example, William Rowe acknowledges that his gripping image of the fawn perishing in a forest fire [40] even though an all-good and all-powerful God could end its suffering will leave plenty of rational theists unconvinced.

A fictionalist reading of philosophical thought experiments holds that they are short stories. More generally, fiction is a form of pretense, of as-if reasoning. In Jean-Paul Sartre's case of the missing friend [20], the protagonist comes to meet his friend Pierre at a Parisian café, but is late for the appointment. We are told Pierre is very punctual, and yet Pierre is not there. The props (a punctual friend, a busy Parisian café, the friend who is nowhere to be seen) focus our attention on the fact that we can experience someone's or something's absence (Meynell 2014). One difficulty with the fictionalist reading is that it remains unclear how, if at all, we learn from fiction (see, e.g., Landy 2008). This is an enduring philosophical question, tackled by, among others, Iris Murdoch, Friedrich Nietzsche, and Martha Nussbaum. These philosophers have argued that fictions provide us with knowledge, precisely because they alter and distort some aspects of reality. In this way, they help us to see some truths more clearly, which otherwise might be obscured by our day-to-day preoccupations. For example, Ibn Sīnā's *Flying man* [31] distorts reality by having us imagine a man who has no sensory or even proprioceptive experience, and asks if something would remain in the absence of any external stimulus. If we're still aware of something in this state, it must be that our soul is not merely defined in relation to our body, but rather, is an immaterial, living, rational substance.

This volume provides a wide range of philosophical thought experiments—some are clearly argumentative, others are meant to pump our intuitions and deliver clear verdicts, yet others are imaginative stories without definite answers or morals that can help us to transform our thinking. This broad diversity, which includes also several thought experiments from outside Western philosophical traditions, indicates that philosophical thought experiments serve many different purposes and do many different things.

References

Cooper, Rachel. 2005. "Thought experiments." *Metaphilosophy* 36, no. 3: 328–347.

De Cruz, Helen. 2017. "Religious disagreement: An empirical study among academic philosophers." *Episteme* 14, no. 1: 71–87.

Dennett, Daniel C. 2013. *Intuition pumps and other tools for thinking.* New York: WW Norton & Company.

Gendler, Tamar Szabó. 2004. "Thought experiments rethought—and reperceived." *Philosophy of Science* 71, no. 5: 1152–1163.

Landy, Joshua. 2008. "A nation of Madame Bovarys: On the possibility and desirability of moral improvement through fiction." In *Art and ethical criticism*, edited by Garry L. Hagberg, 63–94. Oxford: Blackwell.

Machery, Edouard. 2017. *Philosophy within its proper bounds.* Oxford: Oxford University Press.

Meynell, Letitia. 2014. "Imagination and insight: A new account of the content of thought experiments." *Synthese* 191, no. 17: 4149–4168.

Miščević, Nenad. 1992. "Mental models and thought experiments." *International Studies in the Philosophy of Science* 6, no. 3: 215–226.

Norton, John D. 2004. "On thought experiments: Is there more to the argument?" *Philosophy of Science* 71, no. 5: 1139–1151.

Schwitzgebel, Eric, and Fiery Cushman. 2014. "Expertise in moral reasoning? Order effects on moral judgment in professional philosophers and non-philosophers." *Mind & Language* 27, no. 2: 135–153.

· PART I ·

Thought Experiments in Ethics

· CHAPTER I ·

The Child at the Well, by Mengzi

The Thought Experiment

Everyone has a heart that cannot bear the suffering of other people. The ancient wise kings were like this, so they had governments that could not bear the suffering of others. Why I say that everyone has a heart that cannot bear the suffering of others is this: suppose someone suddenly saw a child about to fall into a well. Anyone would feel alarm and compassion at the sight of this. That feeling would not be caused by a desire to gain favor with the parents, or to get the praise of neighbors and friends, or by worries about one's reputation. From this we can conclude that if you lack the feeling of compassion, you are not human. Similarly, if you lack the feeling of shame, you are not human. If you lack the feeling of modesty and deference, you are not human. And if you lack the feeling of approving and disapproving, you are not human. The feeling of compassion is the sprout of benevolence. The feeling of shame is the sprout of righteousness. The feeling of modesty and deference is the sprout of etiquette. The feeling of approving and disapproving is the sprout of wisdom. People have these four sprouts in the same way as they have four limbs.

Source of the thought experiment:

Van Norden, Bryan W., trans. 2008. Mengzi 2A6 in *Mengzi: With selections from traditional commentaries*, 45–46. Indianapolis: Hackett. A free online version of the Mengzi, with an older translation and Chinese original, can be found here: https://ctext.org/mengzi

Reflection by Bryan W. Van Norden, Chair Professor in the School of Philosophy, Wuhan University, and James Monroe Taylor Chair in Philosophy, Vassar College

Is human nature good? Bad? Indifferent? Is human nature perhaps good in some people but bad in others? These questions were heatedly debated in ancient Chinese philosophy.

Mengzi, a Confucian philosopher of the fourth century BCE, famously claimed that human nature is good. But before we rush to agree or disagree with Mengzi, we should get clear about what he means by this claim. Mengzi explained that human nature is good in the sense that we have innate but incipient tendencies toward virtues like benevolence. He described these tendencies using an agricultural metaphor as "sprouts." Consider what is implied by this metaphor. The sprout of an apple tree does not yet bear fruit, but it has the potential to do so, if it receives proper nurturing. A sprout also has a potential that is active, rather than passive. A sprout responds to and seeks out water and sunlight in order to grow. The potential of a sprout to become a tree is thus different from the potential of a tree to be carved into cups and bowls. Similarly, our innate tendencies toward virtue are not yet fully formed virtues, but are active tendencies to perceive, feel, think, and act in virtuous ways. These tendencies respond to external stimuli, and they can be nurtured or stunted by environmental influences and by our own efforts.

Mengzi was challenged to provide a reason why we should believe there is something like a "sprout of benevolence." His response was the famous thought experiment of the child at the well. "Suppose," Mengzi said, "someone suddenly saw a child about to fall into a well: everyone in such a situation would have a feeling of alarm and compassion" (Van Norden 2011, 88). Mengzi describes this feeling as the "sprout of benevolence." [See also 2, *The drowning child*, for a related thought experiment.]

That the situations occurred "suddenly" is important: the suddenness of the reaction indicates that our compassion for the child is spontaneous and genuine. There is simply no time for ulterior motives. In addition, Mengzi did not claim that everyone would definitely act to save the child. Mengzi knows that we might freeze or have a second selfish thought about how the death of the child might benefit us. All he thinks the example proves is the existence of the *sprout* of the virtue of benevolence, not the fully developed virtue.

Perhaps Mengzi is right that most people would have a "feeling of alarm and compassion" in this situation. But what if a particular person did not feel any compassion for the child at the well? Mengzi responds to this concern with the metaphor of Ox Mountain: "The trees of Ox Mountain were once beautiful. But because the mountain bordered on a large state, hatchets and axes besieged it. … it was not that there were no sprouts or shoots growing there. But oxen and sheep then came and grazed on them. Hence, it was as if it were barren" (Van Norden 2011, 90). People who look at the mountain now mistakenly believe that it is the nature of the mountain to be barren. Similarly, Mengzi claims, people who appear to be "barren" of the sprouts of virtue have had their true nature effaced by bad influences in their environment, like violence, starvation, and false doctrines that teach them to be selfish.

What stance we take on human nature will influence our views on many other topics. If human nature is bad, our government will most likely need to be authoritarian. However, if human nature is good, the government can and should appeal to our best instincts and coax rather than coerce. Successful education also depends upon matching the practice to human nature. If human nature is good, education is about stimulating the student's natural interests, but if human nature is bad, education must be more about instilling beliefs and values into a recalcitrant subject. What are your stances on these topics and why?

Discussion Questions

1. Give a similar thought experiment of your own to illustrate the sprout of benevolence. Come up with analogous thought experiments for another virtue. For example, what is an example of a situation in which the "sprout of justice" might manifest itself? Or the "sprout of honesty"? Or the "sprout of righteousness"?
2. Explain in your own words the kinds of environmental influences in contemporary society that could lead to people who are like Ox Mountain.
3. What kind of teaching or practices could help transform the sprout of benevolence into the mature virtue of benevolence? How might reading books (philosophy, history, or poetry) help stimulate the growth of the sprouts? How would we think about ethical cultivation (making a person into someone virtuous) differently if our analogy were carving cups and bowls out of wood, as opposed to nurturing a sprout into a mature tree?

Further Reading

Ivanhoe, Philip J., rev. ed. 2000. *Confucian moral self-cultivation*. Indianapolis: Hackett. A helpful overview of Confucian views over time.

Liu, Xiusheng, and Philip J. Ivanhoe, eds. 2002. *Essays on the moral philosophy of Mengzi*. Indianapolis: Hackett. A collection of secondary essays.

Van Norden, Bryan W. 2011. *Introduction to classical Chinese philosophy*. Indianapolis: Hackett. See especially chapters 5: "Yang Zhu and Egoism," 6: "Mengzi and Human Nature," and 10: "Xunzi's Confucian Naturalism."

· CHAPTER 2 ·

The Drowning Child, by Peter Singer

The Thought Experiment

On your way to work, you see a child who appears to be drowning in a shallow pond. There's no one else around. It would not be a problem for you to wade in and pull the child out of the water, but your clothes would become muddy and wet, and your expensive shoes would be ruined. Should you, in spite of this, still save the child? It seems like the costs you incur in your efforts pale in comparison to the death of the child if you do not step in.

Source of the thought experiment:

Singer, Peter. 1972. "Famine, affluence, and morality." *Philosophy and Public Affairs* 1, no. 3: 229–243.

Reflection by Peter Singer, Princeton University

The drowning child in the shallow pond appears in "Famine, Affluence and Morality," which I wrote in 1971, at a time when nine million refugees from what was then East Pakistan had fled across the border into India to escape mass killings carried out by the Pakistani army. India, a much poorer nation then than it is today, appealed for assistance in feeding and housing this vast number of people, but the funds donated were manifestly insufficient.

I asked myself: do I have a responsibility to help people who are dying because they cannot afford food, or even the most basic level of health care? I was a junior lecturer at Oxford University, and my wife was a high school teacher. We were not wealthy, but we had enough money to be able to live comfortably and travel to Italy during the summer holidays. Should we be spending money on luxuries when that money could save lives elsewhere in the world? We went to visit Oxfam, one of the world's leading organizations combating extreme poverty in low-income countries. We found their staff impressive, and started giving 10 percent of our income to them. Over the years, as we have become more financially comfortable, we have increased the proportion of our income we are giving (in part still to Oxfam but to other charities as well) to somewhere between one-third and half.

Although the refugee crisis in India was a big news story, it was occurring against a background of extreme poverty that attracted less media attention, but was, over time, taking more lives. Millions of children were dying every year from avoidable, poverty-related causes. These deaths were preventable, and there were organizations like Oxfam trying to prevent them, but with their limited resources they were able to help only a small fraction of the people in need. So even when the refugee crisis was resolved (as it eventually was by the intervention of the Indian army and the creation of the independent country of Bangladesh), the basic ethical question, about spending on things we don't need when the money could save lives, did not go away.

If I can, at no risk, and no great cost, to myself, save the life of a complete stranger, do I have an obligation to do so? Is it wrong not to save the stranger's life, even if I have no responsibility for the stranger being in danger? The drowning child in the shallow pond seemed the perfect way to test our intuitions on that question, and most people's intuitions are that it would be wrong—quite awful, in fact—to ignore the child and walk on, because you don't want to ruin your expensive shoes.

If we agree that it would be wrong not to save the child in the pond, the next question is: Are there any morally relevant differences between the situation of the person faced with the child in the pond, and the situation of the billion or more people living in rich countries who spend money on things they don't need? They could instead donate that money to an effective charity that will use it to save the lives of children (or adults) who would otherwise die from poverty-related causes. There are differences between the pond situation and the situation we are in. The fact that we cannot see, or even identify, a child whose life we save by, for example, donating to the Against Malaria Foundation (www.againstmalaria.com) so that the child will be protected against malaria-carrying mosquitos, does make it emotionally easier for us to do nothing. Yet it is implausible to think that this difference somehow justifies our failure to act to help the child we cannot see.

"Famine, Affluence and Morality" has been reprinted more than fifty times, mostly in anthologies intended for classroom use in introductory courses in philosophy and ethics. In some countries it is also read in high schools. As a result, it has been read and discussed by hundreds of thousands, perhaps millions, of students. One of them, an Oxford student named Toby Ord, went on to found Giving What We Can (https://www.givingwhatwecan.org/), an organization whose members pledge to give 10 percent of their pre-tax income, until retirement, to the charities that they believe will do the most good. At the time of writing, they have donated more than $231 million to highly effective charities and have pledged to donate, over their lifetimes, more than ten times that amount.

Giving What We Can in turn played a role in starting the movement known as Effective Altruism. Effective Altruism advocates using reason and evidence to do the most good we can, whether by charitable donations, through our choice of career, or by using our time and energy in other ways. I subsequently founded the charity The Life You Can Save (www.thelifeyoucansave.org), which recommends the most highly effective charities helping people in extreme poverty.

Discussion Questions

1. Have you donated to charities, and if so, to which ones? Thinking about the charity to which you have given most, what factors led you to decide to donate to that particular charity?
2. Given that the money we can spend on more fashionable clothes, or a new phone, could restore sight to a blind person, or even save someone's life, is it morally permissible to buy these items?
3. How would you reply to those who say that donating to charities does not solve the structural injustices that cause extreme poverty across the world, or that it is up to governments rather than individuals to address these injustices?

Further Reading

MacFarquhar, Larissa. 2015. *Strangers drowning: Grappling with impossible idealism, drastic choices, and the overpowering urge to help*. New York: Penguin Press.

Singer, Peter. 2015. *The most good you can do: How effective altruism is changing ideas about living ethically*. New Haven, CT: Yale University Press.

Singer, Peter. 2019. *The life you can save: How to do your part to end world poverty*. Revised edition. Bainbridge Island, WA: The Life You Can Save. (Available free as an eBook or audiobook from www.thelifeyou-cansave.org)

· CHAPTER 3 ·

The Impartial Caretaker, by Mozi

The Thought Experiment

Some people object to the idea of impartial care—that we are to care for strangers as much as we would for people close to us. But suppose there are two men, one holding to impartial care, the other to partial care, and they practice what they believe. Now, it is wartime. There you are, ready in armor and helmet to join the battle. Whether and when you will return is uncertain. Would you entrust your parents and family to the care of the partial man, or the impartial one? It seems to me that in such occasions, everyone would entrust their family to the impartial man, even those who object to the idea of impartial care on theoretical grounds.

Source of the thought experiment:
Ivanhoe, Philip J., trans. 2001. "Mozi." In *Readings in Classical Chinese philosophy*, edited by Philip J. Ivanhoe and Bryan Van Norden, 55–109. Indianapolis: Hackett. A free online version with an older translation and Chinese original is available here: https://ctext.org/mozi

Reflection by Hui-chieh Loy, National University of Singapore

According to the ancient Chinese thinker Mozi (late fifth to early fourth century BCE), morality requires that we practice "impartial care"—we are to regard others as we do ourselves, and strangers as we do our associates (i.e., our kin, fellow countrymen, etc.). He believes that all the bad things human beings do to other human beings come about because people generally prioritize themselves over others, their own associates over strangers, so that they have no qualms harming others to advance their own interests. Impartial care, being the exact opposite pattern of behavior, is thus the direct antidote to all those human evils. But both in his own time and in ours, impartial care appears to be an unappealing ideal. While most of us would balk at harming others to advance the interests of one's own, we normally think that it is at least permissible to give greater regard to ourselves over others, our associates over strangers in distributing favors and resources.

In response, Mozi proposed two thought experiments. In the first ("Caretaker"), the interlocutor is to imagine that he needs a caretaker to look after his familial dependents; he is being sent on a mission and unsure if he can return alive. Given a choice between a caretaker who consistently behaves according to impartial care (the impartialist) or one who does the opposite (the partialist), Mozi claims that even those who disapprove of impartial care would rather entrust their dependents to the former rather than the latter.

The second thought experiment ("Ruler") is similar, except that the choice is between an impartialist or a partialist ruler in the circumstance where the country is facing a severe pestilence with many people in misery and privation. Again, Mozi claims that in such a scenario, even those who disapprove of impartial care would choose an impartialist, rather than partialist ruler. (In both cases, we are to assume that the choice is exclusive—you can only have one caretaker, or one ruler.)

On the face of it, Mozi's thought experiments are unpersuasive. Even if we set aside the possibility of some other option that is neither impartialist nor partialist, there remains an ambiguity—it surely makes a difference whether the partial caretaker or ruler is partial toward *me and my own*. If he is, then the caretaker or ruler who counts me as an associate would seem to be the superior choice to the impartial caretaker or ruler, at least under most circumstances, and only after that, the partial caretaker or ruler who counts me as a stranger. Furthermore, if Mozi were right that even those who disapprove of impartial care would choose the impartialist caretaker and ruler, isn't it also because doing so is the efficient way to advance one's own partialist interests? If so, then Mozi has at best shown that even partialists can "approve of" impartial care when it is practiced by *other* people; he did not show that the partialists have reason to practice impartial care themselves.

What can Mozi say in reply? First, notice that both thought experiments involve an unfavorable choice scenario. In Caretaker, the interlocutor chooses on the basis that he is uncertain whether he will come back alive from his mission. In Ruler, he chooses on the condition that the country is facing a famine or drought. The point is that when the circumstances are extreme enough, the partialist caretaker or ruler will prioritize those closest to him—and eventually, himself—over my dependents, while the impartialist will continue to give all equal regard. Choosing the impartial caretaker or ruler is thus analogous to buying disaster insurance—paying premiums (and thus forgoing benefit) in happy times so that a claim can be made in the unlikely event of a disaster, even though one does not know whether those claims will be made in one's lifetime!

We should also not assume that Mozi's intention was to persuade the interlocutor to practice impartial care through the thought experiments. Within Mozi's text, the thought experiments respond to an audience who have already dismissed the earlier argument from the diagnosis of the human evils in the world. Despite their rejection of impartial care, Mozi can still attempt to show them something—even if they are not going to practice impartial caring, it can still be in their interest that *other people* do. This is especially relevant considering that not everyone is going to be partial toward them in particular, and circumstances can arise in which they need the help of others. They thus have reason *not* to oppose Mozi's preaching of impartial caring. If anything, they have reason to encourage others to practice impartial caring or to support social arrangements that instantiate impartial caring.

Finally, a more speculative possibility. When earlier arguing for impartial caring, Mozi observed that if people generally practiced impartial care and organized society in a way that captures its spirit, then the weak and disadvantaged would receive help from the strong and advantaged. Mozi's thought experiments invite the interlocutor to see things from the perspective of someone without the power to shield himself and his dependents from the ravages of circumstance, rather than one with access to social advantages. Here, keep in mind that Mozi's primary audience is the social and political elite. By having the interlocutor vicariously share in the yearning of the disadvantaged for succor from the better off, Mozi thus placed them in a position where they can come to share his intuition that impartial caring is what morality requires.

Discussion Questions

1. Most people seem to have more regard for those who are closest to them (e.g., family members or fellow countrymen) than for strangers. Do you think this is what most people believe and act on? What about yourself?
2. How would you choose in Mozi's thought experiments? If the point is to make sure that those who depend upon your care are looked after in dire circumstances, is it true that an impartialist caretaker is superior to a partialist one?

3. Moralists and social activists often tell us to see things from the perspective of the downtrodden in society. Do you think we really gain any form of moral insight by doing so? If so, what sort of moral insight is that?

Further Reading

Fraser, Chris. 2016. *The philosophy of the Mòzǐ: The first consequentialists*. New York: Columbia University Press.

Van Norden, Bryan. 2003. "A response to the Mohist arguments in 'Impartial Caring.'" In *The moral circle and the self: Chinese and Western approaches*, edited by Kim-chong Chong, Sor-Hoon Tan, and C. L. Ten, 41–58. Chicago: Open Court.

Wong, David.1989. "Universalism versus love with distinctions: An ancient debate revived." *Journal of Chinese Philosophy* 16: 251–272.

· CHAPTER 4 ·

The Experience Machine, by Robert Nozick

The Thought Experiment

The experience machine is a special device that can give you any experience you would like. Do you want to be the world's best jockey? Would you like to be friends with your favorite celebrity? The machine would make you feel like it's really happening, while you are in reality floating in a tank, electrodes attached to your skull. You have the opportunity to plug into this machine for the rest of your life. Your life would be preprogrammed to maximize your pleasure, but you wouldn't remember plugging in, and while plugged in you would have no idea that what you're experiencing isn't real. Should you plug in?

Source of the thought experiment:

Nozick, Robert. 1974. *Anarchy, state, and utopia*. New York: Basic Books.

Reflection by Eden Lin, The Ohio State University

There are at least two questions that thinking about the experience machine might help you answer: What do you value? What is of value? The first has to do with what you care about and what matters to you: it is a question about your personality or psychology. The second has to do with what things are good or valuable—not in the merely monetary sense in which cars are more valuable when new than when used, but in the ethical sense that we have in mind when we say that world peace would be a good thing or that friendship is a valuable part of human life. Because there is no guarantee that everything you value is valuable, or vice versa, these are different questions.

You can start to answer the first question by asking yourself whether you would permanently plug into the experience machine if you were given the opportunity to do so and you were absolutely sure that it would operate as intended, with no glitches. If, like many other people who have considered this thought experiment, you wouldn't permanently plug in, this strongly suggests that what your experiences feel like (e.g., how pleasant, varied, or interesting they are) is not the only thing you care about. For if you did care about literally nothing else, why wouldn't you do something that would ensure that your future experiences will be far more to your liking than they otherwise would be? This doesn't tell us what else you do value, so it isn't a complete answer to the first question. But it's a start, and you can try to figure out what else you value by asking yourself why you wouldn't plug in: is it because you don't want to be totally deluded, because you care about the people you could no longer interact with if you were plugged in, or for some other reason? If, on the other hand, you would permanently plug in, then this suggests either that you value only what your experiences feel like or that you value this more than whatever you would give up by plugging in.

You can start to answer the second question by asking yourself whether you *should* permanently plug into the machine if given the opportunity. If you wouldn't plug in, then unless you believe that this decision would be irrational or unreasonable (in the way that a recovering alcoholic might think that he shouldn't order another drink, even though he predicts that he would if given the opportunity), you also believe that you shouldn't plug in. But if you shouldn't plug in, this suggests that pleasant, interesting, or otherwise desirable experiences are not the only good or valuable things. After all, why shouldn't you do something that will greatly improve your future experiences if you wouldn't thereby give up anything good? This line of thought leads some people to the view that you would have a worse life (i.e., one that would not go as well for you) if you were to plug into the machine than if you were not to do this, even though your life would *feel* better if you were to plug in. In their view, the experience machine shows that what a person's experiences feel like is not the only thing that determines how well their life is going: a person's quality of life (i.e., their *well-being* or *welfare*) is also partly determined by something else that you would no longer have, or would have less of, if you were to plug in—something that is *good for you*, in the sense that it benefits you, is in your self-interest, or makes your life go well. But suppose you believe that you should permanently plug into the machine if given the opportunity. (Perhaps you believe that you would plug in and that it would be rational to do this, or perhaps you believe that although you wouldn't plug in, this choice would be irrational.) If you are right about that, then this might suggest either that your experiences are the only good things or that, although they aren't, what you would forgo by plugging in is less valuable than the experiences that you would thereby acquire.

Some people object to the aforementioned inference from the claim that you shouldn't plug in to the conclusion that your life would go worse if you were to plug in. They argue that perhaps you shouldn't plug in because you owe it to your friends and family to stay with them in the real world, because a life in an experience machine is undignified, or for some other reason that is compatible with the claim that your life would go better (or at least no worse) if you were to plug in. But there is another way in which the experience machine might threaten the view that how well someone's life is going is determined entirely by what it feels like "from the inside." What if, without knowing it, you've been plugged into an experience machine all your life? If your life would be worse if that hypothesis were true than if it were false, then how well a life is going isn't entirely a matter of how it feels. After all, your life would feel exactly the same either way, so something else must explain why it would be worse if that hypothesis were true.

Discussion Questions

1. Would you permanently plug into an experience machine if you were given the opportunity to do so and you were certain that it would function as advertised? Why, or why not?
2. Are there any reasons why a person who is given the chance to permanently plug into an experience machine shouldn't do so? If so, what are they?
3. Because the experiences generated by an experience machine are perfectly convincing, all of the experiences that you've actually had are compatible with the hypothesis that you have been plugged into an experience machine your whole life. Consider the argument that, because your life would have gone worse if this hypothesis were true even though it would have felt exactly the same, how well someone's life is going is not entirely determined by how that life feels "from the inside." How might someone rebut this argument?

Further Reading

Feldman, Fred. 2011. "What we learn from the experience machine." In *The Cambridge companion to Nozick's anarchy, state, and utopia*, edited by Ralf M. Bader and John Meadowcroft, 59–86. Cambridge: Cambridge University Press.

Lin, Eden. 2016. "How to use the experience machine." *Utilitas* 28, no. 3: 314–332.

Weijers, Dan, and Vanessa Schouten. 2013. "An assessment of recent responses to the experience machine objection to hedonism." *Journal of Value Inquiry* 47, no. 4: 461–482.

· CHAPTER 5 ·

The Violinist/People Seeds by Judith Jarvis Thomson

The Thought Experiment

Let's grant that a fetus is a person from the moment it is conceived. Does this make abortion morally objectionable? Judith Jarvis Thomson offers two thought experiments that push back against this idea. First, imagine you wake up in a hospital bed, back to back with a famous violinist. It turns out you've been kidnapped by members of the Society of Music Lovers. They plugged your circulatory system into that of the violinist so you might save him from a terrible kidney ailment. You alone have the right blood type to help—but no worries, it's only for nine months! Are you morally required to agree to this situation? Or is it justified for you to unplug yourself? Second, imagine that people seeds drift in the air like pollen. You don't want children, so you make sure your windows are secured with fine mesh screens, so that no people seeds can drift in when you open your windows. But no mesh is perfect; on rare occasions, a seed drifts in and takes root, slowly growing on your carpet. Are you morally required to let this person grow?

Source of the thought experiments:

Thomson, J. J. (1971). "A defense of abortion." *Philosophy & Public Affairs* 1, no. 1: 47–66.

Reflection by Elselijn Kingma, Peter Sowerby Professor in Philosophy and Medicine, King's College London

In her 1971 "a defense of abortion," Judith Jarvis Thomson asks us to set aside a deeply controversial question: whether the embryo and/or fetus is a person—or to what extent it is like, or has the same moral rights as adult humans or even infants. Thomson does in fact think that there are important differences between adult humans and fetuses. But for the sake of argument she asks us to assume that a fetus has all the rights of an adult human. This allows us to focus our attention on the following question: *if* a fetus/embryo has the same moral standing as human adults, would it *then* be permissible for a woman—the person gestating the fetus—to end its existence through abortion?

To help answer this question, Thomson invokes the now famous thought experiment of the violinist, described earlier. Would it—so asks Thomson—be permissible to unplug the violinist and thereby let her die? Thomson's answer is: yes.

Of course, Thomson recognizes that it would be good of you to *not* unplug the violinist—to save her life. But, she argues, this is not something that you are required to do by morality or justice; the violinist is not entitled to the use of your body, and we are not obliged to rescue anyone we can, at any cost to ourselves. Saving the violinist, Thomson argues, would be heroic or *supererogatory*—that is, it would be doing more than justice requires. It is what a good Samaritan would do. But you are not required to be a good Samaritan—only to be a minimally decent one.

It is therefore permissible, Thomson argues, to unplug the violinist and let her die. By the same reasoning, it must be permissible to unplug an embryo/fetus and let it die, *even if* it were to have the same moral standing as an adult.

The violinist is not depicted in this illustration, however. Instead, the image depicts "people seeds." This thought experiment is devised because many will be tempted to respond to

Thomson as follows: "The violinist and the fetus are disanalogous in important respects. The fetus is not *just anyone*—but your (impending) child. And you did not consent to the violinist's being plugged in, nor did you make a causal contribution to her present state of distress. But when it comes to embryo/fetuses—cases of involuntary intercourse aside—you *did* have a role to play in causing it (and thereby its present state of dependency). Moreover, in having (voluntary) intercourse you did knowingly run the risk that an embryo might be created."

"People seeds" is Thomson's response. It is supposed to show that you are not required to let someone use your house, let alone your body, *even if* you knowingly ran some risk of their coming into an existence that is (temporarily) dependent on you.

The philosophical literature on abortion has grown to be vast, but it seems to me that Thomson's early contribution continues to drive home some important points. Above all: that abortion is deeply unlike an ordinary case of "killing" (although this language continues to be used frequently and—I think—erroneously, to describe abortion in the literature).

Exemplary cases of killing involve *interference:* walking up to another person, and shooting them through the heart (or similar). The question about abortion, by contrast, is not about whether you are allowed to interfere with another to end their life, but rather about whether you are morally obliged to continue constant interference to keep them alive; whether you are obliged to provide and sustain a *dependent* other through your body. Or, and instead, whether you are permitted to withdraw that interference, which means their life will end.

The question about abortion is therefore not about whether the fetus or embryo has some abstract right to life, but about whether it has a much more specific right to the continued use of *this* person's body. And as the violinist case illustrates so well, there are cases where we clearly think there is a right to life, but no right to the use of another person's body.

But Thomson's thought experiment also has clear limitations, which—influential as it is—may continue to distort our philosophical reflection on the permissibility of abortion. There is a reason why the picture chosen is not one of the violinist, but one of people seeds. For it is difficult to depict in a drawing the intimate invasiveness and extended nature of pregnancy; a picture of two people lying next to each other in a hospital bed connected by some tubes just does not convey the length of time; the relentless constancy; the pervasive transformation; or the intimate invasiveness, of sustaining another within oneself. And if the violinist thought experiment cannot convey these and other important aspects of pregnancy in a visual depiction, then perhaps the thought experiment also fails truly to convey them in thought.

The image of people seeds, by contrast, does depict at least some of the horror and the freakishness (though not the length, invasiveness, pervasiveness, and physicality) of pregnancy. (A freakishness that is enhanced by the décor, inspired by *Goodnight Moon* [Brown and Hurd 1947])—a very strange book I only encountered, tellingly, as a parent, and that still freaks me out every single time I have to read it!)

It is a freakishness on which roughly half the population can reflect *in abstracta*, free in the knowledge that they will never have to directly face it. For the, roughly, other 50 percent of the population, by contrast, this possibility is very real: always there, more or less remotely, hanging over their lives. And although this freakiness, when realized, need not cause the horror or despair that I read in the eyes of the woman on the bed, but may instead be warmly welcomed—or more likely cause a vast wave of complex, ambivalent and changing emotions—freaky it is. Every single time.

These issues may matter much more than we are inclined to think. Woollard (2021, 1) explains that after her first pregnancy "the philosophical literature's understanding of what it is to require someone to remain pregnant and of the value of a human foetus—key issues for understanding the ethics of abortion—appeared woefully inadequate." Not only, she argues, is a proper, undistorted understanding of what pregnancy involves essential for an adequate moral reflection on abortion, but she also claims that this understanding is very difficult to achieve. Pregnancy, according to Woollard, is a *transformative experience*: the sort of thing one can only understand in relevantly meaningful ways if one undergoes the experience directly (or listens *very carefully* and in great detail to someone who has) [see also 34, *Becoming a vampire*]. This would seem to prevent—or at least make it very difficult—for those who have not experienced pregnancy, to meaningfully reflect on the morality of abortion.

Another limitation of Thomson's though experiment is that the violinist is a stranger. And whatever we may say precisely about the embryo/fetus and its relationship to ourselves, surely a stranger it is not. Indeed, it is as far removed from *the violinist*—a random stranger—as it is possible to be. Little (1999) thus impresses upon us that pregnancy is not just a transformation and invasion of the body—as the Thomson's violinist emphasizes—but a much deeper and much more wrenching transformation and invasion of the heart: a transformation of relationships, and perhaps even the self—at least in terms of what one takes to be core to one's identity.

None of this is captured by the violinist in image or thought—although a hint is there, perhaps, in the earlier image of the despairing girl staring indecisively at her freaky people seed, which is rapidly growing into a cute, lovable, utterly dependent and demanding but almost unabandonable baby who—if left to grow to fruition—may come to represent a main dimension by which she comes to value and evaluate her "life's work" (Cusk 2008).

We should perhaps finish, then, with a warning: thought experiments, like the violinist, can be vivid and therefore useful in lastingly impressing certain truths. But in their vividness they can equally lastingly impress falsehoods. In re-evaluating her earlier appreciation of the violinist, Overall (2015, 137) writes: "a picture held [me] captive—a picture of the violinist, physically individuated and separate. And that picture is not adequate to represent the fetus." The question is: what picture is?

Acknowledgements: I would like to thank Fiona Woollard and the editor for helpful comments on this piece; this reflection was written while receiving funding from the European Research Council under the European Union's Horizon 2020 research and innovation program (grant agreement no. 659486).

Discussion Questions

1. Do you agree with Thomson that it would be permissible to unplug the violinist?
2. What are your thoughts about people seeds? Are you obliged to provide for them or is it permissible to dislodge them? Why or why not? Are your views affected by changes in the details of the story? (For example: does it matter if you failed to maintain the mesh or put in substandard mesh? What if you can't afford or don't have access to quality mesh? What if a burglar broke in and left your window open, without putting in mesh? Does it make a

difference if you want to dislodge the seed because you already struggle to care adequately for seeds that landed previously? Can you think of other useful ways of adjusting the details?)

3. What do you think of the suggested limitations of the thought experiments? Can you think of any others?
4. Consider the following proposition: *"An adequate ethics of pregnancy, and therefore an adequate ethics of abortion, must take the relevant facts of pregnancy—of physical, metaphysical and emotional intertwinement—seriously."* Woollard argues that you can only properly grasp what pregnancy (and the transition to motherhood) is like by going through the experience itself—or by listening *very carefully* to someone who has had that experience and is willing to share it honestly. If you have been pregnant, then do you think your (unique) experience suffices? If you have not been pregnant, then who do you know who might be able and willing to acquaint you with these facts/experiences? Will they honestly share their experience—and are you able to listen? How else, if at all, might you obtain the relevant knowledge?

Further Reading

Brown, M. W. and C. Hurd. 1947. *Goodnight moon*. Harper & Brothers.

Cusk, R. 2008. *A life's work*. London: Faber & Faber.

Little, M. O. 1999. "Abortion, intimacy and the duty to gestate." *Ethical Theory and Moral Practice* 2: 295–315.

Overall, C. 2015. "Rethinking abortion, ectogenesis, and fetal death." *Journal of Social Philosophy* 46: 126–140.

Thomson, J. J. 1971. "A defense of abortion." *Philosophy & Public Affairs* 1, no. 1: 47–66.

Woollard, F. 2021. "Mother knows best: Pregnancy, applied ethics, and epistemically transformative experiences." *Journal of Applied Philosophy* 38: 155–171.

· PART II ·

Thought Experiments in Political Philosophy

· CHAPTER 6 ·

The Original Position, by John Rawls

The Thought Experiment

If you could choose where in society you would end up, what would you choose? Likely, you'd choose to be born in a privileged situation, wealthy, or at least very talented so you'd be able to work your way up. But what if you did not know where you would end up? This is Rawls's thought experiment of the original position. In this situation, people get to design which principles of justice will govern their society. However, they don't know their class, gender, or any talents or natural abilities they might have. What society would they choose, from behind a veil of ignorance?

Source of the thought experiment:

Rawls, John. 1971. *A theory of justice*. Cambridge, MA: Belknap Press.

Reflection by Marcus Arvan, University of Tampa

Governments impose laws on people. If you violate the law, you may be arrested, tried in court, fined, or imprisoned. What morally justifies this? One philosophically influential answer is the idea of a social contract: an *agreement* among citizens to be governed. Yet, assuming this is correct, what does justice require the social contract to be? In *A Theory of Justice*, John Rawls argues that justice is fairness, and that a fair social contract is one that we would all rationally agree from a situation of perfect fairness: *the original position*.

Try to imagine having no idea who you are. You know you are human being and a citizen of some society. But beyond that, you know nothing else about yourself: not your name, your gender, race, religion, sexual orientation, talents, personality, moral views, and so on. This may seem hard to imagine. Yet consider the famous picture of Lady Justice, who holds the scales of justice while wearing a blindfold. Rawls argues that to be fair—just like Lady Justice—the social contract must be one we would all rationally agree to from behind a "veil of ignorance": an *imaginary* blindfold that prevents anyone from unfairly privileging themselves.

If we were behind the original position's veil of ignorance, what social contract would we rationally agree to? Rawls first argues against an answer influential in his time and still popular among some today: utilitarianism—the theory that society should maximize the overall happiness of its citizenry. Rawls argues that utilitarianism is irrational from behind the veil of ignorance because you would know that utilitarianism could require *sacrificing your happiness* for the sake of the happiness of others. Rawls contends it would be more rational instead to seek particular types of goods: *social primary goods*.

Consider basic political rights and liberties, such as free speech, freedom of association, freedom of religion, and the right to vote. Now consider political and economic opportunities: the ability to run for political office or get a well-paying job. Finally, consider wealth and income. Rawls argues that everyone in the original position has rational grounds to *ensure* that they have these goods. This is because everyone would know behind the veil that no matter who they *might* be in the real world, these goods will enable them to pursue or even change their life goals. For example, if you want to express yourself, the right to free speech enables you to do that, no matter what your race, gender, religion, and so on, might be. Similarly, if you want political reform, then opportunities to run for political office can help you pursue it. Finally, regardless of who you are, wealth and income can help you achieve what you want in life, even if it is simply giving your money away to help others.

Rawls argues that everyone in the original position would agree that a fully just society would distribute these goods according to two principles: a principle of equal basic rights and liberties, and a principle of fair equality of opportunity that permits economic inequality, but only to the extent that it benefits everyone, particularly society's lowest socioeconomic class. Then, in *The Law of Peoples*, Rawls applies the original position internationally, arguing that entire societies behind a veil would agree to particular principles of international law and practice. However, there is ongoing debate about whether justice instead requires a global or "cosmopolitan" original position where every *person* in the world deliberates from behind the veil to principles of global justice—principles that might require global democracy, open borders, and worldwide economic fairness (Miklaszewska 2016).

Finally, Rawls briefly suggested that justice as fairness might be a part of a more general moral theory, "rightness as fairness." Following Rawls, I have argued that the original position may be key to understanding prudence, morality, *and* justice as a unified whole, including how to justly rectify past and present injustice (Arvan 2020). Consider prudence, that is, making good decisions about your own life. Life is long and profoundly uncertain. If you are lucky, you will live to old age. From now until then, your life may undergo all kinds of unexpected twists and turns: you may fall in love, change careers, develop different values, face serious health challenges, and so on. How can you make good decisions *now* given that you do not know how your life will go?

I argue that the original position provides the answer. The veil of ignorance requires you to determine which principles are rational to act on *not knowing* how your life will go. Using this prudential original position, I argue that prudence requires caring about how your actions *might* affect others—both because of potential remorse but also because other people can reward or punish your behavior. I contend this makes a *moral* original position rational, thus making prudence *fairness to oneself*, morality *fairness to others*, and justice *social and political fairness*. Finally, there are interesting scientific questions regarding which principles people prefer in the original position, and how original position reasoning affects moral thinking and behavior (Huang, Greene, and Bazerman 2019).

Discussion Questions

1. If you were behind the original position's veil of ignorance (not knowing who you are), which principles do *you* think would be rational for you to agree to define (a) prudence (making good decisions about your own life), (b) morality (how you treat others), and (c) justice (the morality of governments and laws)?
2. How do you think Rawls might respond to the concerns that life isn't fair and we will probably never actually be in the original position?

Further Reading

Arvan, Marcus. 2020. *Neurofunctional prudence and morality: A philosophical theory*. New York: Routledge.

Huang, Karen, Joshua D. Greene, and Maz Bazerman. 2019. "Veil-of-ignorance reasoning favors the greater good." *Proceedings of the National Academy of Sciences 116*, no. 48: 23989–23995.

Miklaszewska, Justyna. 2016. "Rawls on cosmopolitanism and global justice." In *Uncovering facts and values: Studies in contemporary epistemology and political philosophy*, edited by Adrian Kuzniar, 323–335. Leiden: Brill-Rodopi.

· CHAPTER 7 ·

The Happy Grass-Counter, by John Rawls

The Thought Experiment

Is it okay for a member of a liberal society to do something as frivolous and useless as counting blades of grass? Imagine Geordie, a famed mathematician, who enjoys nothing better than to count and tally up blades of grass in the well-trimmed lawns around Harvard. Should we allow him to do that? His time could be better spent doing something else, after all.

Source of the thought experiment:
Rawls, John. 1971. *A theory of justice.* Cambridge, MA: Belknap Press.

Reflection by Bonnie Honig, Brown University

Rawls's grass-counter tests the limits of justice as fairness, his ideal society, run in accordance with the requirements of his theory of justice [see also 7, *The original position*]. Liberty is important to Rawls but so is what he takes to be its point: to allow everyone the equal opportunity to develop and pursue their own conception of the good, as long as it does not harm others or infringe unfairly on their liberty. So Rawls asks: what should we do when someone in a just society uses their liberty to do something as meaningless as count blades of grass? Rawls answers: if this is really his pleasure, he should be free to pursue it.

> Imagine someone whose only pleasure is to count blades of grass in various geometrically shaped areas such as park squares and well-trimmed lawns. He is otherwise intelligent and actually possesses unusual skills, since he manages to survive by solving difficult mathematical problems for a fee. The definition of the good forces us to admit that the good for this man is indeed counting blades of grass . . . Naturally we would be surprised that such a person should exist . . . Perhaps he is peculiarly neurotic. . . . But if we allow that his nature is to enjoy this activity and not any other . . . this establishes that it is good for him. (Rawls 1971, 432–433)

Justice as fairness is neutral among conceptions of the good, but the grass-counter tests that. In the end he is tolerated, whereas others are respected. We may interrogate him, we wonder whether he might not be neurotic, and if we tolerate him it is because we are "forced" to admit that grass-counting is his good: is this neutral?[1]

Indeed, Rawls struggles with what to call this peculiar pastime. He wants to call it a "pleasure," not "a conception of the good." But sometimes it is hard to distinguish the two. A pleasure can be a way to reject dominant values on behalf of an alternative form of life. We could see the grass-counter as a *farnienete*, part of a long tradition of do-nothings in philosophy, film, and literature, including Melville's Bartleby, Thoreau's saunterer, Baudelaire's flaneur, Chaplin's tramp, Euripides' bacchants, and the sinthomosexual of Lee Edelman's queer theory. All reject the demand that they be socially productive or reproductive in the usual capitalist, nationalist, or heterosexual ways. All "prefer not to," in Bartleby's famous phrase.

---

[1](For more in this vein, see my *Political Theory and the Displacement of Politics*, chapter 5. For a real-life example of a neuro-atypical grass-counter, consider Joseph Fiennes, whose story illustrates connections between neuro-diversity and biodiversity. https://www.newyorker.com/magazine/2020/02/17/can-farming-make-space-for-nature.)

But the best literary partner to the happy grass-counter is the hero of children's book, *The Story of Ferdinand*, who

> liked to sit just quietly and smell the flowers. He had a favorite spot out in the pasture under a cork tree . . . and he would sit in its shade all day and smell the flowers. Sometimes his mother, who was a cow, would worry about him. She was afraid he would be lonesome all by himself. "Why don't you run and play with the other little bulls and skip and butt your head?" she would say. But Ferdinand would shake his head. "I like it better here where I can sit just quietly and smell the flowers." His mother saw that he was not lonesome, and because she was an understanding mother, even though she was a cow, she let him just sit there and be happy.

Ferdinand's mother first inquires—don't you want to run and play with the other little bulls?—and then lets Ferdinand do as he pleases. But Ferdinand explains himself ("I like it better here where I can sit just quietly and smell the flowers"). It is not clear the grass-counter would explain. He might simply "prefer not to," thus challenging the good of justification that underwrites Rawls's justice as fairness.

Critics have wondered whether Ferdinand and Bartleby are gay. Is the grass-counter? It may explain why Rawls takes pains to describe the grass that grips the grass-counter as "geometric" and "well-trimmed"? Does the grass's adjacent straightness somehow forestall or quarantine the queerness of its (gay) blades? With these details, Rawls is surely trying to set up the example so it is only weird, not wild. Why?

Perhaps because the "monogamous family" is one of the "major social institutions" on which Rawlsian justice depends, along with "competitive markets and private property in the means of production" (*Theory of Justice*, 7). Moreover, Rawls casts the subjects of justice as fairness as heads of families or households. This is in order to provide the intersubjectivity and intergenerationality that liberal theorists otherwise have a hard time accounting for. But this reliance on the iconic figure of patriarchy suggests Rawls's theory depends on the heteronormative household whose (re)productive demands are themselves unjustified and nonneutral. Thus, the grass-counter is the spanner in the works of an otherwise "well-ordered society."

Besides, what if the grass-counter's refusal is contagious? Rawls seems vulnerable to it. Worried about how families introduce inequality to a social order determined to lessen it, he asks on p. 511 of *A Theory of Justice*: "Is the family to be abolished then?" Of course not, he replies. But by floating the idea, Rawls risks its circulation, again recalling Bartleby, whose "I prefer not to" soon infects the whole of the office where he works. Maybe Rawls's confinement of the grass-counter to the well-trimmed spaces and straight lines of urban geometry shows that justice as fairness depends on more mechanisms of enclosure than it justifies.

Discussion Questions

1. Is it paternalistic or illiberal to ask people who live unconventional loves to justify them? What if we think they are ill or mad? When does a Good Samaritan turn into an unwelcome source of surveillance or intervention?

2. In *The Life and Death of Latisha King*, Gayle Salamon observes that many people experience trans people's "gender expression . . . as a form of sexual aggression." The habits of heteronormativity seem to mean that some people need to be "forced" to tolerate people who are trans. Could Rawls's theory help, by defending trans people's lives as their "conception of the good"? Would that work? Why (not)?
3. Does justice have to be demoted from the "first" virtue of social institutions, which is Rawls's grounding claim for his theory, to one of several institutional virtues that might even conflict with each other, in order to develop a moral and political theory for the kind of complicated societies we live in now?

Further Reading

Honig, Bonnie. 1993. *Political theory and the displacement of politics*. Ithaca, NY: Cornell University Press.

Melville, Herman. 2004. *Bartleby, the scrivener*. Hoboken, NJ: Melville House.

Wolin, Sheldon. 1996. "The liberal/democratic divide: On Rawls' political liberalism." *Political Theory* 24, no. 1: 97–142.

· CHAPTER 8 ·

The Stag Hunt, by Jean-Jacques Rousseau

The Thought Experiment

Here's how people can acquire some rough ideas on mutual commitments and plans. It's advantageous to follow through on joint commitments, but only if it's in your present interest and if it's sensible to do so. You cannot foresee what will happen, especially not long term. Suppose there is a group of hunters who have agreed to hunt a stag together. Everyone knows that in order to do that successfully, you need to act as a team and faithfully stay on your post. Now imagine that a hare passes by one of them. This hunter could easily abandon his hunting partners and go for the sure but smaller reward. The problem is, if everyone makes the same calculation, then it's impossible to go on a collective hunt for a deer. Everyone then just ends up chasing their own, smaller reward. How do we avoid this situation?

Source of the thought experiment:

Rousseau, Jean-Jacques. (1755) 1997. "Discourse on the origin and foundations of inequality among men *or* Second discourse." In *Rousseau: The discourses and other early political writings*, edited by Victor Gourevitch, 115–229. Cambridge: Cambridge University Press.

Reflection by Christopher Bertram, University of Bristol

The Stag Hunt is an episode in a conjectural history that Rousseau imagined in his *Discourse on Inequality.* The purpose of this history is to venture an explanation, by way of a narrative, of how modern human beings like us, with our unequal institutions with their divisions of rank and fortune and our problematic psychologies could have come to be. For Rousseau, human nature is not some given fixed thing, but something that has developed along with society and has been shaped by and shapes the evolution of the social world in which we live.

In the *Second Discourse* Rousseau begins by imagining us stripped back to a presocial nature. This presocial nature is hardly distinguishable from the life of other animals and shares many of their characteristics. We have basic needs, for food, shelter, warmth, and we have the physical and mental powers sufficient to satisfy those needs and to care for ourselves but also limited to what is necessary for us to do so. We are solitary creatures, wandering through vast forests, living on what we find there, and only reproducing the species by way of chance encounters between proto-humans of different sex to one another.

We differ from the animals only in that we have a capacity for choice that frees us from being limited to one particular form of sustenance and an ability to discover new ways and techniques of making or doing things that we can remember and communicate to others. These capacities for free choice and learning mean that our lives are not limited by our natural instincts as animals are. Our psychological drives are limited to a self-interested impulse to look after our natural needs and a sense of compassion, that Rousseau calls *pitié,* that leads us to be repulsed by suffering and that impels us to alleviate that suffering, if we can do so without endangering our own self-preservation.

Gradually, thinks Rousseau, pressures of survival, the need to overcome nature, and the variation of different environments and seasons lead us to develop primitive technologies. We also start to develop more sophisticated notions about our fellow humans. We notice that they look and act somewhat similarly to ourselves and draw the conclusion that their mental processes also resemble our own and that we should take account of them in our dealings with them, leading to the possibility both of working together with them for the satisfaction of our needs and of taking preventive action in cases of conflict or competition.

This is the moment when the Stag Hunt appears in Rousseau's story when he speculates that:

> Men might imperceptibly have acquired some crude idea of mutual engagements and of the advantage of fulfilling them, but only as far as present and perceptible interest could require; for foresight was nothing to them and, far from being concerned with a distant future, they did not even give thought to the next day. If a Deer was to be caught, everyone clearly sensed that this required him faithfully to keep his post; but if a hare happened to pass within reach of one of them, he will, without a doubt, have chased after it without a scruple and, after catching his prey, have cared very little about having caused his Companions to miss theirs (163).

The structure of the interaction facing the hunters bears some resemblance to the prisoner's dilemma but with the difference that the hunter who makes the selfish choice doesn't benefit from doing so in the case where others remain cooperative. Here, the individual who chases the hare may do worse for himself compared to cooperation with others. He simply lacks the foresight and the self-control to get himself to check his impulses even when it would be better for him to do so.

The psychological changes that would enable the kind of cooperation that would reliably enable teamwork are yet to come in Rousseau's story because they depend upon human beings not simply being able to predict the actions of others, but on acquiring the capacity to see themselves as others see them. The acquisition of this capacity comes with settlement into small communities and competition for the affections and respect of others. Unfortunately, this concern for being valued in the eyes of another, which Rousseau terms *amour propre*, gives rise to a series of attitudes, including pride, jealousy, and resentment and the desire for pre-eminence, that usually leads people into violent conflict with one another.

There is an alternative though, which Rousseau explores in other works, such as his *Social Contract.* Here Rousseau explores the idea of a general will which involves people being able to see cooperation not just as instrumentally useful for themselves as individuals but from the perspective of the group as a whole, and to conceive themselves as playing a part in a more extended scheme of cooperation as a participant in a collective subject, a "we" alongside the "I." If the stag hunters had been able to see themselves as part of such a subject rather than just as individuals with personal interests, they would have been more successful in playing their separate roles in the division of labor that hunting as a group involves. Some modern research in psychology (Tomasello 2009) suggests that this capacity for switching perspective between our individual interests and that of a group we identify with is distinctively human and enables us to engage successfully in extended cooperation.

Discussion Questions

1. Can you explain why a hunter would be tempted to go after the hare, even though hunting the deer cooperatively would result in a much bigger reward?
2. Why does human cooperation require us to be able to control our impulses and to think about future consequences?
3. Can we cooperate successfully just by thinking about how our individual interests are served by us working together?

Further Reading

Neuhouser, Frederick. 2014. *Rousseau's critique of inequality: Reconstructing the argument of the second discourse.* Cambridge: Cambridge University Press.

Rousseau, Jean-Jacques. (1762) 2012. "Of the social contract." In *Of the social contract and other political writings*, edited by Christopher Bertram, translated by Quintin Hoare, 1-134. London: Penguin Books.

Skyrms, Brian. 2004. *The stag hunt and the evolution of social structure.* Cambridge: Cambridge University Press.

Tomasello, Michael. 2009. *Why we co-operate.* Cambridge, MA: MIT Press.

· CHAPTER 9 ·

The Veil, by W. E. B. Du Bois

The Thought Experiment

Do you know what it feels like to be a *problem*? I'll attempt to describe it to you. Growing up, I realized I was not like the others. I seemed to be shut out of their world by a vast veil. I could beat my friends in academic achievements, or other things, but it became clear to me they had lots of opportunities I could only dream of. Black people in the United States are subject to a predicament that W. E. B. Du Bois called "double consciousness," which he saw as a peculiar inner self. He described it as looking at yourself through the eyes of others, measuring yourself by the tape of a world that looks on you with a mixture of amusement, contempt, and pity. According to Du Bois, African Americans feel this twoness, of being both an American and a black person. The history of black people in the United States is the history of this strife, of trying not to lose those two selves, and of trying to merge this double self into a single, true self.

Source of the thought experiment:

Du Bois, W. E. B. 1897. "Strivings of the Negro people." *The Atlantic*, August issue. Reprinted at https://www.theatlantic.com/magazine/archive/1897/08/strivings-of-the-negropeople/305446/

Reflection by Liam Kofi Bright, London School of Economics

W. E. B. Du Bois uses the image of a veil to convey the difficulties of coming to a mutual understanding that white and black Americans face, even when they apparently share day-to-day activities. Black Americans—Negroes, as Du Bois would have put it—come into the world as if born covered by a veil. This veil allows them to look out on the world, but it prevents the external (white) world from ever properly seeing them. In Du Bois's own words:

> the Negro is a sort of seventh son, born with a veil, and gifted with second-sight in this American world—a world which yields him no true self-consciousness, but only lets him see himself through the revelation of the other world. (Du Bois 1903, 3)

As we shall see, this imagery of a veil, and differences in what can and can't be seen by those occupying different social positions, captures much that is core to Du Bois's vision of American life [for a different use of the veil metaphor in a thought experiment, see 6, *The original position*].

Indeed, this metaphor of the veil was important to Du Bois, who would often return to the image, sometimes using it in slightly different ways. To give just one instance, later on within *Souls* Du Bois went on to say this when describing changing religious practices among white and black Americans:

> The worlds within and without the Veil of Color are changing, and changing rapidly, but not at the same rate, not in the same way; and this must produce a peculiar wrenching of the soul, a peculiar sense of doubt and bewilderment. (De Bois 1903, 202)

Here the veil is seen not to cover a particular African American, but rather shrouds an entire world, as Du Bois suggests that black and white Americans lived in entirely different worlds and that the white cannot properly see the black. What then is this veil, separating white from black at the level of both individuals and whole social worlds?

For Du Bois, as a sociologist, one of the most important features for understanding American life at the turn of the twentieth century was understanding the peculiar relationship between the black and white occupants of the country. From the oppression of slavery, with only brief and partial respite during phases of Reconstruction, African Americans had found themselves placed under the cruel oppression of Jim Crow and often suffering in dire poverty. And compounding all this was the fact that white Americans seemed to routinely believe awful falsehoods about black people, about our intellect, propensity for crime, ability to produce art and culture, and so on. These falsehoods were often in and of themselves insulting, and tended to justify the subordinate position African Americans were placed in. Du Bois set himself the task of trying to correct these falsehoods through presenting clear and accurate sociological research on African Americans' situation.

But it didn't work! He found that his work, despite being obviously more methodologically rigorous and better grounded in actual empirical research, was routinely ignored and dismissed. Good work was being passed over in favor of work that was evidently of lower quality yet served to uphold the insulting myths he sought to debunk. The imagery of the veil, then, can be seen as relating his peculiar experience to the broader situation of African Americans. For it is intimately tied to the experience of being ignored and unable to find an audience that perceives you as you actually are.

The imbalance of power and access to resources in America, as well as the mores and customs that had built up around that base, had given rise to the following situation. African Americans, to get by in life, had to actually understand white Americans and their social world. White Americans were their employers, the political class was entirely dominated by white people, the law was set and enforced by white people, and their norms were upheld through sanctions against black people that ranged from loss of employment to brutal mob violence. An African American had to be able to understand the white American world—they could see into it, as it were.

White Americans, however, had no such interest or need to understand black Americans. The very same imbalance of power made it not urgent for them to really understand black Americans. They would never have to travel into the black quarters of town to find work as was frequently done in the opposite direction, and falsehoods about black Americans made it easier to maintain a system of oppression without the stirrings of conscience.

As such, patterns of asymmetric ignorance were formed and engraved in American life. White people felt no need to really see their black compatriots, but black Americans must be watching them and their ways carefully if only to survive. It was as if the latter watched the former through a veil permitting only one-way sight, and this was the metaphor Du Bois reached for.

Exploring the ramifications of this social epistemic situation would take up much of Du Bois's research time. What could pierce the veil? How could black Americans avoid having their self-conception become assimilated to white Americans' (often insulting) view of them, given how closely they must watch the latter? What is to be done? As difficult as these questions are, recognizing that the veil exists and prevents mutual understanding is a vital first step to posing and solving them.

Discussion Questions

1. How would you say your self-conception differs from other people's conception of you?
2. Have you ever noticed yourself internalizing a negative self-image based on dominant cultural ideas of people like you?
3. What can you do to help people better understand (what you take to be) the real you?
4. What sort of social changes would need to occur for us to better understand each other?
5. Are there any social groups you think you are similarly ignorant of?

Further Reading

Du Bois, W. E. B. 1903. *The souls of black folk. Essays and sketches.* Chicago: A.C. McClurg.

Du Bois, W. E. B. 1940. *Dusk of dawn: An essay toward an autobiography of a race concept.* New York: Harcourt, Brace & World.

Gooding-Williams, Robert. 2009. *In the shadow of Du Bois: Afro-modern political thought in America.* Cambridge, MA: Harvard University Press.

Lewis, David L. 2009. *W.E.B. Du Bois: A biography.* New York: Henry Holt.

· PART III ·

Thought Experiments in Epistemology

· CHAPTER 10 ·

Splitting the Bill at a Restaurant, by David Christensen

The Thought Experiment

Suppose you are out together with friends, and it's time to pay the bill. You will split the bill evenly, so you won't worry about who had the more expensive drinks or who had dessert. You all decide on a 20 percent tip. You can see the total clearly, as does your friend. On previous occasions, both you and your friend have worked out how much everyone owes, and you're both roughly equally good at mental arithmetic. Sometimes she makes a mistake; sometimes you do. On this particular occasion, you have calculated that you owe $43 each. However, your friend says everyone should pay $45. Should you remain as confident as you were before that you have it right, or should you now lower your confidence, perhaps recalculate?

Source of the thought experiment:

Christensen, David. 2007. "Epistemology of disagreement: The good news." *Philosophical Review* 116, no. 2: 187–217.

Reflection by David Christensen, Brown University

Most of us have at least some opinions on controversial matters. And this is not just about matters that seem purely subjective. (I think oil-cured olives are delicious; my partner disagrees.) Most of us have opinions on *matters of fact*, while knowing that others disagree. Some economists think that raising the national minimum wage in the United States would increase the well-being of lower-income Americans, while other economists think it would have the opposite effect. Some scientists think that an asteroid impact was responsible for the demise of the dinosaurs, while others blame volcanic ash. And philosophy, of course, is rife with disagreement. Do we have the sort of free will required for moral responsibility? Are minds ultimately physical? Is morality objective? Philosophers have firm beliefs on both sides of all these questions.

When two people disagree about a matter of fact, at least one of them is wrong—that much is obvious. But what's less obvious is this: might both of them be perfectly *rational* in believing as they do, even while knowing that the other person disagrees? Of course, if a five-year-old believes that Santa Claus brought her presents, that's no threat to the rationality of my continuing to believe otherwise. But what about cases where I disagree with someone who is just as well-informed, sophisticated, intelligent, and so on, as I am? In those cases, maybe I should be more worried. After all, I know that one of us has a false belief. And if the other person seems at least roughly my equal in those characteristics that are responsible for reaching accurate beliefs, can it be rational for me to be confident that *they're* the one who got this particular matter wrong?

Naturally, this is a question about which philosophers . . . well, disagree. Let's call people who seem to be my rough equals (in characteristics responsible for reaching accurate beliefs) my *epistemic peers*. *Conciliationist* philosophers think that the disagreement of epistemic peers typically requires me to reduce confidence in my beliefs. *Steadfast* philosophers think that it's often OK to maintain full confidence in one's belief, even if an epistemic peer disagrees.

Here's an argument some have given for supporting the steadfast view (Kelly 2005): Suppose Aisha and Berto are epistemic peers who disagree about some matter. They have the same evidence, and are generally equally good at drawing correct conclusions from that sort of evidence. But today Aisha has drawn her conclusion correctly, and Berto has made an error. Perhaps, steadfast philosophers have argued, the fact that Aisha's belief is *actually supported by their common evidence* means that she has good reason—grounded in that very evidence—for believing that it was Berto who made the mistake this time.

The restaurant thought experiment is designed to support conciliationism against this sort of argument. The description of the case makes clear that you and your friend are epistemic peers: you're equally good at drawing arithmetic conclusions, and you share the relevant evidence (the amount on the bill). Most people find it intuitively plausible that you should lose confidence in your answer because your friend disagrees. And this would apply even if, as it eventually turns out, $43 is actually the right answer (so you are like Aisha in the earlier example)!

The idea behind the restaurant case is that when one makes a mistake in drawing a conclusion from one's evidence, one can't necessarily tell that one has made a mistake. So if peers are, in general, equally likely to have misjudged their evidence, the one who happens to be right can't rationally be confident that she's gotten it right this time. She can't rationally say, "OK, the right answer is $43. My friend got $45, so he must be wrong today!" (Of course, in the restaurant case, you can then check to see who's right. But in other cases of disagreement, there's no calculator you can use to settle the issue.)

Many key features of the restaurant case seem to generalize to more important cases of disagreement. Two doctors recommending different treatments for the same patient may have equally good education and records of curing patients, and they may both have access to the patient's chart. If our intuition from the restaurant thought experiment carries over, perhaps each doctor should become significantly less confident in her recommendation after finding out about her colleague's disagreement. And in science, history, philosophy, and other fields, experts disagree with other experts who have equal training, and who have access to all the same evidence and arguments. Conciliationism says that in many of these cases, parties to the disagreement should be much less confident in their opinions than they would be without disagreement.

There is another way in which the issue illustrated by the restaurant case generalizes. When your friend disagrees with you in the restaurant, you get a reason to suspect you've *misjudged your evidence*. You may also get this sort of reason in other ways—for example, by learning that you're subject to the judgment-distorting effects of fatigue, or drugs, or biases (Christensen 2010). Should you reduce confidence in beliefs that may be affected in these ways? Conciliationists will naturally say yes. But some steadfast philosophers will say no: if your assessment of the evidence happens to be correct, you may rationally retain your confidence. For an interesting, though difficult, defense of this idea, see Lasonen-Aarnio (2014).

Discussion Questions

1. If one is a conciliationist, doesn't that mean that (because of the disagreement of steadfast philosophers) one cannot rationally believe one's own view? And if so, does that mean that conciliationism is false?
2. If one is a steadfast philosopher, and maintains strong opinions on many controversial philosophical issues, how should one explain the fact that one has gotten so many issues right, when one's philosophical colleagues have gotten so many things wrong? Should one consider oneself unusually smart and discerning?
3. Do you have a strong opinion on some factual issue where the people on the other side seem just as smart, careful, and familiar with the evidence as you are? Do you think it's rational for you to remain confident in your opinion?

Further Reading

Christensen, David. 2010. "Higher-order evidence." *Philosophy and Phenomenological Research* 81, no. 1: 185–215.

Kelly, Thomas. 2005. "The epistemic significance of disagreement." *Oxford Studies in Epistemology* 1: 167–196.

Lasonen-Aarnio, Maria. 2014. "Higher-order evidence and the limits of defeat." *Philosophy and Phenomenological Research* 88, no. 2: 314–345.

· CHAPTER 11 ·

Dreaming with Zhuangzi, a Butterfly

The Thought Experiment

Zhuang Zhou (also known as Zhuangzi) once dreamt he was a butterfly, flying about joyfully, as butterflies do. He didn't know at that time that he was Zhou. Suddenly he woke up. Then he was Zhou again. He did not know: was it Zhou who dreamt he was a butterfly? Or a butterfly dreaming it was Zhou? There must be a difference between Zhou and a butterfly. This is what we might call the transformation of things.

Source of the thought experiment:

Ziporyn, Brook, trans. 2020. *Zhuangzi. The complete writings* (chapter 2). Indianapolis: Hackett. A free online version of an older translation and the Chinese original are available here: https://ctext.org/zhuangzi/

Reflection by Julianne Chung, York University

Can we know that things *are* as they *appear* to be? We're often mistaken, after all. What's more, just how *stable* are features of the world, anyway? Zhuangzi tells a story in which he dreams that he's a butterfly—fluttering about joyfully, just as a butterfly would—only to wake up, startled and disoriented. He then asks: Is he *Zhuang Zhou* (Zhuangzi, or "Master Zhuang's," first name) who had dreamt that he was a butterfly, or rather a *butterfly* dreaming that he is Zhuang Zhou? A human and an insect seem distinct things if ever there were any. Yet Zhuangzi and a butterfly are nonetheless intimately connected: so much so that the vignette concludes with what strikes many as a cryptic remark, concerning the story's illustration of "the transformation of things."

I'm not sure how many of us have specifically dreamt that we were butterflies (or, perhaps, humans), but bewildering and affecting dreams like this are common [see also 36, *Al-Ghazālī's skeptical ruminations*]. I remember once dreaming that I ran into an old friend, years after his death, and being upset that he'd not gotten in touch with me for so long. Then, I awoke, only to regret my anger at first. What I would've given for my friend to actually be there, alive, even if I'd still be mad at him! But then, another thought: *Wait . . . am I right—is he really gone—or am I wrong, is it instead that he's just been away for a while? In which event, I'd be right to be annoyed: I've missed him and he really should've called!* Just like Zhuang Zhou, I wasn't sure what was so upon awakening, and my mood shifted dramatically from one moment to the next: in this case, from one of minor irritation to one of profound sadness.

Such mixed and regularly even confused thoughts and feelings can arise not only when we wish that dreams were true but also when we're happy that they (supposedly) aren't. *Phew! I'm so glad that's not actually happening,* I've thought upon waking up from a variety of particularly troublesome ones. *Or . . . is it? I . . . I don't think so; maybe I'd better check just to be sure?* From panic, to relief, to anxiety, to bemusement, such changes are often to be found in transitions between dreaming and waking, waking and dreaming.

As is frequently remarked, the story of Zhuangzi's "butterfly dream" (or, possibly, a butterfly's "Zhuangzi dream") can be read as suggesting (as numerous other reflections on dreams are) that there's very little, if anything, that we can know or be certain about. In contrast with many, however, Zhuangzi—similar to others who are now classified as *Daoist* philosophers—implies that we might be better off embracing, rather than resisting, such a thought. This story may have seemed silly at first, but butterflies are known for *fluttering* from one thing to another: for flitting back and forth, from experience to experience, in a sense *effortlessly*. Instead of struggling against the world in order to impose their will upon it, they work with what we might (perhaps metaphorically) call "the will of the world" to which they belong. In this way, they can live *spontaneously*, *flexibly*, and even *creatively* and *playfully*, free of the sorts of self-imposed restrictions that human beings are prone to place on themselves, others, and other things in the world more generally. The world is an ever-changing place, continually in flux, and we potentially have much to learn from how butterflies navigate it (Wu 1990).

Thus, Zhuangzi can be interpreted as challenging us to think and act differently, by opening us up to fresh points of view and encouraging us to consider unusual possibilities (in the thought experiment at hand, that one could be *dreaming of* a butterfly, or *the dream of* a butterfly). This in turn might allow us to expand our ways of thinking and acting beyond the assorted limited perspectives that we have adopted, often by chance, and that frequently dominate and constrain us without our realizing it—and hence, to spontaneously and productively transform ourselves along with the world of which we are a part.

As Michael Puett explains,

> [B]y offering [the butterfly] story, Zhuangzi proposes an as-if question: What would it be like if I looked at the world as if I were a butterfly dreaming I am a human being? For that moment, we suspend reality and enter an alternate universe where we expand our ability to imagine all sorts of as-if possibilities in the broadest sense. The entire cosmos is open to us; a world in which everything is flowing into everything else. None of this is prescriptive. Zhuangzi doesn't tell us what we should do after we gain this different perspective; what comes from that is up to us. The key is the break of perspective itself. (Puett and Gross-Loh 2016, 152)

In other words, one might think that, in telling this story, Zhuangzi doesn't issue a *demand* as much as he issues an *invitation*: an invitation to think and act differently than we have before, concerning even possibilities that we hadn't yet been able to imagine—much less contemplate—previously.

Discussion Questions

1. Have you ever had a dream that you felt sure—at least, at the time—was real? Could you even be dreaming now, or might indeed all of human life be (or at least be akin to) a dream? What broader significance could your answers to these questions have, regarding, for example, what we can know, or how we should live?
2. Can you think of a situation from your own life in which someone else benefited, or could've benefited, from stepping back and saying: "Maybe I'm thinking about things the wrong way," or "Maybe I'm the one who's got the (supposed) facts wrong?" Now, can you think of a situation in which you benefited, or would've benefited, from doing this?
3. Can you think of an event (either in your life or the life of someone else, real or fictional) that significantly changed your or someone else's perspective on—that is, the way that you or that person thought about—someone or something (actual or possible)? What

happened, and what was it like? What can we learn about how we can work to become more spontaneous, flexible, or even creative or playful, with respect to shifting perspectives from reflecting on this case?

4. Is there such a thing as being too open-minded or being too open to still other kinds of changes? If so, why? If not, why not? (You might find it interesting to try to argue for, and against, *both* of these possibilities.)

Further Reading

D'Ambrosio, Paul, and Hans-Georg Moeller. 2018. "Authority without authenticity: The *Zhuangzi*'s genuine pretending as socio-political strategy." *Religions* 9, no. 398: 1–11.

Mattice, Sarah. 2014. *Metaphor and metaphilosophy: Philosophy as combat, play, and aesthetic experience*. Lanham, MD: Lexington Books.

Moeller, Hans-Georg. 2005. *Daoism explained: From the dream of the butterfly to the fishnet allegory*. Chicago: Open Court.

Puett, Michael, and Christine Gross-Loh. 2016. *The path*. New York: Simon & Schuster.

Wu, Kuang-ming. 1990. *The butterfly as companion: Meditations on the first three chapters of the Chuang-Tzu*. New York: SUNY Press.

· CHAPTER 12 ·

Happiness for a Fish, by Zhuangzi

The Thought Experiment

Zhuangzi and Huizi were strolling on the bridge over the River Hao.

Zhuangzi said, "These minnows are out and playing so freely and easily, that is the happiness of fish!"

Huizi said, "You, sir, are not a fish. How would you know what makes fish happy?" Zhuangzi replied, "You, sir, are not me. How would you know that I do not know what makes fish happy?"

Huizi conceded, "True, I'm not you. Though I don't pretend to know you fully, you certainly are not a fish. So, I can definitely say that you don't know what makes fish happy."

Zhuangzi replied, "Shall we stick to your original question? You asked me 'How do you know what makes fish happy?,' and yet, you knew that I knew it, and still you asked me. I knew it from up above the Hao."

Source of the thought experiment:

Ziropyn, Brook, trans. *Zhuangzi*, chapter 17. Indianapolis: Hackett. A free online version of an older translation and the Chinese original are available here: https://ctext.org/zhuangzi/

Reflection by Ian James Kidd, University of Nottingham

Zhuangzi and Huizi were very close friends, and like many good friends, they disagreed with one another about all sorts of things. They often light-heartedly debated very high-minded philosophical issues. Indeed, after Huizi's death, Zhuangzi sadly remarked that there was "no longer anyone I can really talk to." What he lost was an intellectual companion, a very special sort of friendship which offered intimate philosophical company bound up with genuine affection.

Notice three features of the "happy fish" passage. First, the setting is totally ordinary—two friends enjoying a walk, strolling along a river, quiet and mellow. None of the formality of a seminar room, no public audience to impress, no clashing of egos. Just a pair of friends walking and talking at ease. Second, their attention is caught by the fishes in the river. This reflects an attractive feature of the loose group of figures—Daoists—with whom Zhuangzi is grouped. They enjoyed nature and animals, for sure, but also thought they offered deep philosophical lessons. Notice the fish as admired for their "free and easy" behavior, those being features of the good life for human beings who overcome the oppressive demands and pressures of the artificial human world.

A third feature is the use of very *personal* ways the two philosophers interact. There is teasing and provocation—they're obviously enjoying the philosophical banter. Zhuangzi provokes Huizi with a bold claim about knowing what happiness is for fish. Huizi takes the bait, while teasing his friend—while Zhuangzi can't *know* what happiness means for fish, Huizi *definitely* knows that his friend is not a fish! Such features might make the story seem just a bit of fun.

Provocation, teasing, and two friends enjoying each other's company. I see the happy fish story as a masterclass in how serious thinking can be done *lightly*. But there's a deeper set of issues at work, too.

One popular reading is that the happy fish story is about *relativism*. Daoists usually challenged claims to objective knowledge or certainty. Judgments and experiences always reflect certain presuppositions, needs, and values. (What's attractive and hospitable to a fish or frog won't be so for a human being, which is one reason we don't live in ponds and rivers). Sometimes, this is called *perspectivism*. Zhuangzi claims knowledge of the perspective of fish, which Huizi sees as quite radical. Let's construct some of the philosophical back and forth:

1. Zhuangzi knows what happiness is for fish.

Huizi questions whether Zhuangzi knows what happiness is for fish, because he thinks that you have to be a fish—to inhabit its perspective on the world—to know what happiness means for them.

2. Huizi knows that Zhuangzi is not a fish.

Zhuangzi accepts this, of course! But then turns the point back. How does Huizi *know* that Zhuangzi doesn't know what happiness means for fish? After all, even though they are both humans, Huizi doesn't share his *friend's* perspective on the world, and on those fish in the River Hao.

3. Huizi knows all along that Zhuangzi knows what happiness is for fish, since his initial question was "How do you know that"—or, better, "How did you come to get that knowledge?"

We can puzzle over all of these claims. Is it true, for instance, that one must *be* a fish to gain knowledge of what makes fish happy? Zhuangzi seems unsure—when watching the minnows swimming about, "playing so freely and easily," perhaps he recognizes them as continuous with other creatures, humans included. Fish, dogs, young babies, and even old friends all enjoy playfulness, freedom, and ease of movement.

Sitting on that bridge, looking at the fish, perhaps what Zhuangzi knew came not from sophisticated theorizing and chains of argument. His knowledge comes from attentiveness, exercises of the imagination, and a sense of empathy for other creatures. Maybe he notices commonalities across different species, appreciating that creatures naturally take pleasure in using their bodies—swimming, flying, galloping, running. Maybe he sadly remembers the ways that animals always suffer when their movements are limited—when they're cruelly caged, penned, chained. Such knowledge doesn't require Zhuangzi to actually be a fish or to possess any magical, Dr. Doolittle-style abilities. It requires our virtues, not our powers of reason.

Perhaps Zhuangzi called attention to the fish to gently teach his friend an important lesson—that when it comes to understanding other creatures, our powers of reason are of only limited value. Sometimes we need to attend imaginatively and sensitively to the other creatures following their own ways of life. Maybe that's what was clear from up above that bridge that afternoon over the River Hao.

Discussion Questions

1. What point do you think Zhuangzi was trying to make when he was commenting on the happiness of fish?
2. Some skeptics argue that we can't *know* whether animals experience happiness, joy, boredom, pleasure, or sadness. This sort of skepticism is rejected by many people—vets, animal trainers, pet owners—who are closely engaged with animals. Can the happy fish story help us find ways to respond to these skeptics?
3. Friendship gives us special knowledge about the inner feelings, moods, and concerns of other humans. Is this true of our friendships with animals, too?

Further Reading

Cantor, Lea. 2020. "Zhuangzi on 'happy fish' and the limits of human knowledge." *British Journal for the History of Philosophy* 28, no. 2: 216–230.

Hansen, Chad. 2003. "The relatively happy fish." *Asian Philosophy* 13, no. 2–3: 145–164.

Thompson, Kirill O. 2016. "Philosophical reflections on the 'fish happiness' anecdote." *Philosophy East and West* 66, no. 4: 1307–1318.

· CHAPTER 13 ·

The Creationist Teacher, by Jennifer Lackey

The Thought Experiment

Can we acquire knowledge from someone who doesn't have it herself? Stella is a fourth-grade teacher who teaches her class that *Homo sapiens* evolved from *Homo erectus*, which is a generally accepted scientific view in evolutionary biology. In spite of this, Stella does not believe, and so doesn't know, that human evolution occurred. She is a deeply devout fundamentalist Christian who believes in Young Earth Creationism: she thinks that the world only came into existence six thousand years ago, and that all species (including humans) were created in their present form by God. Do Stella's students come to know that *Homo sapiens* evolved from *Homo erectus* on the basis of Stella's teaching, in spite of her not knowing that this is the case?

Source of the thought experiment:

Lackey, Jennifer. 1999. "Testimonial knowledge and transmission." *The Philosophical Quarterly* 49: 471–490.

Reflection by Jennifer Lackey, Northwestern University

Our dependence on testimony is as deep as it is ubiquitous. We rely on the reports of others for our beliefs about the food we eat, the medicine we ingest, the products we buy, the geography of the world, discoveries in science, historical information, and many other areas that play crucial roles in both our practical and our intellectual lives. Even many of our most important beliefs about ourselves were learned at an earlier time from our parents and caretakers, such as the date of our birth, the identity of our parents, our ethnic backgrounds, and so on. Were we to refrain from accepting the testimony of others, our lives would be impoverished in startling and debilitating ways.

The standard view understands the process of acquiring testimonial knowledge as being much like a bucket brigade: in order to get a full bucket of water from me, I must have a full bucket of water to pass to you. Similarly, in order for you to acquire knowledge via my testimony, I must have the knowledge in question. In both cases, I cannot give to you what I don't have myself. In this way, testimony and memory are said to be alike as sources of knowledge, and different from other sources such as perception and reason. Perception and reason are capable of generating new knowledge in their own right: I can come to have new knowledge that there is a fox in my backyard by seeing it, or that 2 + 2 = 4 by reasoning to this conclusion. But testimony and memory are denied this capacity: memory is said to only *preserve* knowledge from one time to another, and testimony is thought to merely *transmit* knowledge from speaker to hearer. For instance, just as I cannot now know something on the basis of memory unless I knew it at an earlier time from a source other than memory, the thought here is that I cannot know something on the basis of your testimony unless you know it.

The case of the creationist teacher challenges this standard view of testimony. A necessary condition on knowledge is belief: I cannot know that today is Friday unless I at least believe that it is Friday. But now suppose, as the case asks us to, that a devout creationist who does not believe in the truth of evolutionary theory nonetheless researches the topic extensively. She does so because she fully recognizes that there is an overwhelming amount of scientific evidence in favor of evolutionary theory, and she readily admits that she is not basing her own commitment to creationism on evidence but, rather, on the personal faith that she has in an all-powerful creator. Given this, she doesn't think that religion is something that she should impose on those around her, and this is especially true with respect to her students. On the basis of her research, she constructs extremely reliable lecture notes and uses them to teach science to her elementary school students. When she testifies in the classroom that *Homo sapiens* evolved from *Homo erectus*, the teacher is able to impart knowledge to her students that she fails to possess herself. In particular, the teacher doesn't know that *Homo sapiens* evolved from *Homo erectus* because she doesn't believe this; her creationist commitments conflict with the truth of this claim. At the same time, she is a reliable testifier of this information because she did extensive research on the topic and drafted notes on this basis.

What this shows is that contrary to the standard view, testimony does not merely transmit knowledge from one person to another since the creationist teacher is able to generate new knowledge in her students about *Homo sapiens* evolving from *Homo erectus*, despite not having it herself.

Instead of requiring that the speaker knows what she testifies to, my view focuses on the reliability of the testifier. Obviously, one way to be a reliable testifier is to have the knowledge in question and to be a sincere testifier: if I know that whales are mammals, and I sincerely report this to you, I'm clearly a reliable source of information. However, as we've seen with the creationist teacher, beliefs and reports can crucially come apart. This is clear when I am trying to lead you astray, but this can also happen when I recognize that my own beliefs are not matching up with the best available evidence. Acquiring testimonial knowledge requires that the *statements* of speakers be reliably connected with the truth, not necessarily their mental states. The upshot of this is that we learn from one another's words, not from their personal beliefs.

Discussion Questions

1. Is the creationist teacher lying to her students? Why or why not?
2. Is the creationist teacher functioning merely as a sort of parrot with respect to her testimony about evolutionary theory? Why or why not?
3. Should the creationist teacher's students trust her testimony? Why or why not?

Further Reading

Carter, J. Adam, and Philip J. Nickel. 2014. "On testimony and transmission." *Episteme* 11: 145–155.

Greco, John. 2020. "The transmission of knowledge and garbage." *Synthese* 197: 2867–2878

Peet, Andrew. 2018. "Testimonial knowledge without knowledge of what is said." *Pacific Philosophical Quarterly* 99: 65–81.

· CHAPTER 14 ·

Fake Barn Country, by Carl Ginet, featured in Alvin Goldman

The Thought Experiment

Henry and his son live in the city. One day, Henry decides it would be nice to drive around in the nearby countryside. For the boy's edification, he points out several features in the landscape: "That's a silo, that's a cow, that's a tractor, ..." He spots a red barn, such as you often see on American farms. Henry can see the barn clearly and has no doubt that it is in fact a barn when he says, "That's a barn." Normally, we would think that Henry knows that the object he's pointing out to his son is in fact a barn. Unbeknownst to Henry, the area he's driving in was turned into a filmset. All the barn facades are fake; they are made out of cardboard, scaffolding, and papier mâché. However, Henry just so happens to have pointed out the *one* real barn in the vicinity. He was just lucky he happened to pick out the one barn that wasn't a facsimile. He could just have picked out any other, and it would have been a fake. Given that information, would you still say that Henry knows the object he's pointing at is a barn?

Source of the thought experiment:

Goldman, Alvin l. 1976. "Discrimination and perceptual knowledge." *The Journal of Philosophy* 73, no. 20: 771–791.

Reflection by Clayton Littlejohn, Australian Catholic University

We learn early (and often the hard way) that belief isn't the same thing as knowledge. They might feel the same from the inside, but no matter how firmly convinced we are that, say, our side will win or our friends will flourish, reality needn't match our expectations. Once we recognize that what we know is so and what we believe needn't be, we might wonder what distinguishes knowledge from mere opinion.

Truth is a start, but only a start. If we were to convince two gullible relatives into believing, respectively, that there is an afterlife and that there is not an afterlife, we know that one of our relatives now has a true belief about the afterlife. We do not, however, have a relative who knows if we'll see our pets again after we die. There must be more to knowledge than mere true belief. People "in the know" have a kind of rational authority. Here's a way to cash this out. When someone knows, they aren't just right; they have good reasons to believe.

If we think of knowledge as involving a belief that is both true and that is held for good reasons, we seem to accommodate the idea that when we try to acquire knowledge we have to try to form an accurate belief about some matter and that knowledge differs from beliefs that just happen to be true in that it has a kind of rational authority that a lucky guess might lack. It was largely thanks to Gettier's (1963) paper that most contemporary philosophers realized that knowing differs from being justified in believing something true. One problem with this JTB account (i.e., knowledge as justified true belief) might be put like this. When you know, it's not an accident that you have the right answer. When you believe something that is true even if you have a justification to believe this, it still might be an accident that you have the right answer.

To see why, let's think about what it takes for someone to be justified in believing something. This might be nothing more, say, than relying on a testimonial source known to be reliable. Let's imagine that *The Guardian* reports that Arsenal lost a match to Manchester City. It seems that you should be justified in believing this given what you know about the reliability of reports in the sports section. When a team loses and another team wins, the winning team will move up three points in the league table and the losing team will remain where they are. So you deduce that Manchester City will move ahead three points in the table. Knowing what you now know about football league tables, you surely would be justified in believing that Manchester City moves up three points if you are justified in believing that they just defeated Arsenal. As it happens, however, *The Guardian* made a mistake that they might only make once every few decades. It was Manchester *United* that beat Arsenal, not Manchester City. (They are different teams from the same city.) You have justification to believe that Manchester City has just earned three points, but this is based on the mistaken belief that they earned this by beating Arsenal. If it just happens to be the case that Manchester City also won their match (e.g., against Chelsea), it doesn't seem that your belief that they have earned three points is knowledge. It seems to be true as a matter of luck.

One lesson epistemologists take from such cases is that when we know, it cannot be an accident that we're right. Another is that being justified or having good reasons does not preclude an accidental connection between belief and fact. In the example sketched earlier, it seems that there was a surprising lack of causal connection between events on football pitches and reports in newspapers. Under normal conditions, we assume that there is a causal connection between the match that just finished and the testimonial reports we receive, but that broke down in our example and it seems to help explain why we think that a salient true belief (i.e., that Manchester City just earned three points) fails to constitute knowledge.

If we take this idea and run with it, we might say that you know that something is true when the fact that something is true is causally connected to your belief in a suitable way. In the normal case, *The Guardian* only says that a team won or lost because some reliable people were there to see for themselves, who, in turn, sent through the information through the normal channels until it was printed on the page in your hands. If we think about ordinary perceptual cases, we might say that in the ordinary case of visual knowledge, you know that this building is a barn because this belief is causally explained by various visual cues (e.g., the building's shape, size, coloration, etc.). The fake barn case causes trouble for this simple causal view. In the normal case (i.e., the case where there are no nearby convincing fakes), you can know by sight that something is a barn (or a bank, a courthouse, a grocery store, etc.). In the abnormal case (i.e., the case where there are lots of nearby convincing fakes), you cannot know by sight that something is a barn. Since your belief seems to be caused by a real barn and not a fake, it is hard to see how to explain this difference in what can be known in terms of a difference in causal connections between you and your environment.

Discussion Questions

1. Philosophers often disagree about the fake barn cases. There is some disagreement about whether the relevant beliefs constitute knowledge and about whether the relevant beliefs are justified. What do you think about the case? If you think that this is a case of knowledge, are there ways of modifying the example to make it more persuasive?

2. It is important to the example that the protagonist sees a barn and knows generally what barns look like. What does the case teach us about the connection between knowledge and perception? Can the protagonist see that the building is a barn just by looking? Do things change if they were shown a large array of similar looking structures where only one building in that group is a real barn and the rest are fakes?
3. If you think that the protagonist does not know that the building is a barn, what is missing? What distinguishes this case from cases where we can know what something is by looking at it?

References

Gettier, Edmund L. 1963. "Is justified true belief knowledge?" *Analysis* 23, no. 6: 121–123.

Goldman, Alvin. 1976. "Discrimination and perceptual knowledge." *Journal of Philosophy* 73: 771–791.

Matilal, B. K. 1986. *Perception: An essay on classical Indian theories of knowledge*. Oxford: Oxford University Press.

Nagel, Jennifer. 2014. *Knowledge: A very short introduction*. Oxford: Oxford University Press.

· CHAPTER 15 ·

Neurath's Boat, by Otto Neurath

The Thought Experiment

Imagine a boat that is on the open sea, forever traveling. We, as people who try to acquire knowledge (through science and other means), are like sailors who can never dock in a harbor to repair the boat, or start afresh. Rather, we have to make gradual improvements, replacing one rotten beam at a time, slowly changing our boat (our beliefs) over time.

Source of the thought experiment:

Neurath first mentions the boat in this article: Neurath, Otto. (1921) 1973. "Anti-Spengler." In *Empiricism and sociology*, edited by Marie Neurath and Robert S. Cohen, 158–213. Dordrecht: D. Reidel. However, his 1932 paper in *Erkenntnis* is the one cited by Quine and hence the most commonly referred to (see Further Reading, first entry for an English translation of that paper).

Reflection by Zoe Drayson, University of California, Davis

Each piece of knowledge we have of the world seems to depend on further pieces of knowledge. Our understanding of planetary orbits, for example, is partly justified by our understanding of gravity, and our understanding of gravity is in turn justified by our understanding of mass and force. Many philosophers have assumed that this process bottoms-out when we reach a basic level of knowledge that doesn't require further justification: a set of foundational claims that are indubitably and unquestionably true. On Moritz Schlick's view, for example, scientific knowledge is like a pyramid in which each piece of the structure rests on the level below, except for the lowest level which needs no support of its own. Parts of the pyramid of knowledge might have to be rebuilt in light of new discoveries, but always on the same solid and unquestionable foundations. For Schlick ([1934] 1979), the foundations of the pyramid are basic claims about our sensory observation from which all other knowledge can be derived.

Schlick's contemporary, Otto Neurath, rejected the "pyramid" view of scientific knowledge. Neurath instead compared our scientific knowledge to a raft made up of many planks, each of which contributes to our total knowledge in a similar way. Neurath suggested that there are no indubitable or unquestionable truths: all of our scientific claims are revisable, just as any plank is replaceable without threatening the structure of the raft. Importantly, Neurath thinks that we don't have the luxury of rebuilding our raft from scratch on dry land, in the way that we might rebuild a pyramid from its foundations. He suggests that "we are like sailors who have to rebuild their ship on the open sea, without ever being able to dismantle it in dry-dock and reconstruct it from its best components" ([1932] 1983, 92).

Neurath's boat features in discussions of several different philosophical ideas. One of these is the problem of justification: if each belief is justified by other beliefs, how can we avoid an infinite regress? There are two traditional ways to address this problem: foundationalism and coherentism. Foundationalists avoid the regress by positing a basic level of beliefs that require no further justification themselves, while coherentists argue that each belief can be justified by its fit within a larger system of beliefs. Foundationalism can be captured by the metaphor of Schlick's pyramid, while coherentism is often characterized in terms of Neurath's boat.

Neurath's boat, and the associated coherentist approach to justification, feature prominently in the ethics literature on reflective equilibrium: the state we achieve when there is no conflict among our moral beliefs. Many ethicists propose that we should adjust our individual moral judgments in light of our moral theories, and adjust our moral theories against our individual moral judgements, until we reach a stable and coherent set of moral beliefs.

The metaphor of Neurath's boat can also be used to make a claim about the relationship between science and philosophy. Many foundationalist philosophers, including Descartes, have proposed that all of our scientific knowledge ultimately rests on indubitable truths that we can know by philosophical reflection, prior to any empirical observation of the world. On this view, philosophy uses nonempirical methods to arrive at necessary truths, whereas science uses empirical methods to arrive at contingent truths about the world. This distinction between science and philosophy is called into question by philosophers like Willard van Orman Quine, who propose a "naturalistic" view of philosophy as continuous with science. Quine (1960) suggests that philosophers, like scientists, are in the position of the sailors aboard Neurath's boat: just as Neurath's sailors can't rebuild their boat on dry land, so philosophers don't have a privileged independent position from which to evaluate scientific methodology and knowledge. On Quine's view, there is no difference between the kinds of knowledge sought by scientists and by philosophers, and philosophy has no distinctive nonempirical methodology.

Discussion Questions

1. Are all of our beliefs about the world justified by other beliefs? How would this lead to an infinite regress? Foundationalism and coherentism are two strategies for avoiding infinite regress. Can you think of any others?
2. How do you understand the difference between philosophy and science? Descartes proposed that reflecting on our own thoughts can provide us with truths that are more certain than any of our empirical knowledge. Do you agree?

Further Reading

Neurath, Otto. (1932) 1983. "Protocol statements." Reprinted in *Philosophical Papers 1913–1946*, edited and translated by Robert S. Cohen and Marie Neurath, 91–99. Dordrecht: Reidel.

Quine, Willard Van Orman. 1960. *Word and object.* Cambridge, MA: MIT Press.

Schlick, Moritz. (1934) 1979. "On the foundation of knowledge." Reprinted in *Philosophical papers Vol. II (1925–1936)*, edited by Henk. L. Mulder and Barbara van de Velde-Schlick, translated by Peter Heath, 370–387. Dordrecht: Reidel.

Sosa, Ernest. 1980. "The raft and the pyramid: Coherence versus foundations in the theory of knowledge." *Midwest Studies in Philosophy* 5, no. 1: 3–26.

· PART IV ·

Thought Experiments in Philosophy of Mind

· CHAPTER 16 ·

The Extended Mind, by Andy Clark and David Chalmers

The Thought Experiment

Otto enjoys art. He wishes to visit the Museum of Modern Art (MoMA). Otto has mild Alzheimer's. As his biological memory began to decline, Otto has increasingly relied on a notebook that he always carries with him. In the notebook, he writes down addresses, facts about his family, friends, wider environment, important dates, and so on, so that the notebook has come to play a role that's importantly similar to his biological memory. To get to the museum, Otto consults his notebook and reads that it is on 53rd Street. Inga also wants to visit MoMA, but unlike Otto, she does not have Alzheimer's. She recalls, using her brain, that MoMA is on 53rd Street. Now we would normally say that Inga *already knew*, even before she consulted her biological memory, where the museum was situated. But what about Otto? Though the retrieved fact "MoMA is on 53rd Street" was not stored in his brain, but in his notebook, the information in the notebook was poised to guide his behavior in a way that is relevantly similar to that of Inga's biological memory. Thus, we should also say that even prior to looking at his notebook, Otto knew that MoMA was on 53rd Street. Otto's notebook is part of his memory. The machinery of Otto's mind is not all inside his head.

Source of the thought experiment:

Clark, Andy, and David J. Chalmers. 1998. "The extended mind." *Analysis* 58, no. 1, 7–19.

Reflection by Andy Clark, University of Sussex, and David Chalmers, New York University

We developed the Inga/Otto thought experiment to argue for the extended mind thesis: the mind can extend outside the head to include tools in the environment. When these external tools play the same sort of role as the brain, they are equally part of the mind. Otto's notebook is playing the same role as Inga's biological memory, so it is part of his mind.

When we wrote "The Extended Mind" in the 1990s, mobile computing technology was not nearly as developed as it is today. Today, the obvious illustration would be a smartphone. Hardly anyone uses biological memory to remember phone numbers anymore. We all use smartphones instead. The smartphone is playing the same role that our biological memory used to play. According to the extended mind thesis, our smartphones have become part of our minds.

Of course, there are many differences between the way memory works in Inga and Otto. But there are also differences in the ways biological memory works in different species. Memory in crows is quite different from memory in humans. But this does not mean that crows cannot remember. To allow that would be to base our concepts of mind too closely on the human in-head case, perhaps thereby ruling out much of the in-the-head processing of intelligent Martians!

One common response to the thought experiment is to say that Otto's notebook cannot be part of his mind because it is outside his head, or perhaps because it is not biological. We think that this is a sort of "skin and skull chauvinism" (in the first case) or biological chauvinism (in the second). There is nothing magical about the boundary of the skull that makes it a privileged boundary for the mind, and there is nothing magical about biology as a substrate for the mind.

Another common objection is that all Otto knows in advance of the moment of retrieval is that the right information is stored in his notebook. By contrast, Inga, even before accessing biomemory, counts as having a memory-based belief (sometimes called a standing belief) that the museum is on 53rd Street. We think this is too restrictive, because the whole point of ascribing knowledge and beliefs is to get a grip on the patterns that matter in our own and other people's behaviors. In terms of my getting a grip on the patterns that matter, Otto and Inga are in much the same boat—they each reliably navigate to the same place and for the same underlying reason.

With that in mind, our aim was to argue for parity of treatment. So if you insist that all that Otto believed prior to accessing the notebook was that the address was stored in the notebook, then you should also say that all that Inga believed *before* retrieving the address was that the information was stored in her memory. We don't usually say this about Inga, of course. Some philosophers have suggested that we should shrink the notion of what we believe to include only what we believe consciously in the here and now. But this shrinks the mind to a very small set of contents indeed. However you slice it, we argued that it is unprincipled to count Inga's memory as part of the mind, while denying that status to Otto's notebook.

You might also be concerned that Otto could lose or mislay his notebook. But biological memory, too, is fragile, as the case of Otto himself suggests! What's more, Inga, after one martini too many at lunchtime, might be temporarily unable to retrieve MoMA's address. So what counts is not guaranteed success but robust and reliable success, most of the time. Once again, rough parity of behavior-guiding role is the key.

One of the strongest responses to our argument turns on the roles of perception and action. It looks like Otto has to perceive and act upon the notebook to find the information, whereas Inga simply retrieves it without "looping out" through perception and action. Someone could suggest that it is perception and action, not skin and skull, that serve as the boundary of the mental. In response, we have argued that what looks like perception from one perspective can look like memory from another, and that even perception and action need not be a boundary for the mental. In fact, part of the mental processes can extend outside this boundary, too.

As technology develops, it is likely that our minds will keep extending further. Already it is arguable that much of our minds reside on the servers for Google and other corporations. With augmented reality technology, smart glasses may enable us to recognize faces far better than we did before. Brain–computer interfaces may incorporate our devices ever more closely into our minds. In this way we will continue to see that minds like ours are not brain-bound after all.

Discussion Questions

1. Suppose you come to rely upon another person—a long-term partner, for example—to recall certain kinds of information. Does that make some aspects of their brain activity count as part of the machinery of your beliefs?

2. What about conscious experiences such as a feeling of anger or a thought about the future? Can the machinery of conscious experience extend beyond skin and skull?
3. Aren't brains special? If minds are extended, how can we best accommodate the (currently) unique role that brains seem to play in supporting our mental life?

Further Reading

Chalmers, David. 2020. "Extended cognition and extended consciousness." In *Andy Clark and his critics*, edited by Matteo Colombo, Elizabeth Irvine, and Mog Stapleton, 9–20. Oxford: Oxford University Press.

Clark, Andy. 2010. "Out of our brains." *New York Times Opinionator*, December 12, 2010. Appears with 191 comments: https://opinionator.blogs.nytimes.com/2010/12/12/out-of-our-brains/. For Clark's replies, see https://opinionator.blogs.nytimes.com/2010/12/14/extended-mind-redux-a-response/

Gertler, Brie. 2020. "Overextending the mind." In *Philosophy of mind: Classical and contemporary readings*, 2nd ed., edited by David J. Chalmers, 192–206. Oxford: Oxford University Press.

· CHAPTER 17 ·

The Missing Shade of Blue, by David Hume

The Thought Experiment

A man has seen all colors, except one particular shade of blue. But he has seen all the other shades of blue, and if he were to arrange them in his mind, it would become clear that there's a gap. Would he be able to fill in this shade using his own imagination? Hume says that he would be able to do so.

Source of the thought experiment:

Hume, David. (1739-1740) 2000. *A treatise of human nature.* Edited by David Fate Norton and Mary J. Norton. Oxford: Oxford University Press. Book I, part I, section 1, paragraph 10. He repeats it again in Hume, David (1748) 1999. *An enquiry concerning human understanding.* Edited by Tom L. Beauchamp. New York: Oxford University Press. Section 2, paragraph 8. The *Enquiry* was originally published by Andrew Millar of the Strand, London, under the title *Philosophical essays concerning human understanding* in 1748. Hume changed the title in the 1758 edition.

Reflection by Liz Goodnick, Metropolitan State University of Denver

Do you think you could know what pineapple tastes like without trying it? David Hume said no. He was an empiricist, who thought that all of our knowledge—in fact, every single idea we have—must be ultimately grounded in sensory experiences.

Hume believed that humans are trapped behind a "veil of perception." When you look at a tree, you're only indirectly aware of the tree itself, and directly aware of a mental image of a tree produced by your mind. While some people use the term "perception" to refer to images, smells, sounds, and other sensory phenomena, Hume used the term to describe anything that's present to the mind—sensory phenomena but also feelings, emotions, thoughts, and so on.

He divided perceptions into two categories: ideas and impressions, which only differ in their vivacity. Vivacity captures the difference between feeling pain (vivid) versus remembering pain (less vivid). Impressions are the more vivid perceptions we experience when we use our senses or have feelings or desires, such as the sound of a trumpet or the feeling of anger. Ideas are the less vivid perceptions we experience when we reflect on or remember any of our impressions, such as the memory of the feeling of the sun on your face or imagining your favorite color.

Ideas can be either simple or complex. Simple ideas are those that "admit of no distinction or separation." Complex ideas "may be distinguished into parts" and are composed of simple ideas. All of our experiences are complex—when you examine an apple, you see the shape and color, feel the smoothness of the skin, smell the delicious aroma. However, when you reflect on that experience, you can separate all the components—roundness, redness, smoothness, and the smell—into distinct simple ideas in your mind, even if they can't be separated in reality.

Hume claimed that every simple idea is an exact copy of an impression: "all our simple ideas in their first appearance are deriv'd from simple impressions, which are correspondent to them, and which they exactly represent" (T 1.1.1.7; SBN 4). Don Garrett dubbed this thesis the Copy Principle (CP) (Garrett 1997). CP entails that all ideas must ultimately be based on experience. If you have never seen a golden mountain, you couldn't think of one without first having impressions of the simple ideas that make it up (by, for example, seeing a mountain and a golden ring). CP also explains why Hume thought that to have an idea of what pineapple tastes like, you would need to have tasted it before.

Hume's main argument for CP is based on his claim that if someone cannot use one of their senses, then they do not have ideas that come from that sense since they are missing the appropriate impressions: someone who was born blind wouldn't have any color ideas. He uses CP to argue that if there are no impressions which could produce an idea, then that idea should stop being used to avoid confusion. Some of the ideas used by other philosophers that Hume attacks in this way include necessary connection, substance and attribute, and personal identity.

Hume presented the Missing Shade of Blue (MSB) as a counterexample to the CP—the thought experiment suggests that, in certain circumstances, you could have a simple idea without first having the corresponding impression. He dismisses the example as something "so particular and singular" that we shouldn't pay it any attention. But readers of Hume have noted that there are more cases—missing tones in a series of musical notes or missing temperatures in a series of heated water—that also seem to violate the CP.

Some Hume scholars deny that MSB is really meant as a counterexample to CP. They claim that shades of colors are complex, not simple ideas, or argue that we can acquire the idea of the MSB similarly to how we invent fictional ideas like golden mountains. While this interpretation saves CP, it is odd that Hume repeats the counterexample in a later work and never explains how someone could acquire the idea of the MSB without violating CP.

Others think that the MSP is a merely possible counterexample—not an actual one—revealing not that CP is actually false, but only that it could have been false. And this is no problem, since Hume seeks to study human nature through scientific means and many scientific truths are contingently true without being necessarily true. For example, while it is true that DNA encodes our genes, other encodings are possible. However, Hume seems to think that the counterexample is actual, not merely possible.

Finally, some, including myself, think that Hume is right to dismiss the counterexample because the cases where he applies CP are not affected. The MSB shows that we can have ideas without corresponding impressions. However, we can only do this in unusual scenarios, such as when we are considering qualities that come in gradients (like colors or temperatures). This reading fits with what Hume says in the text, allows him to use CP to dismiss the use of ideas like substance or personal identity, and also fits in with Hume's empiricism and methodology.

Discussion Questions

1. Some philosophers think that humans can have ideas that are not based on experience. Instead, we are born with them. For example, Descartes thought they are placed into our mind by God, though others have suggested that they are coded into our DNA. Proposed innate ideas include the idea of God, the basic logical truths (such as the law of noncontradiction), and more. What do you think? Do you think that Hume is correct that our ideas are limited by our experience? Or do you think that there are some ideas that we are just born with? How could you tell one way or the other?

2. Do you think that Hume's thought experiment is correct—that is, could someone fill in the missing shade of blue without previously seeing it? How might you construct a scientific experiment to figure out the answer? Could you run this experiment with your classmates? (See Finch 2015 for an attempt at doing so.)

Further Reading

Finch, Jonathan. 2015. "A test: Hume's missing shade of blue." *The Journal of Scottish Philosophy* 13, no. 3: 219–228.

Garrett, Don. 1997. *Cognition and commitment in Hume's philosophy*. New York: Oxford University Press.

Kelahan, Emily. 2016. "Simple ideas and Hume's missing shade of blue." *Philosophia* 44: 809–825.

Kendrick, Nancy. 2009. "Why Hume's counterexample is insignificant and why it is not." *British Journal for the History of Philosophy* 17, no. 5: 955–979.

· CHAPTER 18 ·

The Cube and the Sphere (Molyneux's Question), Addressed by John Locke

The Thought Experiment

Imagine that you were born without sight, and that early in your life you learned to identify the shapes of solid objects by touch. You could, for example, identify a cube by counting its six square-shaped sides, or a round globe by feeling the continuous curvature of its surface. And you could also identify a person you knew, not just by hearing their voice but also by touching their face with your hands and recognizing its familiar shape. Now imagine further that your missing sight was restored, either miraculously or through medical intervention. When this happened, and the objects whose shapes you had previously known only through touch were presented to your eyes, would you be able to identify those shapes immediately?

Source of the thought experiment:
Locke, John. (1690) 1996. *An essay concerning human understanding.* Edited by K. M. Winkler. Indianapolis: Hackett. Book II, Chapter IX, §8.

Reflection by John Schwenkler, Florida State University

The philosopher John Locke posed this question in the second edition of his *Essay Concerning Human Understanding*, crediting the question to a letter he received from the Irish writer William Molyneux. Both Locke and Molyneux thought that the answer to this question was "No": it would not be possible for a newly sighted person to identify immediately through vision the shapes that they had previously known only through touch. Molyneux supported his reasoning as follows: while a person in this position will have "obtained the experience of how a globe, how a cube affects his touch; yet he has not yet obtained the experience, that what affects his touch so or so, must affect his sight so or so; or that a protuberant angle in the cube, that pressed his hand unequally, shall appear to his eye as it does in the cube" (*Essay*, Book II, Chapter IX, §8).

Molyneux's question is connected to many important concerns in the philosophy of perception, some of which are outlined later. But another way that the question is valuable is in helping us to think about the relationship between philosophical ideas and scientific discoveries. While Locke and Molyneux approached the question just as a philosophical thought experiment, in 1728 the physician William Cheselden published a description of how he had successfully restored the sight of a thirteen-year-old boy who had been born with congenital cataracts. (For discussion of this case, as well as two others that took place during the twentieth century, see Sacks 1995.) According to Cheselden, the boy was entirely perplexed by how things appeared to his newly restored vision:

> When he first saw, he was so far from making any judgment about distances, that he thought all objects whatever touched his eyes, (as he expressed it) as what he felt, did his skin . . . He knew not the shape of any thing, nor any one thing from another, however different in shape, or magnitude; but upon being told what things were, whose form he knew before from feeling, he would carefully observe, that he might know them again; but having too many objects to learn at once, he forgot many of them. (Cheselden 1728, p. 448)

This result seems to confirm Locke's negative answer to Molyneux's question: the boy could recognize shapes by touch but was unable to extend this knowledge to the visual appearances of things. But a closer look reveals that matters are more complicated than this. After all, if Cheselden's boy couldn't even use his sight to tell "any one thing from another, however different in shape," then perhaps it's just because the boy couldn't *see* things very well that he couldn't tell what shapes those things had.

More recent attempts at addressing Molyneux's question experimentally face similar difficulties. In one much-discussed study (reported in Held et al. 2011), the experimenters tested congenitally blind individuals whose sight had just been restored by having them feel a solid shape with their hands, without being able to see it, and then judge which of two seen shapes matched the one they had previously felt. At first the patients were at chance on this task, but within a week their performance averaged close to 80 percent. By contrast, in a similar task in which all the shapes were presented visually, the patients were able to succeed right away—a result that seems to rule out the idea that it was because they couldn't *see* well enough that they weren't able to match seen shapes to felt ones.

But that conclusion is too hasty. (For a more detailed version of this argument, see Schwenkler 2013.) How clearly do you need to see two things in order to tell if they have the same shape? Imagine that you are looking through distorting glasses or a dirty pane of glass: as long as both things are displayed from the same viewing angle, you might be able to tell if their shapes are the same or different, even if you can't make either of them out very clearly. That's because in a task like this you can rely on low-level visual cues like the objects' overall contour and shading instead of a clear perception of their three-dimensional shapes.

However, this last strategy wouldn't work if you had to match a seen shape with one that you felt in your hands. To do this, you'd need to compare the objects in terms of their overall shapes, and this would require perceiving them much more clearly than if you were making a vision-to-vision or touch-to-touch comparison. And other experiments provide good evidence that the patients in the study described earlier simply couldn't see well enough to perceive three-dimensional shapes in this way.

Could other scientific experiments provide a more decisive answer to Molyneux's question? It is hard to say—and the answer seems to depend in part on facts about the human visual system that it is the business of science to discover. If we can't answer the question empirically, then to what extent can we support an answer on philosophical grounds? The discussion questions that follow should help you to work out your own view of these matters.

Discussion Questions

1. *Is perception "direct," or is it mediated by inference? And to what extent is it influenced by prior experience?* Locke wrote that when we see a round globe, "the idea thereby imprinted in our mind, is of a flat circle variously shadowed," and that through a "settled habit" we come to perceive things as three-dimensional solids only because this is how we have *learned* them to be (*Essay* II.IX.8). Is this a correct description of how we see the world? Is it supported by any of the experiments discussed earlier? What other experimental or philosophical evidence would tell for or against this position?

2. *What is the relation between perceiving in one sense and perceiving in any others?* If the look of a person tells you something about how their voice will sound, or the texture of a piece of fruit tells you something about how it will taste, that is probably only because you have learned to associate these things in the past. But does the same hold when the very same feature of an object, such as its shape or size, is perceived in two different modalities, such as sight and touch?
3. *How can the philosophy and science of perception inform one another?* Perception is at once a biological phenomenon and a topic of philosophical discussion. Can scientific evidence help us resolve philosophical puzzles about the nature of perceptual experience? And can philosophical reasoning make positive contributions to the scientific study of perception?

Further Reading

Cheselden, Willliam. 1728. "An account of some observations made by a young gentleman, who was born blind, or lost his sight so early, that he had no remembrance of ever having seen, and was couch'd between 13 and 14 years of age." *Philosophical Transactions of the Royal Society* 35: 447–450.

Evans, Gareth. 1985. "Molyneux's question." In *Collected Papers*, 364–399. Oxford: Clarendon Press.

Held, Richard, Yuri Ostrovsky, Beatrice Gelder, Beatrice deGelder, Tapan Gandhi, Suma Ganesh, Umang Mathur, and Pawan Sinha. 2011. "The newly sighted fail to match seen shape with felt." *Nature Neuroscience* 14: 551–553.

Sacks, Oliver. 1995. "To see and not see." In *An anthropologist on Mars*, 108–151. New York: Vintage Books.

Schwenkler, John. 2013. "Do things look the way they feel?" *Analysis* 73: 86–96.

· CHAPTER 19 ·

Mary in the Black-and-White Room, by Frank Jackson

The Thought Experiment

Mary is imprisoned in a black-and-white room. She learns about the outside world only through books printed in black and white, a black-and-white computer, and a black-and-white television screen. Mary learns all the relevant facts about color vision that can be learned in this way. She becomes an expert not only in neuroscience but also in physics and chemistry, and thus gains theoretical knowledge about all the relevant facts involved in color vision. She knows, for example, that what we see as red is caused by the excitement of long-wavelength cones in our eyes, and how the brain translates this into red. One day, Mary is released from her cell, and she sees the color red for the first time. Now it seems if physicalism is true—that is, if it is true that all our knowledge can be reduced to knowledge about physical facts—that Mary learns nothing new when she sees a red flower just outside the prison door. But Mary does learn something new. From this, we can conclude that physicalism is false.

Source of the thought experiment:
Jackson, Frank. 1986. "What Mary didn't know." *The Journal of Philosophy* 83, no. 5: 291–295.

Reflection by Martina Fürst, University of Graz

Think of the first time you had a particular experience: the first time you tasted an exotic fruit, felt snow on your skin, or smelled the ocean. Maybe some of your friends or family had already enjoyed this kind of experience, they told you about it, and they tried to describe it—nevertheless, having the experience was something completely different. No description, comparison, or information about the causes of the experience conveyed to you what you gained by having the experience yourself: knowledge of what the experience is like, of the experience's so-called phenomenal character.

The thought that there is something special about experiences, namely, that their phenomenal character cannot be conveyed by descriptions, is already present in C. D. Broad (1925). He argued that even a logically omniscient archangel, endowed with the power to perceive the structures of atoms, could not find out that a substance with a particular structure has, for example, the distinctive smell of ammonia to humans. If Broad was right, then it is not our limited knowledge about physics or chemistry that explains why we cannot figure out what an experience is like before having it. Rather, theoretical descriptions are *fundamentally* unable to convey what experiences are like. Jackson's thought experiment about Mary the scientist elaborates in detail the idea that no theoretical knowledge suffices for knowing the phenomenal character of experiences—not even complete physical knowledge (broadly understood to encompass neurophysiological, chemical, and other knowledge). Notably, the thought experiment does not only reveal that *knowledge* about experiences is special. It also aims to show that the very *nature* of experiences, and of consciousness in general, is special.

The nature of consciousness and how it relates to the body is one of the fundamental questions in the philosophy of the mind. In the past century, many philosophers aimed at reducing consciousness to a physical phenomenon. For instance, on one view, conscious states such as red experiences are just brain states. On another view, experiences are states that play a particular role (e.g., of detecting red objects in the environment), and various physical systems (e.g., brains, computers) can realize this role. What is common to these accounts is that consciousness is ultimately physical and can be explained in physical terms. But wait: didn't we just see that no physical theory can tell us what an experience is like?

Mary's room is based on this insight, but it aims higher: at elucidating the very *nature* of experiences. To reach this aim, Jackson assumes that Mary knows *all* physical facts; that is, he ascribes knowledge of a complete physical theory to a subject. This combination highlights perfectly the puzzling relation between objective theory and experiencing subject. On the one hand, Mary knows all the physical facts about color experiences, but, on the other hand, she still cannot deduce what the color experiences will be like. Therefore, some facts about consciousness—in particular, facts about what experiences are like—are not physical facts, Jackson concludes.

The intuition that physically omniscient Mary learns something when having her first color experience is compelling. Some philosophers (for example, Daniel Dennett) reply that this intuition is misleading, that Mary learns nothing. Others take the intuition seriously, but reject the conclusion about the nonphysical nature of consciousness. They ask: What is it that Mary learns? Does she really learn new *facts* about color experiences? Accordingly, alternative explanations of what Mary learns have been proposed that do not entail the nonphysical nature of experiences: for example, David Lewis and Lawrence Nemirow think that Mary just acquires a new capacity, such as knowing how to recognize red experiences. Others, for example, Katalin Balog, Terence Horgan, and Brian Loar argue that Mary relearns a fact she already knew, but in a new way: in her achromatic room, she grasped facts about red experiences from an objective perspective, and now she grasps the very same facts, but from her subjective perspective.

On my view, the latter explanation is particularly interesting, since it elucidates a feature of consciousness that makes its investigation very special. With regard to consciousness, we have two ways of accessing it: from our inner, subjective perspective, and from a third-person, objective perspective. But which of these two perspectives reveals the nature of experiences?

I think Jackson is right in that enjoying an experience from the subjective perspective reveals something significant about this experience. In particular, I suggest the following analysis of experiences: what makes an experience the very experience it is, is its phenomenal character. If so, the subjective perspective directly reveals *essential* properties of experiences (see also David Chalmers, Martine Nida-Rümelin). Accordingly, theories of consciousness that are stated in objective, physical terms cannot adequately account for experiences, since they have to leave out facts about the essential properties of experiences; facts about what experiences are like. Recall again the experience of tasting an exotic fruit for the first time, an experience that until then you only knew by description. On my view, by having this experience, you did not just grasp the experience in a new way. Rather, you gained direct insight into an essential property of this experience—an insight that you could not have gained in any other way. If this analysis is correct, then the nature of experiences, and more generally, of consciousness is not (entirely) physical.

The question of whether science ever can account for what it is like to have an experience is known as the "puzzle of consciousness." Mary's room helps us to understand more deeply this philosophical puzzle. Thinking through various analyses of the scenario opens the door to possible solutions to one of the deepest puzzles in the philosophy of mind.

Discussion Questions

1. Think of the first time you had a particular experience. Prior to having it, could others have conveyed to you what the experience would be like? What, if anything, changed when you enjoyed the experience yourself for the first time?
2. Do you think that (future) science will explain consciousness just as a well as other (for example, biological or physical) phenomena, or do you rather think that consciousness is a special topic of investigation? If so, in what sense is consciousness special, and what would a full explanation of it require?

Further Reading

Alter, Torin, and Robert J. Howell. 2008. *A dialogue about consciousness*. Oxford: Oxford University Press.

Broad, C. D. 1925. *The mind and its place in nature*. London: Kegan Paul.

Coleman, Sam, ed. 2019. *The knowledge argument*. Cambridge: Cambridge University Press.

Fürst, Martina. 2014. "A dualist account of phenomenal concepts." In *Contemporary dualism: A defense*, edited by Andrea Lavazza and Howard Robinson,112–136. New York: Routledge.

Nida-Rümelin, Martine, and Donnchadh O Conaill. 2019. "Qualia: The knowledge argument." In *The Stanford encyclopedia of philosophy*, Winter 2019 edition, edited by Edward N. Zalta. https://plato.stanford.edu/archives/win2019/entries/qualia-knowledge/.

· CHAPTER 20 ·

Pierre's Absence from the Café, by Jean-Paul Sartre

The Thought Experiment

I am in a French café, looking for my friend Pierre; I've made an appointment to meet him at 4 p.m. today. Unfortunately, I'm about fifteen minutes late. Pierre is always on time; will he have waited for me? I enter the café and I scan its interior, its tables, its booths, its mirrors, its light, the sound of voices, the clinking of glasses and plates on the waiters' serving trays, but Pierre is not to be seen. This situation is not uncommon: you expect something or someone to be present and they are not. You discover their absence.

Source of the thought experiment:

Sartre, Jean-Paul. (1943) 2018. *Being and nothingness: An essay in phenomenological ontology.* Translated by Sarah Richmond. London: Routledge.

Reflection by Sarah Richmond, University College London

Sartre proposes this thought experiment at an early stage in his lengthy and most important philosophical work, *Being and Nothingness* (hereafter BN). That book was first published in France in 1943 and, although some of Sartre's famous vignettes are now dated, the type of café described in this scene remains an important element in French culture to this day.

In the first instance, Sartre's example aims to persuade us that the perceiving of Pierre's absence from the café is irreducible; the experience differs from a straightforward perception of what is materially present, before one's eyes, such as the furniture and the people. At a theoretical level, Sartre borrows terms from Gestalt psychology to characterize this difference: Gestalt psychologists claim that human experience is always organized, such that its structure adds something to the component parts. We can apply this model to the perception of Pierre's absence. Despite his absence, *Pierre* is the intended focal figure and the expectation that he will be present organizes everything else in the person's visual field into the "ground," the backcloth for Pierre's appearance. This point is also effective in response to the objection (which is often voiced in philosophical discussions of perceptual illusion) that the person who is looking for Pierre doesn't *really* perceive his absence; if the person is looking at an empty chair, for example, what he perceives is just that chair, and Pierre's absence is simply inferred.

At a more phenomenological level (concerning the description of the experience itself) Sartre notes that the person looking for Pierre perceives his absence in relation to the café in its *entirety*: although every spatial point in the room is surveyed, Pierre's absence is not found to be at any *particular* spatial point; it is experienced instead as "haunting" the café, everywhere and nowhere. This haunting quality also explains why Pierre's absence is *distinctive*, for his waiting friend, from any potential *abstract* absence, such as that of the poet Valéry or the Duke of Wellington. Valéry and Wellington have no haunting quasi-presence.

Sartre's example is presented in Part One of BN, "The Problem of Nothingness," and its importance derives from its role in establishing the concept of nothingness, one of the two key terms in Sartre's title. Inspired in large part by the German philosopher Martin Heidegger,

Sartre aims to establish an ontology (the study of what there is, in the broadest terms) which, due to its recognition of nothingness, is not exhausted by what exists. This poses a challenge; if, as a matter of definition, nothingness (or, synonymously, nonbeing) is nonexistent, how can it make any difference to ontology, let alone to philosophy? Moreover, Henri Bergson—a French philosopher whose influence was at its height in Sartre's student days—had argued that no intelligible conception of nothingness is possible and that apparently negative judgements, such as "This table is not white," fail to correspond to any genuinely negative state of affairs. Bergson's point is that if the table is "not white," then it is some other color. Suppose the table is in fact brown; then one could say, instead, "The table is brown," thereby dispensing with any negative terms. Given this, the *point* of the negative terminology, Bergson claims, is not to record an ineliminably negative property of the table (because there is no such property) but rather to register some attitude on the part of the speaker, such as expectation or surprise. Someone who had (incorrectly) believed that the table was white might, once she saw it, register her surprise at its color by saying "But the table is not white!" Against Bergson, Sartre insists that some negative judgments are not reducible to affirmative ones and are based on an actual *experience* of nonbeing or nothingness, such as Pierre's nonbeing in the café. The logical or judgmental function of negation, for Sartre, depends on nothingness.

Sartre's argument remains controversial and within analytical philosophy its critics—for many of whom its paradoxical character is unacceptable—probably outnumber its supporters. Nonetheless, the argument is of the utmost significance because, if it fails, Sartre's distinctive claim about human beings (i.e., that we are radically free in a manner that is quite incompatible with determinism) will also fail.

Sartre moves from the putative experience of Pierre's absence to his affirmation of freedom in the following way. To Bergson, he concedes that the experience is person-relative: the experience of Pierre's absence is in some way dependent on the fact that his friend expected him to be there; it is not available to the other people in the café. Then, more generally, Sartre asserts that the possibility of nothingness derives from the existence of human beings or, more specifically, of human *consciousness*. For Sartre, nothingness can enter the world only if there exists a type of being which is "its own nothingness" because it nihilates *itself*. In other words, nothingness rests on a *process*—nihilation—which, Sartre argues, is intrinsic to human consciousness. Human freedom obtains precisely because we are the bearers of nothingness, by virtue of existing as conscious, self-nihilating beings.

The example of Pierre's absence is designed to show that we can experience nothingness, and to defuse Bergsonian doubts. The ontological importance of nothingness is that it underwrites human freedom. In response to this claim, a question naturally arises about our *awareness* of this radical freedom. Do we feel, or know, ourselves to be free? According to Sartre, we register it—at least sometimes—through our experience of anguish. Sartre illustrates this with a further famous example, the gambler who wants to give up gambling. He resolves to stop. But then he immediately discovers that *keeping* his resolution is a further task; unhappily, the resolution lacks the power to determine its own consequences. It continues to exist only as an element in the gambler's nihilated past, separated from the present by nothingness, which renders any causal relationship between his resolution and what he does *now* impossible.

In Sartre's view, causal determinism and freedom are incompatible. But nothingness makes it impossible for anything in consciousness to be causally determined. Radical human freedom exists, and we should not be surprised at the intense anguish it occasions, as we realize we are entirely responsible for what we do with it.

Discussion Questions

1. How successful is Sartre's thought experiment in showing that we can have a perceptual experience of absence (in this instance, of Pierre's absence)?
2. Do you agree that the concept of nothingness is intelligible? Is it a concept that you think you already use and, if so, in which circumstances?

Further Reading

Richmond, Sarah. 2007. "Sartre and Bergson: A disagreement about nothingness." *International Journal of Philosophical Studies* 15, no. 1: 77–95.

Richmond, Sarah. 2013. "Nothingness and negation." In *Jean-Paul Sartre: Key concepts*, edited by Steven Churchill and Jack Reynolds, 93–105. Stocksfield, UK: Acumen.

Sorensen, Roy. 2020. "Nothingness." In *The Stanford encyclopedia of philosophy*, Spring 2020 edition, edited by Edward N. Zalta. https://plato.stanford.edu/archives/spr2020/entries/nothingness/

· CHAPTER 21 ·

Skywalk, by Tamar Gendler

The Thought Experiment

Situated a dizzying four thousand feet above the Grand Canyon is Skywalk, a horseshoe-shaped transparent glass balcony. As a tourist, you can walk onto it and witness the sweeping vistas of the Grand Canyon nearly a mile beneath your feet. As you venture on the sturdy glass on your surgical booties (that protect Skywalk from getting scratches), you are as secure as you can be. Nevertheless, if your experience is like that of most visitors, you will feel a sense of vertigo. You know the glass is solid and safe, and yet there you are, desperately grabbing the railing, thinking "It's a long way down! This is dangerous! Get me off!" How can we describe the cognitive state of someone who visits the walkway?

Source of the thought experiment:
Gendler, Tamar. S. 2008. "Alief and belief." *The Journal of Philosophy* 105, no. 10, 634–663.

Reflection by Tamar Gendler, Yale University

When you step out on the skywalk, you believe that you are safe. If you genuinely thought you might fall through the glass, you wouldn't stay out there on the platform, asking a fellow tourist to take your picture. And you certainly wouldn't let your children, or your parents, or your spouse stand there beside you!

But if you are sure that you are in no danger, why are you trembling? Why aren't you standing calmly, as you would be in any other location with a solid floor beneath your feet?

You are trembling because even though you *believe* that you are safe, you *alieve* that you are in danger. Your *belief* is your reason-based assessment of the situation; it's your judgment of what is actually the case, given all the information you have. Your *alief*, by contrast, is your automatic response to the situation's salient features; it's the way you respond—out of instinct or out of habit—to the features of the situation that awaken those instinctive or habitual responses. (You're right: you haven't heard that word before. *Alief* is a novel term, coined by Tamar Gendler—that's me!—to describe this sort of mental state.)

When you are standing on the transparent skywalk, your belief that you are safe takes into consideration all the information you have—that the glass is two feet thick, that the balcony is supported by strong steel girders, that thousands of people have stood there without incident. But your alief responds to a much narrower set of cues—it's an instinctual response to the visual stimulus of seeing almost a mile of empty space beneath your feet.

Alief and belief come apart in all sorts of cases (though—as we will see in a minute—they also often coincide). Suppose that a chef, with gloved hands, takes a delicious piece of fresh fudge and reshapes it before your eyes so that it takes the form of dog feces. Even though you *believe* that it is still a tasty dessert, your *alief* will cause you to hesitate before indulging. Or suppose that you set your watch five minutes fast because you tend to run late. When you look at your wrist and see "10:00," you *believe* that is it only 9:55. But—still—your heart beats a bit faster, and you start to rush. You can't help your *alief*: oh no, it's already 10:00!

Alief explains why you are hesitant to throw a dart at a photograph of someone you love, why audiences scream when they watch horror movies, and why baseball teams put cardboard fans in athletic stadiums during the COVID-19 crisis. Because these depictions have appearances that are associated with certain automatic responses, they tend to elicit those responses even though their audience believes that they are fictional.

But alief isn't just about automatic responses to movies or fudge or glass balconies. Alief also lies at the heart of the phenomenon known as *implicit bias*. Resumés bearing a stereotypical Black name like Jamal or Lakisha are less likely to result in interviews than otherwise identical resumés bearing a name like Emily or Greg; resumés of women are less likely to be judged as scientifically competent as otherwise identical resumés of men—even among evaluators who are explicitly egalitarian. The evaluators may *believe* that the candidates' qualifications are equal, but their overlearned stereotypical associations, their instinctive or habitual automatic responses—their *aliefs*—are activated. And like the trembling skywalker, or the reluctant fudge-eater, or the rushing watch-setter, the belief cannot fully keep the alief at bay.

So why do people have aliefs? People have aliefs because our minds are complex. There are many ways to describe this complexity. The ancient Greek philosopher Plato suggested that the human soul is composed of three parts: a charioteer, which he called *reason*, and two horses, which he called *spirit* and *appetite*. The Buddhist tradition expresses a similar division as involving a rider (reason) and an elephant (instinct or habit). Modern dual processing theorists—such as Nobel Prize–winning psychologists Daniel Kahneman and Amos Tversky—distinguish between System 2, which is deliberative and rational, and System 1, which is quick and automatic. Contemporary neuroscience tells us that a small portion of our actions and reactions are governed by the relatively slow controlled processes in the front part of the brain (prefrontal cortex), while most are governed by habits and associations and automatic responses from more primitive parts in the back. All of these theories predict that we would have both beliefs (slow reflective responses) and aliefs (quick automatic ones).

But here's the really interesting thing. Although the earlier examples feature cases where our aliefs and beliefs come apart, most of the time, they coincide. When I touch-type, my aliefs guide my fingers to the keys, but my typing is accurate because I correctly believe that I am typing on a QWERTY keyboard. When I drive, my aliefs govern most of my behaviors, but my driving is safe because the habits I have developed are responsive to the way I correctly believe things actually are.

My aliefs and my beliefs usually coincide because—for the most part—the way the world seems to me is the way the world actually is. Much—though not all—of the time, the way I respond automatically or through habit is the way that I *would* respond if I had the time to slow down and reflect.

Because alief and belief usually coincide, we might not recognize how much of our action is governed by alief. By showing us a case where alief and belief pull in different directions, the glass skywalk thought experiment helps us recognize that these are two different sorts of mental state. And this in turn allows us to discern the role that alief plays in our responses even in the ordinary cases.

Discussion Questions

1. What are some cases from your own experience where your aliefs and your beliefs have pulled in different directions? How are they similar to, or different from, the examples listed in the Reflection?
2. What are some cases from your own experience where your aliefs and your beliefs have pulled in the same direction? How are they similar to, or different from, the examples listed in the Reflection?
3. Why do alief and belief usually coincide? Why do they sometimes come apart? What does this show about the human mind and our relation to the world around us?

Further Reading

Brownstein, Michael. 2019. "Implicit bias." In *The Stanford encyclopedia of philosophy,* Fall 2019 edition, edited by Edward N. Zalta. https://plato.stanford.edu/archives/fall2019/entries/implicit-bias/

Gendler, Tamar. 2014. "The third horse: On unendorsed association and human behavior." *Aristotelian Society* Suppl. 88, no. 1: 185–218.

Kriegel, Uriah, 2012. "Moral motivation, moral phenomenology, and the alief/belief distinction." *Australasian Journal of Philosophy* 90, no. 3: 469–486.

Mandelbaum, Eric. 2013. "Against alief." *Philosophical Studies* 165: 197–211.

Nagel, Jennifer. 2012. "Gendler on alief." *Analysis* 72, no. 4: 774–788.

· CHAPTER 22 ·

Accidental You, by Ruth Millikan

The Thought Experiment

Imagine that, through some cosmic accident of whirling molecules, a physical copy of you is formed. Molecule for molecule, you and your accidental double would be exactly the same. But would that being have ideas, beliefs, intentions, hopes, and fears? Would she have a liver, heart, eyes, and brain? No—because the evolutionary history of this being would be wrong. Real hearts and real beliefs have been designed to be hearts and beliefs, either by natural selection or by brains that natural selection designed for forming beliefs.

Source of the thought experiment:

Millikan, Ruth. 1984. *Language, thought, and other biological categories*. Cambridge, MA: MIT Press.

Reflection by Ruth Millikan, Distinguished Professor Emerita, University of Connecticut

Around 1960 some new questions began to be asked about what makes mental states such as beliefs and desires be about the things they are about. What is the connection between you and the rain when you think that it's raining, the connection that makes your thought be about the rain? The property of a sentence or a thought that makes it be about something, as the sentence "Dogs bark" is about dogs and barking and your thought that dogs bark is about dogs and barking, might be called "aboutness," but more formally it is called "intentionality."

Before these new questions about intentionality arose, practically everyone assumed that what made your thought, say, of Aristotle be about Aristotle (or about anything at all) was a matter of what the experience of thinking of Aristotle was like. If anyone else were to have exactly that kind of experience, they, too, would be thinking of Aristotle. And it does seem as though thinking of Aristotle, or of anything else, is a matter of having something in or before your conscious mind, a matter of being mentally aware of something. If you were thinking of something else, the experience would be different. Not that there is only one way to think of Aristotle, but to think of him must involve being aware of something that is distinctive about him so that the thought of him is different from the thought of anything else. Thus Bertrand Russell (1912, 58) said, ". . . it is scarcely conceivable that we can make a judgment or entertain a supposition without knowing what it is we are judging or supposing about." Similarly, what you mean when you speak seems to be fully determined within your consciousness.

As this view began to be questioned, Hilary Putnam (1973) produced a slogan for his own developing position that neatly fit the movement underway: "Meaning is not in the head," not *entirely* in the head, that is." This view is sometimes called externalism (in the philosophy of mind). [See 24, *Twin Earth*.]

Philosophers such as Wilfrid Sellars, Jerry Fodor, and Daniel Dennett began to urge that philosophy of mind needs to be integrated with the findings of science such as psychology and cognitive science. Human minds must be understood as continuous with the rest of nature.

Thinking is some kind of physical process. It was proposed, for example, that what made a thought *red* be about red or a thought *horse* be about horses was, at least in part, that the thinker had a disposition to respond with that thought when observing something red or observing a horse. Causal connections to things not in one's head were needed to determine what these thoughts were about.

Tyler Burge and Hilary Putnam argued that what you are thinking of when you use a word is sometimes determined not just by your inner thought but by what that word means in the language you are speaking. When you use the word "kangaroo," for example, you mean kangaroos, even though (I'll bet) you don't yourself know what distinguishes a kangaroo from a wallaby. If you encountered a wallaby, you might say and think that it was a kangaroo, thus misusing not only the word "kangaroo" but your own thought *kangaroo*. The language community outside you helps to determine what your very thoughts mean. Donald Davidson argued that the meanings of your idiolect words and sentences and of your corresponding thoughts has been determined in a complicated way by your past interactions with many things in your world, including, most importantly, your communicative interactions with other people who use your language.

David Papineau, Fred Dretske, and Ruth Millikan started a tradition called "biosemantics" or "teleosemantics" that argued that natural selection during your evolutionary history determined what your liver, heart, and eyes are designed to do and how your brain and your beliefs are designed to function. Add that what makes a functional item such as a screw driver or a car or a shoe be a screw driver or a car or a shoe is not what it actually does or can do but what it was designed to do. Think, for example, of a can opener that is defective or broken so that it cannot open cans. Maybe it has been run over, squashed, or its handle is broken off. Why is it a can opener if it cannot open cans? It is a can opener because it was designed for opening cans, not because it can open cans. Similarly, biosemantics argues that what makes a thought, say a belief, into a belief is that it was designed to be a belief, not directly by natural selection of course but by mechanisms designed by evolution for producing well-functioning beliefs, that is, true beliefs. Central here was the need for a theory of intentionality that would explain what produces the intentionality and the contents not just of true thoughts but also of false thoughts. When belief-producing mechanisms fail to work correctly, they may produce false beliefs, but false beliefs are beliefs nonetheless.

Discussion Questions

1. Would the accidental you be a human? Suppose that accidental you differed from real you just a little bit. Sadly, her "heart" didn't work very well. Her "liver" didn't work very well either. She only had half a "brain" and so forth. Is there some point at which accidental you would not be a human?
2. Accidental you's "heart" was not designed *by* anything or *for* anything, so there is no way it could fail to do what it was designed to do. If it couldn't pump blood, would that be a heart failure or just something it doesn't happen to do? (Lots of things don't pump blood.)
3. Would accidental you have memories?

4. Suppose that all of your beliefs were true. Would accidental you have only true beliefs, too? Her beliefs about where she was born and who her mother is? (Or would those particular beliefs of hers be beliefs about where *you* were born and who *your* mother is?)
5. No offence, but you probably have at least one false belief. Would the corresponding thing in accidental you's head be a *false* belief? Why?

Further Reading

Millikan, Ruth. 2008. "Biosemantics." In *The Oxford handbook in the philosophy of mind,* edited by Brian McLaughlin, 394–406. Oxford: Oxford University Press. A preprint copy is available on Ruth Millikan's website, https://philosophy.uconn.edu/faculty/millikan-2/

Putnam, Hilary. 1973. "Meaning and reference." *Journal of Philosophy* 70, no. 19, 699–711.

Russell, Bertrand. 1912. *The problems of philosophy*. London: Williams & Norgate.

Stalnaker, Robert. 1989. "On what's in the head." *Philosophical Perspectives* 3: 287–319.

· PART V ·

Thought Experiments in Philosophy of Language

· CHAPTER 23 ·

The Morning Star Is the Evening Star, by Gottlob Frege

The Thought Experiment

According to the story, the Ancient Greeks noticed one celestial body—the star that shines brightly in the evening—and named it "Hesperus." They also noticed what they thought was a different celestial body—the star that shines brightly in the morning—and named it "Phosphorus." What they didn't realize, however, was that Hesperus (the evening star) and Phosphorus (the morning star) were one and the same celestial body (in fact, they are both just the planet Venus). Frege showed that this type of case gave rise to an interesting puzzle. Consider the two sentences "Hesperus is Hesperus" and "Hesperus is Phosphorus." Since "Hesperus" and "Phosphorus" are both just names for the planet Venus, it seems that the two sentences are saying the same thing: they both claim that a certain planet is identical to that very planet. Yet the two sentences also seem to be making very different types of statements. It's very easy to figure out that "Hesperus is Hesperus" is true: you can do so by simple reflection. However, it's much harder to find out that "Hesperus is Phosphorus" is true: that requires significant astronomical observation.

This motivated Frege to distinguish between two facets of meaning: the *reference* of an expression which is roughly the object it picks out, and the *sense* of an expression: the way the expression represents its referent. The names "Hesperus" and "Phosphorus" have the same referents—they both pick out the same object (the planet Venus). But the names have different senses: one represents this object as *the evening star*, and the other represents this object as *the morning star*. The two sentences "Hesperus is Hesperus" and "Hesperus is Phosphorus" are, in a way, both stating the same thing (the truth of both requires simply that the planet Venus is identical to that very planet). But the two sentences represent this claim in very different modes or ways: in one we are thinking of it as the claim that whatever celestial body happens to be the evening star is identical to the celestial body that is the evening star (that's trivially true). In the other, we are thinking of it as the claim that whatever celestial body happens to be the evening star is identical to the one that is the morning star (that's a substantive, interesting truth).

Source of the thought experiment:

Frege, Gottlob. (1892) 1948. "Sense and reference." *Philosophical Review* 57: 209–230.

Reflection by Ofra Magidor, University of Oxford

At the heart of Frege's Puzzle is the observation that language is *compositional*: the meaning of a sentence is composed from the meaning of its parts. This entails that if two sentences are built up from expressions with exactly the same meanings (arranged in the same way), the two sentences should also have the same meanings. For example, if "physician" means the same as "doctor," then "Jane is a doctor" means the same as "Jane is a physician" and consequently the two sentences cannot differ in truth-value (they are either both true or both false). Similarly, on the face of it, "Hesperus" and "Phosphorus" have the same meaning: they both pick out the planet Venus, and indeed, "Hesperus is bright" must have the same truth-value as "Phosphorus is bright." However, consider the sentences "Hesperus is Hesperus" and "Hesperus is

Phosphorus." Although they are apparently built out of expressions with the same meanings, the sentences seem crucially different: they are both true, but in the former sentence we can immediately recognize its truth upon simple reflection, whereas the latter expresses a substantive empirical fact.

Frege's own solution was to distinguish two facets of meaning. First, there is the *reference* of an expression; this is the aspect of meaning which goes into determining the truth-value of sentences. Second, there is the *sense* of an expression, which is roughly the way in which the reference is presented. "Hesperus" and "Phosphorus" have the same referents: both names refer to Venus. However, they have different senses: one name represents Venus as *the evening star*, while the other represents Venus as *the morning star*. The fact that the two different names have the same referent explains why the pair "Hesperus is Hesperus" and "Hesperus is Phosphorus" must have the same truth-values. And the fact that the two names have different senses explains how the two sentences containing them can nevertheless differ in cognitive significance.

However, as Frege recognized, this proposal does not fully address the problem. For consider the two sentences "The Greeks believed that Hesperus is Hesperus" and "The Greeks believed that Hesperus is Phosphorus." The two sentences are built out of expressions with the same referents, so if we follow the earlier proposal, we should expect the two sentences to have the same truth-values (even if they differ in sense). Unfortunately, this prediction does not seem correct: while it is true that early Greeks believed that Hesperus is Hesperus, they didn't realize that Hesperus and Phosphorus were identical. Frege's own proposed solution was to add another complication to his theory, maintaining that in special indirect contexts (for example, reports involving "believes that") expressions can receive a different referent than their ordinary one (in fact, in these cases the special referent turns out to be their ordinary sense). Frege's solution has since come under a variety of criticisms, in part objecting to the idea that words have a different referent inside and outside of indirect contexts. Various other solutions have also been proposed: according to one, believing that Hesperus is Hesperus is precisely the same as believing that Hesperus is Phosphorus, and consequently, even the sentence "The Greeks believed that Hesperus is Phosphorus" is true. However, it's a pragmatically misleading way to report a belief that the Greeks themselves would have expressed by saying "Hesperus is Hesperus." According to another proposal, the words "Hesperus" and "Phosphorus" themselves have the same referents both inside and outside of indirect contexts, but the belief report sentences contain some additional unpronounced elements that differ in reference, which explains how the two sentences can differ in truth-value.

Although Frege's Puzzle is primarily an issue in the philosophy of language, it has profound implications to many other areas of philosophy. Consider, for example Moore's *open question argument* in moral philosophy. This argument is intended to show that the property of *being good* cannot be reduced to or identical to any nonmoral property. Suppose, for example, that you think *being good* is really the same as *bringing about the most pleasure*. Moore argued that the question "Is being good the same as being good?" is one that we can trivially give a positive answer to, while the question "Is being good the same as bringing about the most pleasure?" is an open question, one that is hard to answer. The two questions therefore have different meanings. But since the second differs from the first only by replacing the final occurrence of "good" with "bringing about the most pleasure," then it seems that these two terms must pick out different properties. One response to Moore's argument, however, is to claim that it is a variant of Frege's Puzzle: if we think that "Hesperus" and "Phosphorus" can refer to the same planet even though the question "Is Hesperus the same as Hesperus?" is trivial, while "Is Hesperus the same as Phosphorus?" is (or used to be) an open question, then arguably the same might hold in the moral case.

For another example, consider the case of Mary the color scientist [see 19, *Mary in the black-and-white room*]: Mary is a scientist who knows everything there is to know about the physics of color but has never experienced color herself. This entails that for any physical property *P* for which "Red has *P*" is true, Mary knows that red has *P*. However, Mary doesn't know what red looks like. This suggests that the mental property *what red looks like* has to be distinct from all physical properties, which means some mental properties are special, nonphysical properties. However, again we need to consider the possibility that this is another instance of Frege's Puzzle: just as Mary can know that Hesperus is Hesperus even though she doesn't know that Hesperus is Phosphorus, her different knowledge states don't rule out that "P" and "what red looks like" ultimately refer to the same property.

Discussion Questions

1. Can you think of other cases, whether in everyday life or in philosophy, that might be instances of Frege's Puzzle? How do we decide if a case is or isn't an instance of Frege's Puzzle?
2. Does Frege's Puzzle show that words behave in a special way in indirect contexts such as "The Greeks believe that Hesperus is Phosphorus," or does the puzzle arise even when we consider simple sentences such as "Hesperus is Phosphorus"?
3. In philosophy of language, it is common to think of the meaning of a term as something that is part of the public and shared aspects of language: the words of English have the same meaning in the mouths of different speakers (indeed, Frege himself thought both sense and reference are shared). Does accepting this claim make it harder to solve certain versions of Frege's Puzzle? Conversely, does Frege's Puzzle show that we must reject the claim that meanings are shared among different speakers?

Further Reading

Crimmins, Mark, and John Perry. 1989. "The prince and the phone booth: Reporting puzzling beliefs." *Journal of Philosophy* 86: 685–711.

Kripke, Saul. 1979. "A puzzle about belief." In *Meaning and use*, edited by Avishai Margalit, 239–283. Dordrecht: Reidel.

Magidor, Ofra. 2015. "The myth of the De Se." *Philosophical Perspectives* 29: 249–283.

Richard, Mark. 1993. "Attitudes in context." *Linguistics and Philosophy* 16: 123–148.

Salmon, Nathan. 1986. *Frege's puzzle*. Cambridge, MA: MIT Press.

Saul, Jennifer M. 1997. "Substitution and simple sentences." *Analysis* 57: 102–106.

· CHAPTER 24 ·

Twin Earth, by Hilary Putnam

The Thought Experiment

Is meaning something that is purely in our heads? Imagine two worlds that are very similar: Earth and Twin Earth. Twin Earth looks exactly like our world, and both have liquid running in rivers that falls from the sky, that animals drink, and that plants need to grow. People on Earth and on Twin Earth call what they see and taste "water" (or the equivalent word in other languages). However, there is a crucial difference between the two worlds. In our world, water is composed of H_2O molecules. On Twin Earth, it is composed of a much more complex chemical substance, which we will call XYZ. Imagine someone called Oscar, who lived in 1750, a time when the chemical structure of water was not yet discovered. On Twin Earth, there is someone who looks and behaves exactly as Oscar does. Oscar and Twin Oscar both drink, swim, and bathe, and they both call the liquid they use for this "water," and what's in their heads—their mental representation—is of something similar, namely water is a tasteless, odorless liquid that makes up rivers, rain, turns into ice when frozen, and so on. Do they both mean the same thing with "water"? If meaning is purely in the head, they do. But when Oscar talks about "water," he talks about H_2O, and when Twin Oscar talks about "water," he talks about XYZ. So the chemical composition of the stuff we're actually interacting with matters to what our words mean, even if we don't know what it is. If that's true, what something means is not purely in the head.

Source of the thought experiment:

Putnam, Hilary. 1975. "The meaning of 'meaning'." *Minnesota Studies in the Philosophy of Science* 7: 215–271.

Reflection by Antti Kauppinen, University of Helsinki

Unless you're Finnish, you probably don't know what the word "vesi" means. But what exactly would it take for you to learn its meaning? One natural thought is that you come to know it when you acquire the ability to tell whether something is "vesi" on the basis of some of its features. I can teach you that: "vesi" is the clear and potable liquid that, among other things, fills the lakes and oceans on our planet. Now, in one sense, you know what it means.

Sometimes, though, we say that the meaning of a word is what we talk about when we use it. In the case of "vesi," that's water, or H_2O, as science tells us. Putting these together, we get an appealing picture, according to which there are two aspects of meaning. First, there's something like a description in our minds (like "clear, potable liquid") and second, there's whatever it is that fits the description (in this case, H_2O). Frege called them "sense" and "reference" [see 23, *The morning star is the evening star*].

This is a neat story, but Hilary Putnam thinks it's all wrong. In his most famous thought experiment, he asks us to imagine visiting a distant planet in our galaxy that happens to be almost exactly like the Earth. Indeed, the only difference is that on Twin Earth, the watery stuff in the lakes is *not* the same as on Earth, but a substance Putnam labels XYZ, which happens to share all the surface properties of H_2O. If we take a swim on Twin Earth and say, "Boy, this water sure feels nice after the quantum jump!," we're mistaken, because the stuff isn't water, although it seems just like it.

This is a big deal, because it follows that what we have in our minds doesn't determine what we're talking about—"meanings just ain't in the head," as Putnam's famous slogan goes. But where are they, then? Why is that when I use the word "water," I refer to H_2O and not to XYZ, even if I can't tell the difference between the two substances? Here Putnam appeals first to what he memorably calls the "linguistic division of labor": at least when it comes to *natural kind terms* like "water" or "elm," I tend to defer to experts, whom I treat as authorities on the actual nature of the stuff I'm talking about. Putnam himself confesses he doesn't know the difference between a beech and an elm. Nevertheless, the two words have a different meaning in his mouth, because when he says "beech," he means to talk about the tree that botanists recognize as beech, and likewise for "elm." So meanings are *social.*

The second crucial thing for Putnam is that reference depends on the environment in which we acquire the term. When we here on Earth talk about "water," we mean to talk about the very substance that we can point to and that we interact with when we drink it or bathe in it. On Twin Earth, the clear liquid in the lakes is not the *same stuff,* and that's why it's not water, though it has the same appearance. Meanings are in this sense also *environmental,* at least for natural kind terms. That is, they depend on the nature of the things that actually causally influence our thought and talk.

This has many interesting consequences. Consider metaphysical questions about necessity and possibility. It used to be common to think that all necessarily true propositions were *conceptual* or *analytic* truths: you couldn't possibly come across a false belief that amounts to knowledge, because it is part of the very concept of knowledge that only truths can be known. This is something we can learn a priori, without empirical investigation, just by reflecting on our concepts—and indeed *only* that way. In contrast, our concept of water is the same one our ancestors used before modern chemistry was born, so no matter how hard we reflect, we can't learn that water is H_2O. Instead, it's empirical science that reveals that the watery stuff around here is H_2O. But suppose that Putnam is right and our term "water" refers *in any possible situation* to the watery stuff around here. In that case, "water is H_2O" doesn't just happen to be true—rather, water is *necessarily* H_2O. This is philosophically groundbreaking, because it seems we've learned something about the *nature* or *essence* of water by conducting an a posteriori empirical investigation.

OK, in the case of water, this may not sound that exciting, but what about "knowledge" or "rightness"? Some have thought that they, too, are natural kind terms, so that we can discover their nature via scientific investigation into the things that as a matter of fact causally regulate their use.

But hold on. Suppose that the term "morally right" plays the same role in the social life of Twin Earth as it does in ours—for example, they approve of what they call "right" actions, feel guilt for the "not right" ones, and teach children to do what's "right." However, they don't call "right" quite the same things most of us do. They say it is "right" to sacrifice the innocent when it makes many people happy and "not right" to give your own children preference over strangers. It turns out they call "right" only actions that result in as much total welfare as possible, even if it involves using someone as a mere means or rules out personal relationships. Should we conclude that just like they talk about XYZ when they use "water," they talk about maximizing welfare when they talk about "right"? If they did, there would be no straightforward disagreement between my Twin Earth counterpart and me when he says that "It's right to sacrifice the elderly if it helps the economy enough" and I say, "No, that's not right!" But as Mark Timmons and Terence Horgan point out, that's implausible. Rather than talking past each other, we genuinely disagree. And that suggests that while Putnam may be right about how natural kind terms like "water" work, we shouldn't rush to conclusions about other kinds of expression, like moral terms.

Discussion Questions

1. If Putnam is right, it is not *metaphysically possible* for water to be anything other than H2O, if it indeed is H2O. Nevertheless, it is easy enough to *imagine* that water had some other chemical composition. As philosophers like Frank Jackson and David Chalmers (2001) put it, it is *epistemically possible* that water is something else—it is not ruled out by what we can know just by reflecting on our concept. But consider again morality. Can we imagine, even in a story, that smothering a baby because its crying interrupts one's Zoom call is morally right? (See Gendler 2000.) If not, what does it tell us about the difference between natural kinds and morality?
2. Putnam says at one point that natural kind terms turn out to be covertly *indexical*, like the words "I" and "here." Why do you think that is?
3. When Twin Antti and I encounter watery stuff, we will engage in the very same sort of reasoning and action, and will both jump in the lake for a refreshing swim, for example. Some philosophers, like Jerry Fodor (1987), argue that this shows that what we believe and want must after all be the same thing—how else could we end up *doing* just the same things?—in spite of our having acquired our terms in different environments. The claim is that our thoughts must have at least some content that does *not* depend on the environment. But does this follow?

Further Reading

Chalmers, David, and Frank Jackson. 2001. "Conceptual analysis and reductive explanation." *Philosophical Review* 110: 315–361.

Gendler, Tamar S. 2000. "The puzzle of imaginative resistance." *The Journal of Philosophy* 97, no. 2: 55–81.

Horgan, Terence, and Mark Timmons. 1991. "New wave moral realism meets moral Twin Earth." *Journal of Philosophical Research* 16: 447–465.

Kripke, Saul. 1980. *Naming and necessity.* Cambridge, MA: Harvard University Press.

· CHAPTER 25 ·

Gödel and Schmidt, by Saul Kripke

The Thought Experiment

Students of logic have learned that Gödel proved an important mathematical result, the incompleteness of arithmetic. They understand the theorem and its significance, but the only thing many of them know about Gödel himself is that he proved that theorem. Suppose that Jazmin is one of those students. Now, imagine the following: suppose that Gödel was not really the author of the proof. Some student of his, called Schmidt, who was found dead under mysterious circumstances, was really the person that proved the incompleteness of arithmetic. Gödel simply got hold of the manuscript and published it. Now, when Jazmin uses the name "Gödel," is she referring to Schmidt, the real author of the proof, or to the person who got hold of the manuscript and claimed credit for the work?

Source of the thought experiment:

Kripke, Saul. 1972. *Naming and necessity.* Cambridge, MA: Harvard University Press.

Reflection by Genoveva Martí, ICREA and University of Barcelona

How do words connect to things? What makes it possible for speakers of a language to utter a sound or make some marks on a piece of paper and refer to a thing or a person? This is a fundamental question for the philosophy of language and in particular for the theory of reference, the theory that discusses how that connection between words and things takes place. It is not surprising that an important part of the discussion in the theory of reference has revolved around the mode of operation of *singular terms*, expressions that purport to designate one individual, such as proper names ("Hypatia," "Aristotle") and definite descriptions ("the tallest building in New York," "the author of *The Human Condition*"). The Gödel/Schmidt thought experiment was proposed by Saul Kripke as part of an argument against *descriptivism*, a theory of the reference of proper names that had been, until 1970, almost universally accepted.

According to the descriptivist approach, a competent speaker associates a proper name with a definite description, and her uses of that name refer to the thing that satisfies the associated description. A speaker that associates the definite description "the first person to receive Nobel Prizes in different fields" with the name "Marie Curie" refers to Marie Curie because she is the person that satisfies the definite description [see 23, *The morning star is the evening star*].

Descriptivism may not be, prima facie, an appealing position. After all, names and definite descriptions are very different kinds of expressions. Names do not have internal meaningful structure; definite descriptions have component expressions that have themselves independent meaning. Names can be bestowed on things simply by agreement; for a definite description to refer to an object, the object in question must satisfy uniquely the attributes mentioned in the description. Nevertheless, descriptivism is a plausible position. It explains in a natural way how we learn names: we learned the name "Aristotle" probably in a class where we were told that he was a Greek philosopher, who tutored Alexander the Great and made the distinction between matter and form. That information, in the form of a description, is what gives life to the name for us. Descriptivism seems to explain also very naturally how we manage to refer to things with which we have never had any contact. Aristotle has long been dead, but when a speaker uses "Aristotle," the description she associates with the name does the work of connecting the utterance of the name to its bearer. For these and other reasons descriptivism used to be the dominant perspective in the philosophy of language.

But in his 1970 lectures Saul Kripke (first published in 1972) presented powerful arguments against descriptivism. Kripke observed that often speakers do not have enough information to single out a person. All that many people know about Christina Koch is that she is a female astronaut; but that information does not distinguish Koch from Stephanie Wilson or Mae C. Jemison. Still, when people use the name "Christina Koch" to utter sentences such as "Christina Koch must be a very brave person," they do refer. According to descriptivism that could not happen, since the name has to be associated with a uniquely identifying, definite description in order to refer. Hence, Kripke concludes, having a backup of descriptions is not necessary to refer when using a name. This argument has come to be known as the *ignorance* argument.

Kripke also observed that people do refer to what is intuitively the "right" referent even when they associate erroneous descriptions with names. Most people associate the description "the first Westerner to arrive in America" with the name "Christopher Columbus." However, the description most likely applies to some Viking conqueror from the eleventh century. Yet, when these people use "Columbus" to ask "Was Columbus Italian?," they do refer to Columbus. So the description they associate is not sufficient to make their uses of the name "Columbus" refer to the satisfier of the description. This argument is known as the *error* argument.

The Gödel/Schmidt case is a fictional case that illustrates the error argument. According to Kripke, the only thing many of us know about Gödel is that he proved the incompleteness of arithmetic. But even if Gödel had stolen the proof from one of his students, our uses of "Gödel" would not refer to that student. So, if we said "Gödel proved the incompleteness of arithmetic," we would be referring to Gödel and saying something false. We would not be saying something true about Schmidt. As in the "Columbus" case, the fact that we attach a description to a name does not make uses of that name refer to the person that satisfies the description.

The ignorance and error arguments are meant to show that descriptivism does not provide the right explanation about how we use names and how names refer. Recently some philosophers such as E. Machery, R. Mallon, S. Nichols, and S. Stich have questioned the intuitive appeal of Kripke's arguments, in particular the universality of the reaction to the Gödel/Schmidt thought experiment. According to some studies, although Westerners tend to agree with Kripke in their intuitions as regard the Gödel/Schmidt case, East Asians tend to give descriptivist responses as they are inclined to conclude that uses of "Gödel" in the circumstances described in the story refer to whoever proved the theorem and hence that they refer to the person that had the proof stolen from him. Other authors have cast doubt on the significance of these results.

Discussion Questions

1. Descriptivism is not just a view about proper names. It is a general view about the way in which words connect to the world. On a descriptivist approach a term such as "tiger" applies to the things that satisfy some description such as "large yellow striped felines" and

"water" applies to samples of liquid that satisfy the description "transparent and odorless liquid that fills our rivers and lakes" (or something similar). Try to construct ignorance and error arguments for these types of terms.

2. Two sentences that have the same meaning have the same *truth conditions*; that is, they have the same truth-value (true or false) and would coincide in truth-value even if the world were different. For instance, "Mary Apgar was a doctor" and "Mary Apgar was a physician" must have the same truth-value. The sentences are, in fact, both true. But if Apgar had decided to become a chef, both sentences would be false. Do the sentences "Aristotle was a philosopher" and "the tutor of Alexander the Great was a philosopher" have the same truth conditions? What does that tell us about the meaning of "Aristotle" and "the tutor of Alexander the Great"?

Further Reading

Devitt, Michael, and Kim Sterelny. 1987. *Language and reality: An introduction to the philosophy of language*, chapters 3 and 4. Oxford: Basil Blackwell.

Donnellan, Keith. 1970. "Proper names and identifying descriptions." *Synthese* 21: 335–358.

Machery, Edouard, Ron Mallon, Shaun Nichols, and Stephen Stich. 2004. "Semantics, cross-cultural style." *Cognition* 92: B1–B12.

Martí, Genoveva. 2009. "Against semantic multi-culturalism." *Analysis* 69: 42–48.

· CHAPTER 26 ·

Gavagai!, by W. V. O. Quine

The Thought Experiment

You are a field linguist, visiting a society with a language that has never before been translated or encountered. Your task is to translate their utterances into English. This is the project of *radical translation.* How do you proceed? Suppose you are taking a walk with one of the speakers of this language, and he says "Gavagai!" as a white rabbit scurries past. You take your field notebook and tentatively write, "Gavagai = rabbit?" You test this hypothesis by trying to see if it holds up in different cases where rabbits are involved. The problem is that you can never be sure. There are always alternative possible translations, such as "animal," "white," or even "dinner." You can never make a definite decision.

Source of the thought experiment:
Quine, W. V. O. 1960. *Word and object.* Cambridge, MA: MIT Press.

Reflection by Dorit Bar-On, University of Connecticut, Storrs

Imagine that you find yourself one day in a completely unfamiliar land, surrounded by speakers of a language you do not recognize. You can tell that they are saying things, but you have absolutely no idea *what* they are saying. If you're going to be able to communicate with them, you'll need to learn their language. But suppose there are no existing translation manuals between the alien language and English and no one around who understands both languages. (We can also imagine that there are no recognizable similarities between the alien language and any language you know.) So you have to figure out their language from scratch. The philosopher Willard Van Orman Quine (1908–2000) describes this as the task of *radical translation*: mapping words and phrases of one language onto those of another, with no help of dictionaries, bilinguals, or any prior knowledge of the language to be translated.

The task of the radical translator is without a doubt very difficult; but it cannot be an impossible one. After all, children learn their first language "from scratch." And explorers of new territories have been translating "alien" languages all over the world for millennia. But where can a "radical linguist" begin with her task? Here is how Quine describes a possible early step in this process:

> A rabbit scurries by, the native says "Gavagai," and the linguist notes down the sentence "Rabbit" (or "Lo, a rabbit") as tentative translation, subject to testing in further cases. (Quine 1960, 29)

Quine is here imagining that, if you have heard an alien speaker exclaim "Gavagai!" just when a rabbit came by, you could tentatively assume that she meant to say: "Rabbit!," or "There's a rabbit!," or something along these lines. But is this a safe assumption? Perhaps the speaker was really saying: "There's *my* rabbit," or "Look—something for dinner!," or "There's an eagle!" (maybe she noticed an eagle flying in the distance), or even "Pass me the bow and arrows!," or . . . use your imagination. The evidence for translating "Gavagai!" as "Rabbit!" mentioned so far seems too slim; one would need more observations. But just sitting and waiting to hear more utterances of "Gavagai!" might take too long.

Suppose, however, that you could somehow tell when the alien speakers agree or disagree with you (by somehow recognizing the equivalents of our "Yes" and "No"). Then you could take a much more active role: you could start volunteering the sound "Gavagai" in various situations and actually *test* your translation hypotheses. For example, you could point to an eagle and see whether speakers assent or dissent when you ask "Gavagai?." If they dissent—by saying, or gesturing, something equivalent to "No"—then you could rule out the hypothesis that "Gavagai" means "There's an eagle." The same applies to the hypothesis that "Gavagai!" means "Look—something for dinner!" or just "Animal!." (You could rule out the last hypothesis, for example, by pointing to pictures of *different* animals to see whether all of them get a "Yes" when you say "Gavagai?" or only those that have rabbits in them.)

But this method of testing translation hypotheses by assent and dissent has its limits. Even if you could establish that speakers assent to "Gavagai!" whenever—and only when—rabbits are pointed to, this will at most tell you that, *as a sentence*, "Gavagai!" says *something that concerns rabbits*. You cannot yet conclude that the speakers are using a *word that means what our word "rabbit" means*. This is because, for all you know, their word "gavagai," used in isolation, stands for something quite outlandish, like "rabbit-spirit"—perhaps the alien speakers have some odd beliefs about (what we think of as) rabbits, and regard them as bodily incarnations of rabbit spirits. If that were the case, then of course they would still assent to your utterances of "Gavagai!" in the presence of rabbits, since a rabbit-spirit would be present any time a rabbit is. But it would be a mistake to translate their word "gavagai" as meaning the same as our "rabbit."

You *could* rule out the "rabbit-spirit" translation hypothesis, but only by *making lots of assumptions*—both about the alien speakers' background beliefs and about the meanings of *other* words in their language. You could only make legitimate assumptions about meanings of other alien words, it seems, if you could settle on how to translate *those other* words—but you haven't done that yet! And you cannot make specific assumptions about what alien speakers believe without, well, *talking* to them. Understanding what they say depends on knowing what they believe, and knowing what they believe requires asking them questions and understanding their answers. A radical translator must somehow decipher alien beliefs and meanings all at once, since speakers' beliefs and the meanings of their words are *interdependent*.

Quine's well-known thesis of *the indeterminacy of radical translation* says that no amount of observation of the behavior of alien speakers could allow a radical translator to settle on a single, objectively correct mapping between an alien language and hers. This is because it is always possible to adjust what the translator takes the speakers to believe, in order to accommodate alternative ways of translating their words.

Discussion Questions

1. Can you think of additional ways that a radical translator could test hypotheses about what individual words of an alien language mean?
2. We usually assume that, although members of other cultures may differ from us in their religious and moral beliefs, as well as in their customs and habits, they at least see the world around them in roughly the same ways that we do. We assume that, like us, they think and talk in terms of categories and concepts such as "tree," "dog," "clouds," "food,"

"running," "scared," and so on. Does Quine's thought experiment about radical translation present a challenge for this assumption? If so, how?

3. Do you think there are any situations in ordinary communication among speakers of the *same* language that can support Quine's thesis of the indeterminacy of translation?

Further Reading

Gibson, Roger F. 1982. *The philosophy of W.V. Quine: An expository essay*, chapter 3, §3.1–3.2. Tampa: University Presses of Florida.

Lycan, William G. 2008. *Philosophy of language: A contemporary introduction*. 2nd ed. Chapter 8. New York: Routledge.

Martin, Robert M. 1988. *The meaning of language*. Chapter 6. Cambridge, MA: MIT Press.

· CHAPTER 27 ·

The Beetle in the Box, by Ludwig Wittgenstein

The Thought Experiment

I can only say of myself that I know what the word "pain" means from my own experience. Shouldn't I also say that about others? How could I generalize this to other people without being irresponsible? Everyone can tell me that they know only from their own experience what pain is. Suppose now that everyone had a box, and something inside the box which we call "beetle." Nobody is able to peer into anyone else's box, and they all say they only know what a beetle is based on what they can see inside their own box. So it's possible that everyone has something different inside their box. You could even imagine that the thing inside was constantly changing. What can we conclude about the use of the word "beetle" by these people? It would not refer to a thing. Whatever is in the box plays no part in the language-game at all, not even as a "something;" after all, the box might also be empty . . . whatever each of us names "beetle" is of no relevance to it.

Source of the thought experiment:

Wittgenstein, Ludwig. (1953) 2009. *Philosophical investigations*. Rev. 4th ed. §293. Translated by G. E. M. Anscombe, P. M. S. Hacker, and Joachim Schulte. Oxford: Wiley Blackwell.

Reflection by Constantine Sandis, University of Hertfordshire

One of the most natural philosophical thoughts we can have is that we can only know what a sensation like pain *is* (or "is like") from our own case. We are thus inclined to say such things as "What I feel when I have a headache may be different from what you feel when you have a headache," and "we can never know whether what I see as 'blue' is the same as what you see as 'blue'" (*Philosophical Investigations* [hereafter *PI*] §§273–278). Wittgenstein wishes to expunge such statements—to which we return, time and time again, "as if bewitched"— from philosophical language (*On Certainty* §31). This can only be achieved by demonstrating that they are symptomatic of our being in the grip of some untenable picture of the relation between mind and language. The parable of the beetle in the box (*PI* §293) serves as an aid to liberate us from the conception of psychological vocabulary as referring to private, mental sensations.

It is tempting to think that what makes our sensations essentially hidden from others is that they are "inner" things, to be contrasted with our "outer" behavior. But what does it mean to say that something is "inner"? The matchbox in which the schoolchild keeps its beetle seems to be an "outer" object. Yet the parable asks us to suppose that "everyone had a box with something in it which we call a 'beetle'" but that "no one can ever look into anyone else's box." It thereby reveals that what makes something "inner" is not that it lies within us—as opposed to in our hands—but that "no one knows whether other people have *this* or something else" (*PI* §242).

Wittgenstein now asks us to imagine a language-game in which the word "beetle" doesn't mean "a dark, shiny, hard-shelled insect" but, rather, "whatever is in each person's matchbox." We would still all mean the same thing by the word "beetle" even if there were different things inside our respective matchboxes, if these things were constantly changing, or if one or more of the boxes turned out to be empty. This is because the suggested use of the word "beetle" does not depend on the contents of any box. Whatever lies inside the matchbox (the "inner") plays no part in this language-game: "if we construe the grammar of the expression of sensation on the model of 'object and designation,' the object drops out of consideration as irrelevant" (*PI* §293).

At the heart of the parable lies the fact that however greatly our access to things is restricted, the vocabulary we use to talk about them is public and in principle shareable. The workings of our language are thus unaffected by "the inner." *What* we both see as green is that grass or this chair, not some inner sensation of "green." Given that words like "green" and "pain" are public in this way, they cannot derive their meaning from any private sensations we might have while looking at a green object. Whatever "inner" object we try to point at is thus semantically irrelevant. As Wittgenstein puts it: "a wheel that can be turned though nothing else moves with it is not part of the mechanism" (*PI* §271).

In this thought experiment, as in many of his other remarks, Wittgenstein treats the philosophical question as one does an illness (*PI* §255). This methodology stands in stark contrast to that of many philosophers, whose arguments serve to tighten the grip of pre-existing pictures. The precise sense and extent to which his approach constitutes a form of therapy from the maladies of philosophy is contentious. There is nevertheless no doubt that Wittgenstein's aim is to break the spell of certain ways of thinking. This is not a one-off trick. As science and language develop, the same old pictures return under new guises and need to be fought off anew. What was once thought to be hidden in the mind or soul is now said to be hidden in the brain or the AI's "black box." The latter is generally thought to be an impenetrable "neural net," which even its designers and engineers cannot peer into in order to explain how the system "sees" the world (its process of pattern recognition). But if Wittgenstein is right, the picture of AI systems as black boxes is a misleading metaphor that steers us away from a mechanism that is "already in plain view" (*PI* §89).

The parable of the beetle in the box forms part of a series of remarks on "immediate private sensations" (including the infamous "private language argument"), which immediately proceeds Wittgenstein's discussion of rule-following, whereby his interlocutor proposes that "'red' means the color that occurs to me when I hear the word 'red'" (*PI* §239). It contains, in microscopic form, not only key aspects of Wittgenstein's so-called private language argument but also his approach to mental phenomena, rule-following, meaning, nonsense, criteria, pragmatism, language-games, skepticism, solipsism, and the first person.

Discussion Questions

1. Is Wittgenstein denying the existence of the inner altogether, or merely its importance to language?
2. If your color sensations were very different from mine, could we ever come to know this; for example, if your sensation of blue were different from mine, could we find out?
3. What would it mean for a language to be absolutely "private"?
4. The word "beetle" ordinarily means something like "a dark, shiny, hard-shelled insect." What does the word "pain" mean ordinarily?
5. Can two people feel the same pain? Can two people feel the same sadness?

Further Reading

Diamond, Cora. 2000. "Does Bismarck have a beetle in his box?" In *The new Wittgenstein*, edited by Alice Crary and Rupert J. Read, 262–292. London: Routledge.

Finkelstein, David H. *Expression and the inner.* Cambridge, MA: Harvard University Press, 2008.

Hacker, P. M. S. (1990) 2019. *Meaning and mind* (Vol. 3 of an *Analytical commentary on the philosophical investigations*): Part II—Exegesis §§ 243–427. 2nd ed. Oxford: Wiley-Blackwell.

Malcolm, Norman. 1986. *Nothing is hidden: Wittgenstein's criticism of his early thought.* Oxford: Basil Blackwell.

McGinn, Marie. 1997. *The Routledge guidebook to Wittgenstein's philosophical investigations.* London: Routledge.

Mulhall, Stephen. 2007. *Wittgenstein's private language argument: Grammar, nonsense, and imagination in philosophical investigations, §§ 243–315.* Oxford: Oxford University Press.

· PART VI ·

Thought Experiments in Metaphysics

· CHAPTER 28 ·

Plato's Allegory of the Cave

The Thought Experiment

Plato tells us the difference between being educated and not educated. People live in a cavern with a long entrance open toward the light. Their legs and necks are shackled from childhood, so they can only look forward, and the shackles prevent them from turning and seeing what's behind them. Behind them a fire blazes, and between that fire and the prisoners is a road along which a low wall has been built. Along that road walk puppeteers that show all sorts of objects. The prisoners see those shadows, as well as shadows of themselves and their fellow prisoners, cast upon the wall. So the prisoners would conclude that reality is nothing but those shadows. Suppose one of the prisoners was released from her fetters, and could stand up and look about, and leave the cave. At first, the light would be so dazzling it would be painful, and she would be unable to discern the objects she formerly perceived as shadows. She'd have to get accustomed to the sight of the upper world gradually, at first looking at shadows, then reflections in water, and later, the things themselves. Then, she would gaze upon the sky at night, and finally the sun itself. Such a person would think back about her life in the cave, and her fellow prisoners, and would count herself happy and pity them. But suppose she were to be cast back into the cave. Because her eyes would still be accustomed to the brightness above and not able to see the shadows quite as well as before, the other prisoners would find her ridiculous, and they would conclude that it would be better to not even think of escape.

Source of the thought experiment:

Plato. (around 375 BCE) 1992. *Republic.* Translated by G. M. A. Grube. Revised by C. D. C. Reeve. Indianapolis: Hackett.

Reflection by Taylor Carman, Barnard College, Columbia University

Plato's Cave Allegory is the most famous short piece of writing in the history of Western philosophy. It presents, in a single unforgettable image, an account of what is most true and real, of what we can (and cannot) know, and of the attainment of wisdom or enlightenment by means of what the Greeks called culture or education, in Greek *paideia*. More generally, it tells us how we should live our lives—what we should admire and strive for and what we should set aside as shallow and unimportant. The allegory itself takes up just three or four pages, but it is extraordinarily rich.

What are the shadows on the wall of the cave? Appearances, obviously. But what are appearances? And what do the statues or puppets being paraded above the wall represent? Something *more* real—more "true," Plato says—than the shadows. The puppets, however, are in turn less true or real than things outside the cave, things illuminated not by the fire burning behind the prisoners, but by the sun. So the allegory describes a gradual progression from the shadows, to the puppets, and finally out of the cave into the broad daylight.

Plato drew a sharp distinction between what we can perceive with our senses and what we can grasp with our minds, a distinction between the sensible and the intelligible. But although the distinction itself is sharp, what it points to is a difference of degree: a visible thing (an ordinary physical object) is not *un*real, but merely *less* real than something intelligible (what Plato called a "form" or "idea," in Greek *eidos*). Likewise, the error or ignorance of the prisoners in the cave lies not in their taking the shadows to be "true," but merely in their assuming that "the true is *nothing other than* the shadows." Plato did not believe that the visible world is an illusion, only that it has a lesser degree of being than the world of ideas, which is accessible only to thought—visible only to the "mind's eye," so to speak. After all, there really *are* shadows on the wall of the cave. They are, however, mere shadows, mere reflections and distortions of the puppets, which the prisoners cannot see directly.

The allegory also asks what we can know. The question places a high premium on knowledge and sets the bar high on claims anyone might make to *know* something, rather than merely believe it or take it on faith. Just as Plato does not deny the reality of appearances, neither does he deny that we can have beliefs about them. But as appearances are mere shadows, so, too, our beliefs are mere opinions. Knowledge, which must be certain and infallible, can only be of intelligible things, which are permanent and unchanging. Plato thought that the visible world as a whole is constantly in flux, and trying to *know* it is like trying to draw a precise picture of a flickering flame or of clouds changing shape as they move across the sky. By contrast, we can know that 2 + 2 = 4 just by thinking about it, and we can be sure we will always be right, for it will always be true.

Plato also tells us that the prisoners in the cave cannot turn their heads and look around, so they can see neither themselves nor their fellow prisoners, but again only their shadows. What this means is that they do not know themselves, nor do they know each other, only their dim and distorted appearances. Plato is suggesting that we all have, for the most part, superficial and inaccurate conceptions of ourselves and the people around us, just as we grasp only the fluctuating surface of things, not their unchanging essences.

Plato returns to this point a little later when he says, very movingly, that when we see "a soul disturbed and unable to see," we should never laugh thoughtlessly, but remember that we can be blinded in two ways: by emerging from darkness or by emerging from a brighter light. Anyone who has walked into or out of a movie theater on a sunny day knows what Plato is literally describing. The force of the metaphor, though, is to challenge our assumption that we know whether we are dwelling in the light or in the darkness, and so whether someone who struggles to see what we can see knows less or *more* than we do. That poignant word of warning cautions us against presuming that our own talent or success constitutes genuine wisdom; perhaps it is just a kind of glib cleverness, richly rewarded by our peers but in fact flimsy and insubstantial. It also reminds us that the seeming awkwardness or ignorance of others might, for all we know, conceal a deeper wisdom. Those who have trouble seeing in our midst might be fools, but—for all we know—they might know something profound or "divine." Here Plato is clearly referring to his beloved friend and mentor, Socrates, whom many dismissed as a clumsy (and irritating) buffoon, though he was in fact an enlightened genius who was tried and put to death some twenty years earlier for challenging the conventional assumptions and values of his fellow Athenians.

Finally, Plato says that climbing out of the cave and coming to see things in the light of day requires not just turning one's eyes but one's "whole soul" toward the light. True education—wisdom in place of ignorance, light in place of darkness—is not the mere acquisition of information and demands more than just a momentary shift of attention. It must instead be a sustained and wholehearted commitment of the entire person.

Discussion Questions

1. What kinds of things in the world of your own experience do you think Plato might say are mere shadows, rather than substantial things? Talk radio, reality TV shows, spelling bees, and sporting events might be obvious candidates. But what about things we take more seriously like prestigious prizes for scientific and artistic achievement, election to public office, and technological progress? Are such things of real value or are they just show?
2. Is it true that the world of appearance is a kind of chaos or flux, that it cannot be known or described any more accurately than shadows flickering on the wall of a cave? Mathematical problems can be solved objectively, but disputes about which flavor of ice cream, or which film, or what kind of music is the best can be interminable. Are we condemned to a mere cacophony of opinion and disagreement when it comes to such things as culture, politics, society, and morality? Can we know anything at all without knowing it with absolute and final certainty?
3. If it is true that we live most of our lives like prisoners in a cave, what should we do about it? Plato says everyone can learn, but not everyone can attain true wisdom. What about those who can? Do they have an obligation to try to become educated, which is to say, cultivated and enlightened? Or is wisdom just another talent they might have, like running a marathon or playing the piano?

Further Reading

Annas, Julia. 1981. *An introduction to Plato's Republic.* New York: Oxford University Press.
Blackburn, Simon. 2008. *Plato's Republic: A biography.* New York: Grove Press.
Havelock, Eric A. 1982. *Preface to Plato.* Cambridge, MA: Harvard University Press.
Pappas, Nickolas. 2013. *The Routledge guidebook to Plato's Republic.* New York: Routledge.
Santas, Gerasimos. 2006. *The Blackwell guide to Plato's Republic.* Malden, MA: Blackwell.

· CHAPTER 29 ·

The Prince and the Cobbler, by John Locke

The Thought Experiment

What makes our identity the same over time? Clearly, there are lots of things that change about us, for example, when we grow older. To grapple with this question, John Locke asks us to imagine the soul of a prince, which enters the body of a cobbler. In Locke's version of the thought experiment, it's not clear where the soul of the cobbler goes—anyway, the prince's soul is now in the cobbler's body. Would the prince still be the same person? He would still have all his princely thoughts, but he'd still look to everyone else like the cobbler. Also, if we agree it is the same person, would we still say that the cobbler's body with the prince's soul was the same *man*?

Source of the thought experiment:

Locke, John. 1694. *An essay concerning human understanding* (second edition). London: Thomas Bassett.

Reflection by Jessica Gordon-Roth, University of Minnesota, Twin Cities

Questions about diachronic identity—or what makes an individual *the same individual* over time—were not at all new by the time John Locke (1632–1704) was writing *An Essay Concerning Human Understanding* in the late seventeenth century [see also 30, *The self and the chariot*]. Philosophers long before Locke were devising thought experiments to test our intuitions about whether an individual at a later time is identical to an individual at an earlier time, and if so, *why*, or if not, *why not.* But Locke was the first philosopher to construct thought experiments intended to explicitly test readers' intuitions about the identity of *persons* over time.

According to Locke, a person is "a thinking intelligent Being, that has reason and reflection, and can consider it self as it self, the same thinking thing in different times and places" (Locke 1694, 2.27.9). Moreover, Locke takes "person" to be a "forensic term" (2.27.26). Persons are thus thinking intelligent beings that have the ability to reason, reflect, and recognize that they persist over time. Insofar as this is the case, persons are moral agents, or entities that are held responsible for their actions, with whatever punishment or reward that may follow.

With Locke's conception of "person" in hand, we can turn to the question of what makes any person the same person over time. Locke says that "consciousness always accompanies thinking, and 'tis that, that makes every one to be, what he calls *self*" (2.27.9). Consciousness is what distinguishes selves, and thus, "in this alone consists *personal Identity*, i.e. the sameness of rational Being: And as far as this consciousness can be extended backwards to any past Action or Thought, so far reaches the Identity of that *Person*; it is the same *self* now it was then; and 'tis by the same *self* with this present one that now reflects on it, that that Action was done" (2.27.9). The key to personal identity, then, is sameness of consciousness, according to Locke.

Locke devises numerous thought experiments to drive this point home. One of the most vivid thought experiments Locke offers is the "prince and the cobbler" thought experiment. As Locke puts it:

> … [S]hould the Soul of a Prince, carrying with it the consciousness of the Prince's past life, enter and inform the Body of the Cobler as soon as deserted by his own Soul,

> every one sees, he would be the same Person with the Prince, accountable only for the Prince's Actions: But who would say it was the same Man? (2.27.15)

Locke asks us to imagine that the soul of a prince enters and informs the body of a cobbler, taking all of its "princely thoughts" with it. There are many things we might be intended to get out of this passage, but at the very least Locke thinks we will conclude that the person we are calling "prince" will wake up wondering where his royal attendants are, and why customers are asking him for their shoes. In other words, the person we are calling "prince" now persists in the body of the cobbler.

It is important to realize that in this thought experiment, the person we are calling "prince" ends up not just in a new body, but in a new human being (or man). This comes through when Locke asks rhetorically, "But who would say it was the same Man?" (2.27.15). It is additionally important to realize that the prince and the cobbler thought experiment works in tandem with the other thought experiments Locke employs throughout his discussion of personal identity, and examining this passage in isolation might leave us with some misconceptions of Locke's view. In particular, it is worth noting that although the prince has the same soul throughout the scenario that Locke describes, having the same soul is not required for personal identity, according to Locke. The reason the person we call "prince" goes where his soul goes—into the body of the human being we call "cobbler"—is because the prince's *consciousness* remains annexed to his soul. Indeed, some of Locke's other thought experiments show a person can survive a change in soul (2.27.13), and still others show that having the same soul isn't enough to ensure personal persistence (2.27.14, 23, 24). It is always the sameness of *consciousness* that does the job of maintaining personal identity, according to Locke.

Finally, we ought to consider the thought experiments Locke devises in light of the bigger picture that Locke paints and the context within which he is working. Just looking at the thought experiments alone could suggest that Locke thinks that persons pop in and out of existence—jumping from one body or soul to another—on a regular basis. But it is baked into Locke's definition of "person" that persons are the kinds of entities that persist. This is what Locke means when he claims that persons are entities that can consider themselves as themselves in different times and places (2.27.9). Moreover, Locke is just as keen to show what personal identity consists in—consciousness—as he is to show why other competing theories fail. Locke is thus using thought experiments to challenge the *preconceived notions* of his readers. Many readers are going to assume that tracking persons necessarily means tracking souls, while others are going to assume that tracking persons necessarily means tracking human beings. Locke devises the prince and the cobbler thought experiment in an effort to challenge the latter.

Discussion Questions

1. Why does personal identity matter, and what is important about it?
2. Do you think you will be the same person when you are eighty years old as you were when you were five? If so, why? If not, why not?
3. Is Locke onto something when he argues that the identity of persons lies in sameness of consciousness? How might consciousness be different from memory?

Further Reading

Gordon-Roth, Jessica. 2020. "Locke on Personal Identity." In *The Stanford encyclopedia of philosophy*, Spring 2020 edition, edited by Edward N. Zalta. https://plato.stanford.edu/archives/spr2020/entries/locke-personal-identity/

LoLordo, Antonia. 2012. *Locke's moral man*. Oxford: Oxford University Press.

Martin, Raymond, and John Barresi. 2000. *Naturalization of the soul: Self and personal identity in the eighteenth century*. London: Routledge.

Weinberg, Shelley. 2016. *Consciousness in Locke*. Oxford: Oxford University Press.

· CHAPTER 30 ·

The Self and the Chariot, by Nāgasena

The Thought Experiment

The monk Nāgasena had an audience with King Milinda. The King asked Nāgasena what his name was, and Nāgasena replied, "I'm known as Nāgasena, but that is just convention. The name does not refer to any permanent individual."

The King expressed his disbelief. "If you are not a permanent individual," he protested, "then how can you be said to be righteous, or not righteous? If someone were to kill you, there would be no murder."

Nāgasena then asked the King how he had come to their meeting place.

"By chariot," the King replied.

"What is the chariot?" Nāgasena asked, "Is it the axle? The wheels? The chassis? The reins? The yoke? All these things together, or yet something different?"

The King replied, "It's none of those things."

"Ah, then it seemed you were lying when you said you came with a chariot, since you can't show it," Nāgasena concluded.

"No, I spoke the truth," the King retorted, "It's called a chariot because it has all those parts."

"You are right," Nāgasena said, "My body is composed of the physical stuff that makes up human bodies, and that is why I am called "Nāgasena."

Both King and Monk were pleased with this solution, of how you can have a name that refers, even though there is no permanent self.

Source of the thought experiment:

Pesala, Bhikkhu, ed. (1991) 2001. *Milindapañha. The debate of King Milinda*. The new revised edition. Penang: Inner Path. http://www.buddhanet.net/pdf_file/milinda.pdf

Reflection by Alexus McLeod, University of Connecticut

The *Milindapañha* is a Buddhist text dating likely to the first or second century CE (the oldest extant version of which is in the Pali language). It was written as a dialogue between the Buddhist monk Nāgasena and the Greco-Bactrian King Milinda (Menander I), who ruled a region comprised of parts of modern-day Afghanistan and Pakistan during the second century BCE.

Milinda had a reputation for philosophical debate and challenged various teachers in his kingdom to debates, asking them to resolve difficult philosophical questions. None of the esteemed teachers Milinda questioned over the years had been able to resolve his questions. He learned of Nāgasena, a wise elder Buddhist monk at a distant monastery, and immediately set out visit Nāgasena in the hopes of having his questions finally answered sufficiently.

While the discussion between Milinda and Nāgasena covers almost all aspects of Buddhist thought, the most well-known section of the text deals with the Buddhist view on the self, the doctrine of *anatta* (or in Sanskrit, *anatman*). The Pali term *anatta* translates as "no-self" or "non-self." This core early Buddhist view holds that there ultimately is no permanent and unchanging entity belonging to a person and through which we maintain identity through time. There is no permanent self, soul, or other such enduring element of the person. When we think or talk about ourselves, we do not refer ultimately to any such entity. Rather, we refer to a set of changing and impermanent mental and physical "aggregates" (*skandhas*) that constantly come into being and go out of being.

As we can see in the dialogue of this thought experiment, Milinda asked Nāgasena: if there is ultimately no self, what is it that you refer to with the name "Nāgasena"? Moreover, what is the thing that can be deluded or enlightened? Doesn't the doctrine of "non-self" thus undermine the entire Buddhist project? The primary aim of Buddhism is to end the suffering brought about through continual cycles of birth and death, arising and decay, ultimately brought about through grasping and attachment to things. Through following the Buddhist teachings, which enjoin morality, concentration, and recognition of truths about the world, individuals can overcome suffering, attaining what the Buddhists refer to as enlightenment (*nibbana*, better known in its Sankskrit form, *nirvana*). But if there is no self, there is no Nāgasena, no Milinda, and ultimately no one to be enlightened.

Nāgasena responds to this by asking Milinda to consider the chariot that he rode to their meeting. What, Nāgasena asks, is the chariot? Is it the axle? The wheels? Is it all the parts combined? Or something altogether different?

Milinda responds that the chariot is none of those things.

Nāgasena says: "If that is the case, then is there is no chariot? But if there is no chariot, what are you referring to when you talk about the chariot?" Nāgasena goes on to explain that what we call a chariot is a collection of parts. The chariot is nothing above and beyond these parts, but rather a way of referring to these (changeable and changing) parts. When we refer to the chariot, we refer to the collection of parts that include the wheels, axle, and so on. In the same way, Nāgasena says, when we refer to "Nāgasena" or "Milinda," we refer to the changing and impermanent set of mental and physical aggregates causally connected with one another.

If this is the case, however, why reject that there is in fact a "self"? Perhaps there is no single *part* of the chariot that can be identified with the chariot, but the *collection* of parts can be so identified. The problem with this, according to Nāgasena, is that the parts of the individual, like the parts of the chariot, are not permanent and thus the set of parts "self" or "chariot" refers to is itself constantly changing. There is nothing in the set of parts that can be said to endure and be the source of the chariot's identity. Nor can the changing set itself be identified with an enduring thing. I can change the wheels, axle, seat, or other parts of my chariot, yet still refer to it as the same chariot. Likewise, the person I call "Nāgasena" changes in its parts. Not only can it change in its bodily composition—it can lose a leg or an arm, the cells in its body are continually replaced through regeneration—but its mental composition also changes. Thoughts, attitudes, and other mental contents change throughout our lives. When I refer to "Nāgasena," then, I do not refer to any unchanging entity that endures throughout a life. I do not refer to a "soul" in the sense of Plato or the Brahmanist philosophers with whom the Buddhists disagreed [see 31, *The flying man* for a contrasting perspective].

If "Nāgasena" simply refers to the set or bundle of changing mental and physical aggregates, and these aggregates continually come into and go out of existence, then there is no permanent and unchanging entity referred to by the name. "Nāgasena" is a *convention* we use to talk about parts and their activities. When we talk about the chariot, we use a convention to refer to a collection of parts. But we should not, the Buddhist argues, be tricked by our conventions into thinking that there are unchanging, enduring, and ultimately existing entities that we refer to when we use language like "I," "me," and "mine."

Discussion Questions

1. Could a chariot as a *whole* be a distinct entity from the set of parts of a chariot? What would have to be the case concerning parts and wholes for this to be so?
2. How might rejecting the idea that we have permanent and enduring selves be useful in helping to achieve the Buddhist's ultimate goal of eliminating suffering?

Further Reading

Collins, Steven. 2008. *Selfless persons: Imagery and thought in Theravāda Buddhism*. Cambridge: Cambridge University Press.

Siderits, Mark. 2007. *Buddhism as philosophy: An introduction*. Indianapolis: Hackett.

· CHAPTER 31 ·

The Flying Man, by Ibn Sīnā (Avicenna)

The Thought Experiment

Suppose a man is created by God all at once. He is perfect, fully grown, but does not have any sensory input, and floats in the air, in such a way that he does not feel the air, and his limbs are separated so they don't touch each other. So he is not aware of the outside world nor is he aware of his own body. Lastly, since God has just created him, he has no memories whatsoever. Would such a person affirm the existence of his own essence, even though he does not affirm the existence of his own body? Yes, such a person would affirm that his essence exists apart from any relation to his organic human body.

Source of the thought experiment:

Avicenna (Ibn Sīnā). 2007. "On the soul." In *Classical Arabic philosophy: An anthology of sources*, translated by Jon McGinnis and David C. Reisman, 175–209. Indianapolis: Hackett.

Reflection by Scott M. Williams, University of North Carolina, Asheville

Avicenna's (Ibn Sīnā's) flying man thought experiment is intended to help us become aware of who we are and how we relate to our own organic bodies that we use all of the time for many kinds of activities (e.g., seeing, hearing, desiring). Avicenna was concerned that we misunderstand the relationship between ourselves and our organic bodies, and this thought experiment—what he calls a "pointer and reminder"—is supposed to guide us. If the story succeeds, then it shows that each of us is an immaterial, living, rational substance (something that exists in itself). The name for this immaterial, living, rational substance is the "human soul." With other arguments, Avicenna claims that such a soul bestows life and various powers (capacities for nutrition, growth, sensation, and imagination) on our organic bodies. And, if the story succeeds, then it may transform how you understand yourself in relation to your organic body. It may help you to understand yourself as yourself—perhaps for the first time.

Avicenna tells this story several times to establish different claims. On the first occasion (*On the Soul*, 1.1) he intends to show that the human soul in itself is different than the organic body to which it bestows life and various capacities. Before telling the story, Avicenna reports Aristotle's definition of soul as the form or perfection of a living organic body. Although Avicenna agrees with Aristotle that the soul bestows life and various capacities on an organic body, he contends that Aristotle only described the soul in relation to something else (the organic body) but failed to define the soul in itself. In this context, the flying man story is intended to show us that the human soul is not defined merely in relation to an organic body. Rather, the human soul is something in itself, distinct from its relation to an organic body.

Like an inside joke, the background is crucial for interpreting the story in the way that Avicenna intends. Avicenna presumes that a nature or essence (what something is) is the same thing whether it exists outside a mind (e.g., your existing human nature) or exists as a concept in someone's mind (e.g., your concept of your human nature); and an essence as such can only exist either as a concept in someone's mind or in a really existing thing. So, if human nature exists as a concept in my mind, then it corresponds to human nature existing in human beings. This assumption is perhaps the most contentious background for the story.

Now, the flying man understands his own essence as it exists in itself, and without reference to his organic body. Given this, and Avicenna's claim that a true concept of an essence corresponds to a really existing essence, it follows that the human soul in itself is a different essence than the essence of an organic body that it animates. Consider an analogous case: compare a triangle in itself and, for example, an equilateral triangle. If you have the concept of a triangle in itself, then this would not include its relation to an equilateral triangle. This suggests that being a triangle is different than being an equilateral triangle. Likewise, your human soul in itself is different than any relation it has to your organic body.

Some have asked how the flying man's awareness of his own existing essence fits in the story. Should the story be interpreted as suggesting that, for example, I am a thinking thing? Descartes believed that about himself. This is likely the wrong way to interpret Avicenna's story because the point about the flying man's act of thinking of his own essence (or soul) is that he needs to be consciously aware of his own essence in order to be aware of the contents of his essence. Still, there is a similarity with Descartes. Descartes would agree with Avicenna's suggestion that the human soul in itself is not the same thing as the organic body to which it is related.

Avicenna puts the flying man story to another use in a later text (*On the Soul*, 5.7). Avicenna observes that human beings have different kinds of activity (e.g., seeing *X*, desiring *X*) and that these are somehow coordinated with each other. When I see something, I desire (or get angry at) what I see. What explains the coordination of these different kinds of activity? Does one bodily organ, or the whole body, coordinate all of these kinds of activity? Avicenna argues against both of these options and opts for the human soul as the better explanation. I won't rehearse those arguments here. Supposing there are plausible reasons for the human soul as a better explanation compared to the alternative explanations, Avicenna reintroduces the flying man story. With the flying man story, I understand that my human soul is different than my organic body, and with Aristotle's arguments we may suppose that the soul bestows various capacities on the organic body. When I experience my different kinds of activity coordinated with each other, Avicenna contends that this is possible only because the same "I" or soul uses different bodily organs for these different kinds of activity. My soul is the referent of "I," and my soul explains why my different kinds of activity can affect or impede each other. Who am I? The flying man declares, "I am my soul! And I use my organic body for different kinds of activities."

If Avicenna is right, he has given us a way to understand ourselves that is consistent with various religious beliefs, for example, that I could exist even after I die because I am different than my organic body. Today, it remains to be seen whether empirical science, like neuroscience, can give a satisfying explanation of the coordination of our different kinds of activity. But even if neuroscience offers such an explanation, it won't in itself have settled whether there is such a thing as the human soul nor its definition.

Discussion Questions

1. Avicenna takes the flying man to be a real possibility (because God has the power to do so), and he thinks it can teach us about ourselves in relation to our own bodies. Understanding that this story is a starting point for future discussion about the relation between one's soul and one's organic body, how do you think the argument could be developed in favor of a real distinction between the human soul and the organic body? What reasons might there be for believing that there are immaterial human souls that are related to human organic bodies?
2. Have you ever wondered why it is that when you see or taste or hear something, that that experience somehow affects another "part" of you? You taste a delicious Fuji apple, and find yourself desiring more Fuji apples. What's the best explanation for why a taste experience informs or affects your desires? After all, tasting is one thing, and desiring is another thing. What connects or coordinates these different kinds of experience? Does it make sense to say that some other part of your organic body can explain this? Or, with the flying man, do you think it is at least possible that your immaterial soul is the subject of these different kinds of experience and it best explains the coordination?
3. Can you imagine yourself just like the flying man? What would you learn about yourself? How might your background beliefs about yourself, or about what's possible, inform what you might learn about yourself? What would it be like to gain a completely new understanding of yourself in relation to your own organic body? Can you know what it would be like to have a completely new understanding of yourself *before* having this totally new understanding of what you really are?

Further Reading

Adamson, Peter, and Fedor Benevich. 2018. "The thought experimental method: Avicenna's flying man argument." *Journal of the American Philosophical Association* 4, no. 2: 147–164.

Black, Deborah L. 2008. "Avicenna on self-awareness and knowing that one knows." In *The unity of science in the Arabic tradition: Science, logic, epistemology and their interactions*, edited by Shahid Rahman, Tony Street, and Hassan Tahiri, 63–87. Dordrecht: Springer.

Marmura, Michael E. 1986. "Avicenna's flying man in context." *Monist* 69: 383–395.

· CHAPTER 32 ·

The Spear at the End of the Universe, by Lucretius

The Thought Experiment

Is the universe finite, or infinitely big? Let's suppose that it had a limit. A far traveler would go to its very edge and hurl a spear with great force further on. Does the spinning spear continue, or does something block it? Whichever option you choose, space is limitless. Either the spear goes on, or it is blocked by some boundary. It seems the end of the world was not the end of the world. The chance for further flight prolongs the spear's flight forever.

Sources of the thought experiment:

Lucretius. (ca. 50 BCE) 2007. *The nature of things.* Translated by Alicia Stallings. London: Penguin. Aristotle. (fourth c. BCE) 1996. *Physics.* Translated by Robin Waterfield. Edited by David Bostock. Oxford: Oxford World Classics.

Reflection by Matthew Duncombe, University of Nottingham

Lucretius's epic philosophical poem *De Rerum Natura*, or *On the Nature of Things*, presents the main tenets of Epicurean physics in Latin, famously including atomism. We can date the poem to the mid-first century BCE. Not only was the poem admired in antiquity for its brilliance, but its re-emergence in early fifteenth-century Italy helped catalyze the Renaissance and, ultimately, modern atomic theory.

The spear argument comes toward the end of the first book of the poem. After outlining the basics of Epicurean atomic theory, Lucretius asks how large the universe is. He answers that the universe is infinitely large. The Spear is both a colorful thought experiment and an argument the universe is infinite. Here is an informal reconstruction. Suppose that the universe were finite. In that case, the universe has a limit. Imagine you fly to the edge of the universe and throw a spear. One of two things happens: either the spear bounces back, or the spear carries on flying. In the first case, there is something beyond the apparent limit, so you have not really found the limit of the universe. In the second case, the spear carries on beyond the apparent limit, so, again, you have not found the limit to the universe. So, either way, you have not found the limit to the universe.

Crucially, Lucretius's reasoning can be repeated over and over. Suppose that you have gone through that spear-throwing once so you realize that "limit 1" was not really the limit. Optimistic, you carry on flying further out and find what you think is the *real* limit, call it "limit 2." You throw your spear at limit 2. But the same alternatives apply: either the spear bounces back, or the spear carries on flying. In the first case, there is something beyond limit 2, so you have not really found the real limit. In the second case, the spear carries on beyond limit 2, so, again, you have not found the real limit. So, either way, you have not found the limit to the universe. It looks like this reasoning can go on and on just like the universe.

Should we be persuaded by Lucretius's argument that the universe is infinite? That would be hasty. For one thing, you might think that physicists, not philosophers, should determine the size of the universe! But there is a more basic problem with Lucretius's spear argument.

The idea behind the spear argument has a long history and, several centuries before Lucretius, Aristotle criticized a similar argument (*Physics* 203b20–22; 208a11–13). Aristotle's criticism is subtle, but worth taking time to understand.

Aristotle points out that "being a limit" is ambiguous. In one sense, having a limit implies that there is something inside the limit and *something* outside the limit. A city limit is a limit in this sense, because a city limit separates what is inside the limit (the city) from what is outside the limit (other places). But in another sense, having a limit implies that there is something inside the limit and *nothing* outside the limit. If my endurance has a limit, that means that I have a certain amount of endurance, but nothing beyond it.

Armed with Aristotle's distinction, we can see that the spear argument trades on the ambiguity in the term "limit." Go back to the step where Lucretius argues that either the spear will bounce back or the spear will carry on flying. In either case, Lucretius argues, there is something beyond the "limit." But if "limit" here means "there is something inside the limit and something outside the limit," then, of course, there is something beyond the limit: that is true by definition. But if "limit" means "there is something inside the limit and nothing outside the limit," there is no reason to think that there is anything beyond the limit. In fact, that is precisely what Lucretius's opponents would hold. Lucretius's opponents argue that "limit" does not imply that there is anything beyond the limit of the universe. Lucretius's spear argument won't persuade you that the universe is infinite unless you already think that the limit of the universe has something beyond it.

Discussion Questions

1. Try to imagine Lucretius's infinite universe. Is it hard to imagine? If it is, does that give you more or less confidence that Lucretius's argument goes wrong?
2. Does it matter if we cannot imagine what such universes would be like?
3. How might Lucretius respond to the sort of criticism of the spear argument that I offered?

Further Reading

Greenblatt, Stephen. 2011. *Swerve: How the Renaissance began*. London: Bodley Head.

Nawar, Tamer. 2015. "Aristotelian finitism." *Synthese* 192, no. 8: 1–16.

Rovelli, Carlo. 2017. "This granular life." *Aeon*, January 23, 2017. https://aeon.co/essays/is-atomic-theory-the-most-important-idea-in-human-history

Sedley, David. 2018. "Lucretius." In *The Stanford encyclopedia of philosophy*, Winter 2018 edition, edited by Edward N. Zalta. The Metaphysics Research Lab: Stanford University. https://plato.stanford.edu/entries/lucretius/

· PART VII ·

Thought Experiments in Decision Theory

· CHAPTER 33 ·

The Russian Nobleman, by Derek Parfit

The Thought Experiment

We are in nineteenth-century Russia. Pyotr, a young count in his twenties, will inherit vast estates upon the death of his father. At present, he is a socialist and fervently wishes to give these lands away to the peasants who currently farm them. So he signs a legal document to the effect that, when his father dies, the ownership of his lands will transfer directly to the peasants. What's more, he ensures that the document can only be voided by his wife, Anna. Pyotr has seen too many young socialists like himself lose their ideals and become bourgeois as they get older, and he fears the same will happen to him. So he asks his wife to promise that if he later asks her to void the document, she will refuse. Anna agrees and makes the promise to her husband. As the years pass, Pyotr's youthful fears are realized, and he becomes bourgeois. When his father dies and the lands are set to transfer to the peasants, in line with the legal document, Pyotr asks Anna to void it to allow him to become the owner of the lands instead. What should Anna do?

Source of the thought experiment:
Parfit, Derek. 1984. *Reasons and persons*. Oxford: Oxford University Press.

Reflection by Richard Pettigrew, Bristol University

This thought experiment is due to the ethicist Derek Parfit (1942–2017). He presents it in his first book, *Reasons and Persons* (1984), which has exerted an enormous influence on ethics since its publication. Parfit thought that a person—an individual like you or me or Pyotr or Anna—is composed of many different selves, just as a jazz band is composed of its players or a country of its residents. When two selves belong to the same person—my current self, for instance, and my self at midday on my fourteenth birthday—we say that the relation of personal identity holds between them.

This relation does not come in degrees. It makes no sense to say that my current self is more part of the same person as my fourteen-year-old self than my current self is part of the same person as my two-year-old self. But there is another relation that holds between two selves, and it does come in degrees. It is what Parfit called the relation of psychological connectedness [for related ideas, see 29, *The prince and the cobbler*]. Two selves have greater psychological similarities the more memories, beliefs, values, or character traits they share.

One of Parfit's most influential and important philosophical claims is that the relation of psychological connectedness is often a more important relation in ethics than the relation of personal identity. That is, often when we state our ethical principles in terms of personal identity, they should really be stated in terms of connectedness. Here's one example: if a major event is about to occur and I am wondering whether I will survive it, the question that matters to me is not whether there is some future self after the event that is part of the same person as my current self—that is, a self to whom I bear the relation of personal identity—but rather whether there is some future self after the event that is psychologically connected with me to a high degree. Here's another: in Plato's *Protagoras*, Socrates argues that it is irrational to prefer receiving some good thing—chocolate, for instance, or a ride on your favorite rollercoaster—in the near future than in the far future; Parfit responds by noting that we are usually less strongly connected to our far future selves than to our near future selves, because we share fewer memories and so on with them, and thus there is nothing irrational in caring less about them.

In the thought experiment of the Russian nobles Pyotr and Anna, Parfit wishes to argue that the relation of connectedness is also important in the ethics of promising and the obligations that promises create. He invites us to agree with him that, when the older, bourgeois Pyotr at his father's grave asks Anna to void the document, she is obliged not to do so—if she does, she will break her promise. And he argues that we can only make sense of this ethical judgment if we accept that what matters in the ethics of promising is connectedness, not identity. We typically think that, if you make a promise to me, then I can also release you from that promise; when I do so, you are no longer obliged to fulfil the promise. However, if we agree with Parfit that Anna must not void the document on pain of breaking her promise, we judge that older, bourgeois Pyotr cannot release her from the promise she made to younger, socialist Pyotr, even though those selves are part of the same person, Pyotr. So, the reason must be that, while bourgeois Pyotr is the same person to whom Anna made her promise, he is not psychologically connected to his earlier socialist self to the degree required to release someone from their promise. His values have changed too much and the degree of psychological connectedness has become too small.

Discussion Questions

1. Frank committed awful crimes in his twenties. By the time has reached his seventies, he has changed completely. He remembers almost nothing of his youth and his moral values have changed dramatically—while he was right-wing then, he is now on the far left of the political spectrum; and so on. Should we nonetheless punish Frank in his seventies for his earlier crimes?
2. I do wrong if I inflict pain on one person in order to gain happiness for another. But my current self doesn't seem to do anything wrong if it arranges for one of my future selves to experience pain so that another of my future selves experiences happiness. For instance, there's nothing wrong with me now arranging for my future self in one week to undergo pain at the dentist so that my future self in a month can live without toothache. Why are the cases different?
3. Parfit himself thought that thinking about yourself as a series of selves might cure you of your fear of death. After all, on this picture, we are forever dying, because our current self goes out of existence to be replaced by a new self. The only difference with the death of the person is that no new self appears to replace the one that has died. Does this thought help you face death?

Further Reading

Parfit, Derek. 1971. "Personal identity." *The Philosophical Review* 80: 3–27.
Pettigrew, Richard. 2019. *Choosing for changing selves.* Oxford: Oxford University Press.
Strominger, Nina, and Shaun Nichols. 2014. "The essential moral self." *Cognition* 131: 159–171.

· CHAPTER 34 ·

Becoming a Vampire, by L. A. Paul

The Thought Experiment

On a summer holiday to Romania, you decide to explore the remains of a medieval castle. Exploring the dark recesses of a former dungeon, you are suddenly confronted by Dracula! He makes you a one-time-only offer: if you like, he will bite you, making you a vampire. If you refuse, you will be banished from the area, never to be approached again. If you accept, the bite will be painless, drawing you effortlessly toward a new kind of being. Your choice, once you make it, is irreversible.

Source of the thought experiment:

Paul, L. A. 2014. *Transformative experience.* Oxford: Oxford University Press.

Reflection by L. A. Paul, Yale University

The possibility is thrilling. If you become a vampire, you'll become immortal. You'll gain immense strength, new powers, and amazing speed. Anything you wear, everything you do, will be imbued with elegance and effortless grace. However, you will lose your humanity. Vampires are Undead. They relish the taste of blood. They can't survive in daylight, they find garlic repulsive, and they no longer empathize in the way that humans do.

As you stand there, reflecting on your options, Dracula tells you that you have until midnight. You are to go back to your room and reflect on what you prefer. If you decide to become a vampire, wait for him at the stroke of twelve with the window open. Otherwise, keep the window closed, and leave when dawn breaks. Never return.

You rush back to your room and immediately contact a friend for advice. You tell her everything. And then she confesses: she is already a vampire! She was bitten last year. You are, quite naturally, surprised, and more than a little afraid. She reassures you: modern vampires don't have to kill anyone—they drink artificial blood. Collecting your thoughts, you ask her what it's like to be a vampire. Laughing, she tells you that mere humans can't possibly understand what it's like. And then she advises you to accept the vampire's offer. She says, "I'm so glad I did it! I'd never go back to being human, even if I could. Now that I'm a vampire, life has meaning and a sense of purpose that it never had before. I've moved past all those stupid, petty, human things I used to care about. They aren't worth my time. It's being a *vampire* that matters!"

The clock is ticking. You must decide. What do you do? How are you supposed to decide? How can you possibly make this life-changing choice in an informed, authentic, and rational way?

To make a rational decision in these circumstances, you need to weigh your different options and choose in a way that will maximize your expected value. But for this choice, you lack the ability to accurately assess what it will be like to become a vampire, and so you can't compare what it would be like for you to be a vampire with what it would be like to remain human. In a dramatic, distinctive, and personally very important sense, the nature of your future life as a vampire is unknowable. If you become a vampire, your very being will mutate. The way you live your life and experience the world will never be the same. You'll leave your old self behind forever, and become a new self, one that relates to the world in distinctively different ways.

Thus, if you choose to transform yourself, you must do so without knowing, in a deep and salient sense, who you will become. This puts you in a unique kind of situation. You are at a crossroads, making a significant choice about what sort of future self to be, and yet, with regard to how you'd experience life as a vampire, you don't know what you are choosing. If you choose based on what you think it would be like to be a vampire, your choice is not rational, because you cannot know what it is like beforehand. If you choose without attending to what it's like despite the fact that this matters to you, your choice does not reflect what you care about. Moreover, because of the way the experience will change you, the self who makes the choice is not the same as the self who will live with the choice, raising the problem all over again: maybe you don't want to become a vampire right now, but you know that if you did become one, you'd be very happy about it. If so, which self's preferences should determine your choice?

These problems arise because the experience of becoming a vampire is transformative, both epistemically and personally. An epistemically transformative experience teaches you something you could not have learned without having that kind of experience—in this example, what it's like to be a vampire. A personally transformative experience alters some of your core preferences, changing what you care about most. An experience is transformative when it is epistemically and personally transformative, bringing about a profound epistemic change that reshapes who you are.

Such experiences, when they can be chosen, raise puzzles for decision making. Because you cannot know ahead of time what it will be like and thus how it will change your lived experience, you can't make your choice based on the lived experience you'd prefer. And because the experience will change, in a very deep way, who you are, the self who makes the choice is not the self who lives with the choice. If the self that must live with the decision is not the self who makes the decision, whose preferences determine the rationality of the choice? The self who makes the choice? Or the self that results from it?

Discussion Questions

1. Should you rely on the testimony of vampires when you make your choice of whether to become a vampire?
2. Which self should determine whether you should decide to transform? The self at the time of decision, the one who makes the choice? Or the self afterward, the one that results from the decision?
3. Does anything change about the structure of the problem when you face a transformative experience that you did not choose, such as an accident, a religious conversion, or a lucky surprise?
4. As it was defined, can an experience be transformative merely because it is new or unexpected?

Further Reading

Bykvist, Krister. 2007. "The benefits of coming into existence." *Philosophical Studies* 135, no. 3: 335–362.

Paul, L. A. 2015. "What you can't expect when you're expecting." *Res Philosophica* 92, no. 2: 149–170.

Ullmann-Margalit, Edna. 2006. "Big decisions: Opting, converting, drifting." *Royal Institute of Philosophy Supplements* 58: 157–172.

· CHAPTER 35 ·

Sleeping Beauty, by Adam Elga

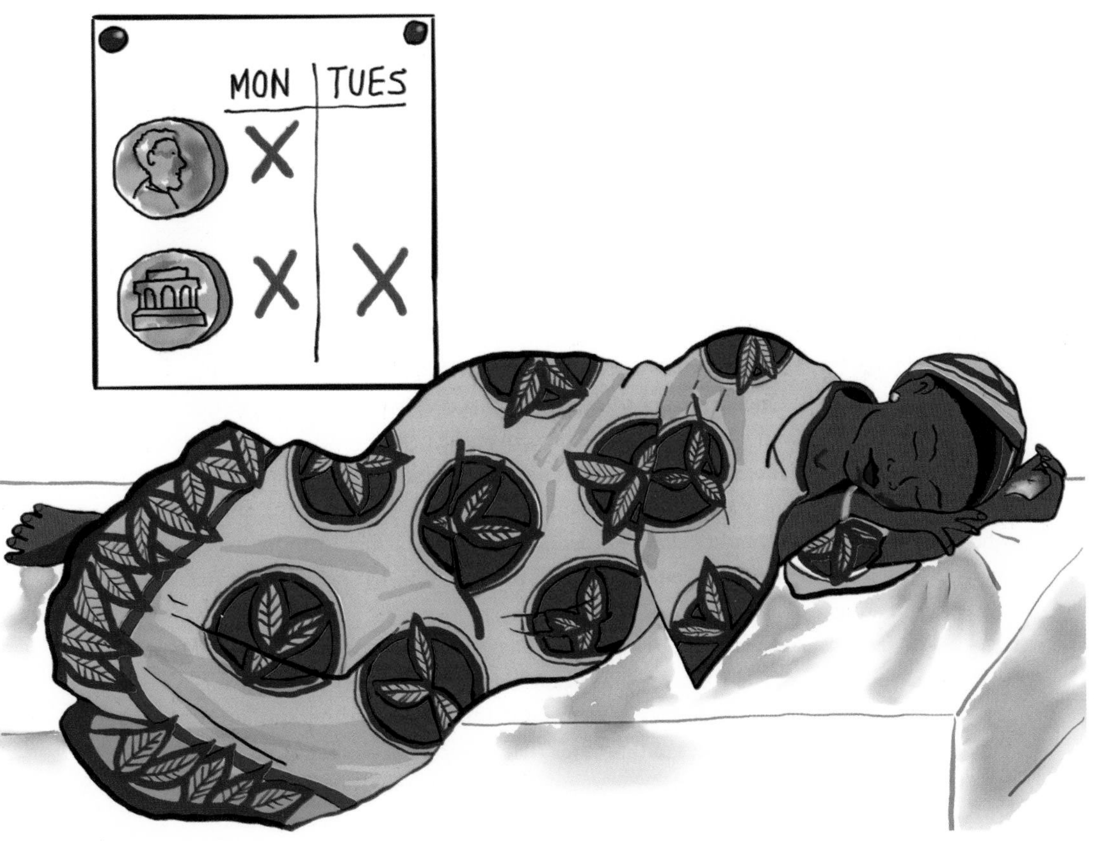

The Thought Experiment

Abebi (also known as Sleeping Beauty) takes part in an experiment, where researchers put her to sleep. She is told that a fair coin will be flipped. At each waking, she is put back to sleep with a drug that will make her forget that waking. If the fair coin lands tails, she will be briefly awakened on Monday and Tuesday. If it's heads, she will only be awakened on Monday. When Abebi awakes on Monday, not knowing what day it is, how confident should she be that the coin has landed heads? You might think her confidence should be 1/2, after all, the baseline chance of a fair coin landing on heads is 1/2, and our sleeping beauty does not receive any new information to change this, as she is awakened anyway. But Adam Elga thinks she should only have confidence 1/3. His reasoning is as follows: she doesn't know whether it's Monday or Tuesday, so she should think that it could be either. When Abebi awakens, there are therefore three possible scenarios: (1) It's Tuesday and the coin landed tails, (2) It's Monday and the coin landed tails, and (3) It's Monday and the coin landed heads. Each of these is equal, so her confidence in each should be 1/3. Therefore, when she is awakened, her confidence in heads should be 1/3. What do you think?

Source of the thought experiment:

Elga, Adam. 2000. "Self-locating belief and the Sleeping Beauty problem." *Analysis* 60: 143–147.

Reflection by Kenny Easwaran, Texas A&M University

Why am I here now? One version of this question is a deep metaphysical question: why does anything exist at all, and why does the universe, over the course of its history, contain all this complexity, including life, and humanity, and my society, and me? But even if we could explain why all this exists, there is a further question: why am I this person, living at this moment in the twenty-first century, rather than a nineteenth-century farmer in India, or a priest at the height of the Mayan empire, or one of the cave painters who left her mark in Australia forty thousand years ago?

Some versions of the question have an easy answer—why am I not a medieval blacksmith in Antarctica? Because there were no medieval blacksmiths in Antarctica! Even when some group isn't totally absent from history, we can sometimes say something similar. Why am I not among the first hunter-gatherer communities that crossed the Bering Strait during the most recent Ice Age? Because there were only a few thousand members of those communities, and there are many billions of other people since then that I could have been instead.

This sort of reasoning can't fully answer the question, but it can give us a good start. Why am I alive near the beginning of the twenty-first century? Because there are over seven billion people alive now, out of the one hundred billion or so people that there have ever been. It was certainly far from inevitable I would have been at this point in history, but it's far more likely than any particular point in history before now.

Here is a related question that is much more mundane. I have just entered a shopping mall, and I see a map in front of me. The map gives the full details of what the building is like, but it doesn't say "you are here" anywhere. I can see a shoe store in front of me, and the map shows five shoe stores in the west half of the mall, and only one in the right half. So I conclude I am probably in the west half. Although this situation is in many ways quite different from the first question I was considering, they are related. In both cases, we have a set of objective facts about what the world is like (the history of the universe, the map of the mall) and want to understand something about our own location within this world. And it looks like in these sorts of cases, there is something we can say. If most shoe stores are in the west half of the mall, and I can tell I am by a shoe store, then I am probably in the west half of the mall. If more people live in the early twenty-first century than any earlier time, and I can tell I am a person, then I am more likely to live in the twenty-first century than any earlier time.

The question that motivates the Sleeping Beauty thought experiment is to understand whether we can do the reverse. Can we use this sort of self-locating information to say something about what the overall facts are like? Sometimes we clearly can. A political prisoner is locked in a cell; she is told that the dictator will flip a coin at midnight and send the execution squad if it comes up heads. The prisoner doesn't have a clock in the cell, so she stays up all night, nervous—she doesn't know whether the future of the world contains a coin that comes up tails, or one that comes up heads. But as the sun's rays start to come through the window, she now knows that the coin must have come up tails. Furthermore, even before dawn, as she becomes more confident that it is well past midnight, she can become more confident that the coin must have come up tails.

The Sleeping Beauty thought experiment makes this tougher by making the discussion of probability explicit. All the examples discussed so far involve uncertainty, but there is no randomness. But in many situations, we want to measure confidence precisely, and probability is a useful tool for this, whether for insurance, gambling, or forecasting rain. Regardless of whether the coin comes up heads or tails, she will wake up. But she will have these thoughts more often if it comes up tails. Does this mean that she should be more confident in tails, now that she is having these thoughts? This reasoning may even affect our beliefs about the future! Even *before* it is actually midnight, the prisoner in the cell should start to wonder if it is midnight, in which case the coin probably came up tails. Even if Beauty's coin is flipped Monday night, Beauty should think on Monday the same way she thinks on Tuesday, because she can't tell the days apart.

Discussion Questions

1. Some people wonder about the future of humanity—will we destroy ourselves in a nuclear war, or will we learn to coexist peacefully and eventually spread out to other planets? We can think of "heads" in the Sleeping Beauty thought experiment as the former, and "tails" as the latter, with people on Monday representing the humans on Earth, and people on Tuesday representing the billions of people that (may) eventually live in other parts of the universe. Does this analogy give us reason to be optimistic? What would Sleeping Beauty's memory erasure represent in this analogy?
2. The "Copernican Principle" is the idea that we should see ourselves as being ordinary, rather than occupying a special place in the universe. How does this principle relate to the reasoning under discussion? What does it suggest to you in the philosophy of mind, in the search for life in the universe, in international politics, and other areas?

3. Some physicists say the universe is vastly larger than we thought, and that what we think of as the emptiness of interstellar space contains matter organized chaotically, according to the thermodynamic principles of Ludwig Boltzmann. Some of this matter will (briefly) be organized into a brain that feels just like your brain does right now, before falling apart in space. Should we find Boltzmann's thermodynamic principles more plausible than others, because they predict the existence of many more brains like ours? Should we worry about *being* one of these "Boltzmann brains"? If we reject this reasoning, should we reject it in all the cases mentioned earlier?

Further Reading

Bostrom, Nick. 2002. *Anthropic bias: Observation selection effects in science and philosophy*. New York: Routledge.

Meacham, Chris. 2008. "Sleeping Beauty and the dynamics of *de se* beliefs." *Philosophical Studies* 138: 245–269.

Moss, Sarah. 2015. "Time slice epistemology and action under indeterminacy." In *Oxford studies in epistemology*, vol. 5, edited by Tamar Szabo Gendler and John Hawthorne, 172–194. Oxford: Oxford University Press.

Titelbaum, Michael. 2013. *Quitting certainties*. Oxford: Oxford University Press.

Wenmackers, Sylvia. 2019. "The Snow White problem." *Synthese* 196: 4137–4153.

· PART VIII ·

Thought Experiments in Philosophy of Religion

· CHAPTER 36 ·

Al-Ghazālī's Skeptical Ruminations, by Abū Ḥāmid Muḥammad al-Ghazālī

The Thought Experiment

As an adult, I realized that many things we think we know are just things we accept uncritically. For instance, Christian children grow up into Christians, Jewish children into Jews, and Muslim children into Muslims. To know that I am justified in my beliefs, I have to scrutinize each one of them. But what is a reliable source of knowledge? Is it the senses? No. It appears that the stars are smaller than a coin, but we know they are in reality huge. Surely, then, I know things through reason, for instance, that 2 and 2 make 4. But what if I am dreaming? We believe a great many false things when we dream. When al-Ghazālī pondered this, he fell into a deep skepticism that lasted for about two months.

Source of the thought experiment:

Al-Ghazālī, Abū Ḥāmid Muḥammad ibn Muḥammad. (Twelfth century) 2000. *Al-Ghazali's path to Sufism. His deliverance from error, al-Munqidh min al-Dalal.* Translated by R. J. McCarthy. Louisville, KY: Fons Vitae. Also printed in Al-Ghazali (1980) along with a useful introduction and related texts (see Further Reading).

Reflection by Andrew Arlig, Brooklyn College (CUNY), and Bilal Ibrahim, Providence College

Did you ever have a dream so vivid that while you are in it, you are *fully* involved [see also 11, *Dreaming with Zhuangzi, a butterfly*]? Perhaps you were being chased by some monster. That monster seemed as real as your nightstand and your pillow. But as you tried to escape, perhaps your legs didn't work as legs should. Maybe the path ahead of you did seemingly impossible things, or the monster moved in impossible ways. But in the dream world, the impossible *was* happening, and it seemed so *real* that when you woke, you were shaking and sweating.

"It was only a dream. It wasn't real." We think we may say such words for two interrelated reasons. First, we wake up; our conscious, thinking selves enter into a different state. Second, we believe that the waking world is more real and that the rules that govern it are truer: those seemingly impossible things really are impossible. But are we right about all this?

Ghazālī tells us that he was incapable of accepting things merely because his elders told him they were true. Ghazālī was living in a tumultuous age. The crumbling vestiges of the Abbasid caliphate were plagued by invasions and vicious sectarian disputes. Numerous groups were clamoring for power and influence, each claiming that they alone had the truth. Ghazālī needed a sure way through this morass, and he thought he found a good one: he would only accept something if it is absolutely certain, and something is only absolutely certain if it is *impossible* to doubt it. This criterion is compelling. But it is also very stringent, and because it is so stringent, Ghazālī eventually succumbs to the "malady" that philosophers sometimes call global skepticism.

Like many who have looked for unshakable foundations for knowledge, Ghazālī isolates two candidates: information provided by the senses and rules of reason (like "something cannot both be X and not X at the same time and in the same manner"). The rejection of propositions based upon the senses follows a well-known trajectory. Taken in isolation, what the senses present seems completely trustworthy. The sun, for instance, really does seem to be the size of a coin. But we know that it is not. Reason tells us this. It is reason that shows us how all the data from the senses fit together to form an account of waking reality that is coherent.

At first it seems that we have found what we are looking for. If anything is certain, the rules of reason are. But *where* is the self when she thinks, "I cannot in any way doubt these"? Ghazālī imagines a dialogue between the senses and reason, and he has the senses point out the obvious: The self is in the realm of reason when she thinks the rules of reason are impossible to doubt. But that very same self, when she was in the realm of the senses, couldn't help but trust what she was seeing. It was only when she "woke up" from that state and entered the realm of reason that she saw that sense impressions are not true representations of reality. Now, isn't it possible that there is another realm above the rational realm, and isn't it possible that if the self were to enter that realm, that she would see that reason's supposedly ironclad rules are just as shaky as the information provided by the senses? Indeed, there are certain individuals, the so-called mystics, who report that when they experience the highest realities, including God itself, their reason cannot make sense of their experiences. When they try to tell us what it was like, their descriptions contain all sorts of things that are deemed by reason to be impossible.

Notice that all the senses need to show is that these mystical experiences are *possible*, not that they are in fact true. The onus is on *reason* to prove that it is impossible for the mystic to be right. But reason cannot, since any proof that reason provides is using the very rules that are now being doubted, and thus, any proof of this sort would beg the question. The self can only say that within reason's realm, she cannot *see* any way for the rules of reason to be false. Yet, when the monster was bearing down on her in that vivid dream, she also could not *see* any way out. When Ghazālī grasped the import of all this, he was confounded, and for some time he was a skeptic.

You might have heard about Descartes's moment of profound doubt as well as his famous way out, which involved the realization that "I think, therefore I am." Descartes thinks that he can *reason* his way out of global skepticism. Yet, given how Ghazālī has set up the problem, human reason by itself and through its own power has no such chance. Instead, Ghazālī must rely on the direct intervention of God. It is only when God illuminates the rules of reason that Ghazālī is able to see that they are indeed certain. Descartes also appeals to the existence of a perfectly good being who guarantees that his faculty of thought is capable of grasping the truth. But whereas Descartes again thinks he can *rationally* prove that there is a divine guarantor of truth, Ghazālī must rely on an immediate experience from above. Human reason, left to its own devices, is trapped.

Discussion Questions

1. Descartes argued that the proposition "I am thinking, therefore I exist" is indubitable; that is, it is a claim that we cannot doubt. Now that you have seen how Ghazālī ends up as a global skeptic (for almost two months before God delivers him from error), what do you think of Descartes's claim? Perhaps there is something indubitable buried in what Descartes sees, but is it precisely that *he* is a thinking thing and that he cannot be deceived about whether *he* exists? Given that mystics sometimes report being "annihilated" when in the presence of God, is anything that reason comes up with indubitable?

2. Suppose that God does not come to Ghazālī's aid. (Perhaps there is no God. After all, from our standpoint, we may not be able to prove the existence of something that is "above" what we take to be obvious, rational, and real. Or, even if there is a God, we still have to rely on *its* decision to bridge the gap and deliver us from error.) Should Ghazālī despair? Could we convince Ghazālī that there is a way to live with skepticism?
3. Or perhaps Ghazālī's skeptical rumination rests on a fundamental mistake. Ghazālī might be right when he claims that reason cannot verify and justify itself—that is, reason cannot provide its own foundations. But perhaps we shouldn't think of knowledge like it is a building, with the higher parts resting on supports. Might there be another model of knowledge, one that might lack ultimate foundations but still allow us to develop a coherent set of rules for determining whether things are true or false, right or wrong?

Further Reading

Al-Ghazālī, Abū Ḥāmid Muḥammad ibn Muḥammad. 1980. *Freedom and fulfillment.* Translated by Richard Joseph McCarthy. Boston: Twayne. Reprinted as *Deliverance from error: Five key texts including his spiritual autobiography, al-Munqidh min al-Dalal.* Louisville, KY: Fons Vitae.

Griffel, Frank. 2009. Al-Ghazālī's *philosophical theology.* Oxford: Oxford University Press

Kukkonen, Taneli. 2010. "Al-Ghazālī's skepticism revisited." In *Rethinking the history of skepticism: The missing medieval background*, edited by Henrik Lagerlund, 29–59 (Studien und Texte zur Geistesgeschichte des Mittelalters, Volume 103). Leiden: E. J. Brill.

Lagerlund, Henrik. 2020. *Skepticism in philosophy: A comprehensive, historical introduction.* New York: Routledge.

Ormsby, Eric. 2008. *Ghazali: The revival of Islam.* Oxford: Oneworld.

· CHAPTER 37 ·

Seeing Color for the First Time, by Ibn Tufayl

The Thought Experiment

Imagine someone who was born blind and grew up in a certain city. Through his other senses he learned about animals, plants, the alleys, markets and squares, and all the other features of his home town, so he could get by without a guide. The only thing he did not know about, but only knew through descriptions and firm command of the sciences, was color. One day that man could suddenly see. He would find everything to agree with the notions he had before. Nothing would look odd or out of place. The colors would be in line with what was sketched to him before. Yet two great changes would happen for him, the one dependent on the other: he would know things with greater clarity as he has now gained the sense of sight, and this would be a source of great joy to him.

Source of the thought experiment:

Goodman, L. E., ed. and trans. 2009. *Ibn Tufayl's Hayy Ibn Yaqzan: A philosophical tale.* Chicago: The University of Chicago Press. For a free online, early modern translation, see *The improvement of human reason, exhibited in the life of Hai ebn Yokdhan*, 1708, written in Arabick above five hundred years ago, by Abu Jaafar ebn Tophail, newly translated from the original Arabic by Simon Ockley. London: E. Powell. http://www.gutenberg.org/files/16831/16831-h/16831-h.htm

Reflection by Eric Schliesser, University of Amsterdam and Chapman University

Modern philosophers and readers are familiar with Molyneux's problem and Frank Jackson's (1986) Scientist Mary (in the black-and-white room) [see for this 18, *The cube and the sphere,* and 19, *Mary in the black-and-white room*]. Let's take them in turn and investigate how Ibn Tufayl's blind man relates to them. In Molyneux's problem, first posed to John Locke in 1688, we imagine somebody born blind who has learned to distinguish and name objects by touch. The question is, would she be able to distinguish and name these objects once her "eyes" are "opened?" Ibn Tufayl's thought experiment assumes that the answer is yes; she "would find everything to be exactly agreeable to those notions which she "had before." Ibn Tufayl's thought experiment may have inspired Molyneux.

Ibn Tufayl's thought experiment assumes that the blind man knows everything scientific about objects, too, much like Jackson's Scientist Mary (in her colorless room). And, in fact, in Ibn Tufayl's thought experiment, and against Jackson's expectation, he asserts that once the blind person can see, *even* "Colours were such as [s/he] had before conceiv'd." If this is true for blind Scientist Mary, it will also hold true for color-blind Scientist Mary, who is at least familiar with the contrast between black and white by acquaintance.

Even so, not unlike Jackson, Ibn Tufayl does not think all that can be articulated in words exhausts all possible experience. For, according to Ibn Tufayl, the blind will experience something new. As he puts it, there will be two new experiences: "a greater Clearness" and "extreme delight." In addition, he claims that such clarity will cause this sense of joy. So Ibn Tufayl is not just making a prediction about what would be experienced, but he is also making a claim about the fact that the change in the *way* of our experience can produce a new emotion.

There are two striking features here. First, Ibn Tufayl is committed to the thought that for a suitably prepared agent, seeing a color for the first time need not be the experience of new content, but rather a *manner* of conceiving. (I return to this later.) Second, this new way of experiencing content can be the source of intense emotion (joy).

Now, Ibn Tufayl's [أبو بكر محمد بن عبد الملك بن محمد بن طفيل القيسي الأندلسي] *Ḥayy ibn Yaqẓān* (حي بن يقظان *Alive, son of Awake*) is an enchanting philosophical allegory. Reading the sparkling prose for the first time produces a kind of shock of the unexpectedly familiar that is not quite identical to what is known. It's also a book that invites rereading; I teach it every year, and each year with my students I find new wonderful connections.

Most of *Ḥayy ibn Yaqẓān* is the description of a precocious boy, Hayy, who grows up alone on an island. The reader follows his physical, intellectual, and spiritual development and so is, thereby, gently taught about the (then) latest natural philosophy (what we would now call "science"). Hayy's quiet life is interrupted by the arrival of a spiritual and political exile from civilization, Absāl. Absāl sees in the purity and of knowledge of Hayy's life a new prophet and brings him to his place of birth. But because Hayy is unfamiliar with human civilization, this ends in failure, and Hayy and Absāl return to the island.

Now, Ibn Tufayl, born in Andalusia, was a twelfth-century court physician. And he would have been familiar with human physiology and with the great Ibn Sina's flying man thought experiment [31, *The flying man*] and suggestions on how to treat the cataracts of blind patients by couching (the standard treatment until the eighteenth century). *Ḥayy ibn Yaqẓān* exhibits wide learning (without being academic), including deep acquaintance with Galenic and Ibn Sina's medical texts. So it's not impossible that for Ibn Tufayl the thought experiment with the blind person was prompted by real experience and expertise.

The thought experiment about seeing colors for the first time occurs in the frame narrative in which the narrator seems to be Ibn Tufayl. This narrator had been asked to explain the mystical elements of the "Eastern philosophy." And the thought experiment itself is used to illustrate Ibn Sina's "Eastern" philosophy. In particular, it is meant to illustrate the possibility and nature of a kind of mystical, intuitive knowledge of the highest truth, or union with God.

Ibn Tufayl's terminology—of more or less clarity—may be familiar from early modern thinkers like Descartes or Hume. But in contrast to a modern philosopher, Ibn Tufayl does not point *to the what it's like part* of experience that is unknowable. From our post-Cartesian perspective, there is a lack of anxiety about any purported opposition between the third-personal (scientific) versus first-personal (private) stances. And this is, in part, so because the way true knowledge with the greatest clarity is conceived by Ibn Tufayl echoing a philosophical tradition stretching back via Al-Farabi to Aristotle's *De Anima* (on the soul), includes the idea that there is no opposition between things known and the knowing object. When the knower knows the most important object (God), he becomes identical to the object known and thereby loses some of his individuality while experiencing mystical bliss. This is, of course, a bit obscure, but the thought experiment is meant to illuminate it.

In fact, Ibn Tufayl's thought experiment is itself building on ideas in Plato and *De Anima* (especially section 3.5) as well other thought experiments within Islamic intellectual thought that are motivated along similar lines. Read in light of that history, Ibn Tufayl's thought experiment is itself a metaphor for the intellectual ascent of the prophetic sage, who, not unlike Hayy, becomes increasingly awake, and so sees with incredible clarity.

The other striking feature about Ibn Tufayl's thought experiment from the perspective of contemporary discussion is that the example is not intended to undermine faith in the transferability of testimony or teaching. On the contrary, it presupposes it. This is not part and parcel of the tradition. For, in his *Deliverance of Error*, al-Ghazālī [see 36, *Al Ghazālī's skeptical ruminations*] had also used a thought experiment about a blind man to motivate belief in prophecy, but that blind man had accepted nothing on testimony. (Al-Ghazālī's book is also mentioned by Ibn Tufayl in immediate context.)

For al-Ghazālī prophecy is a form of guided intuition, an inner faculty or "eye" beyond reason, which makes otherwise unknown phenomena available. In his thought experiment the blind man stands for those of us who lack first-hand knowledge of prophecy and who may doubt testimony about it. For al-Ghazālī it is clear that an unprepared mind is incapable of grasping new experience (and dreams provide this preparation). Ibn Tufayl accepts al-Ghazālī's diagnosis but thinks what's needed is the right sort of previous experience and knowledge.

According to Ibn Tufayl, if one is properly cultivated—and this brings him close to the thought experiments explored by L. A. Paul [see 34, *Becoming a vampire*]—then new experiences that add to one's *way* of knowing can be transformative of one's emotional state. One need not agree with Ibn Tufayl's particular diagnosis that it is joy that will follow the newfound color clarity of experience in order to recognize that such transformative experiences may generate intellectual sentiments (in addition to joy, one can think of wonder, admiration, and surprise).

One may find my classification of joy among the intellectual sentiments a bit dubious. Even so, we may say in Spinozistic terms—and Spinoza was probably familiar with *Ḥayy ibn Yaqẓān*—that for Ibn Tufayl, joy is the mind's movement toward greater perfection.

Discussion Questions

1. Can an individual know everything that there is to know unaided by anybody else?
2. When does a new experience generate joy?
3. Does prior knowledge prevent you from experiencing something as new or is such prior knowledge required to experience it?

Further Reading

Degenaar, Marjolein, and Gert-Jan Lokhorst. 2017. "Molyneux's problem." In *The Stanford encyclopedia of philosophy*, Spring 2017 edition, edited by Edward N. Zalta. https://plato.stanford.edu/archives/spr2017/entries/molyneux-problem/.

History of Philosophy without Gaps, #148 [podcast]. "Fantasy Island: Ibn Bājja and Ibn Ṭufayl." https://historyofphilosophy.net/ibn-tufayl (printed in Adamson, Peter. 2016. *Philosophy in the Islamic world (A history of philosophy without any gaps, volume 3)*. Oxford: Oxford University Press, chapter 24.

Kukkonen, Taneli. 2014. *Ibn Tufayl: Living the life of reason*. New York: Simon and Schuster.

· CHAPTER 38 ·

The Watch on the Heath, by William Paley

The Thought Experiment

You are hiking on a heath, and your foot bumps against a stone. If you were asked how the stone came to be there, "For all I know, it's been here forever" would be a perfectly satisfying answer. But that answer won't do if, instead of a stone, you found a watch on the heath. Now, you need a better explanation for how this watch has come to be there. The answer you gave before ("It's been lying here forever") does not work for the watch, as it did for the stone. Why not? Because the watch plainly shows that it has been made for a purpose. All its parts work together so that the hands move, and that you can read the time. If any part had been shaped differently, or placed differently, the watch would not have functioned. Even if you had never seen a watch made, or had never heard of someone making one, you would still conclude that watches had a designer. Now imagine that you discovered that this device was capable of producing another watch. Would this lessen your belief that the watch is designed? No, if anything, you'd be even more in awe of the ingenuity of the designer of the original watch. You certainly would not conclude that no design was involved in the process. And yet atheists hold something akin to this position.

Source of the thought experiment:

Paley, William. (1802) 2006. *Natural theology: or, Evidences of the existence and attributes of the deity*. Edited by Matthew D. Eddy and David Knight. Oxford: Oxford University Press. The 12th edition (1809) can be found online at the following website: http://darwin-online.org.uk/content/frameset?pageseq=1&itemID=A142&viewtype=text

Reflection by Johan De Smedt

William Paley (1743–1805) was a clergyman in the Church of England. He was a keen outdoorsman who enjoyed hunting, fishing, and hiking. His delight of nature shines through, for example, in his observation of fish that is reminiscent of Zhuangzi's [see 12. *Happiness for a fish*]:

> These [fishes] are so happy, that they know not what to do with themselves. Their attitudes, their vivacity, their leaps out of the water, their frolics in it (which I have noticed a thousand times with equal attention and amusement), all conduce to show their excess of spirits, and are simply the effects of that excess. (Paley [1802] 2006, 238)

Paley was an influential author. His *Principles of Moral and Political Philosophy* was a set textbook at Cambridge University well into the Victorian age when Charles Darwin read his work, including *Natural Theology*. The latter book went through many editions; it still remains in print.

Paley's analogy of a watch found on the heath is one of the better-known design arguments: if one is pressed to provide an explanation for a watch as an intricate object that serves a specific purpose, the best explanation is that someone designed it for that purpose. For Paley, organisms were the most compelling examples of divine design in nature; *Natural Theology* is replete with detailed case studies, including the swim bladder in fish and the mammalian eye.

The design argument draws on deeply seated human intuitions: young children already recognize complexity in nature and discern that animals and plants have features that are there for a reason; for example, claws are for scratching or digging. This intuitive teleological thinking remains strong in adults (see De Cruz and De Smedt 2015 for an overview). It's therefore not surprising that the design argument appeals across cultures and religions; for example, the Roman polytheist Cicero (first century BCE), the Advaita Vedānta (nondualist Hindu movement) Śaṅkara (fl. eighth century), and the Muslim Ibn Tufayl (twelfth century) [see 37, *Seeing color for the first time*] have defended influential design arguments. In Christianity, it became especially popular in the seventeenth and eighteenth centuries. Early modern scientists such as Newton and Hooke described the world as an intricate machine, subject to definite laws that humans could discover; for example, newly described laws of physics elegantly explained the motions of inanimate bodies such as planets. During this period, biological organisms seemed to resist such explanations in terms of laws.

Natural Theology is one long inference to the best explanation (Schupbach 2005, 498); Darwin would follow a similar way of reasoning in his *Origin of Species*. Paley looked at both classic arguments and contemporary hypotheses that organisms came about through some chance process and rejected them in favor of the hypothesis of design, with God as the designer of living beings. He rejected arguments by Empedocles, Democritus, and Lucretius that describe the world as filled with creatures that self-assemble by accident, and where those with improbable features (or combinations thereof) are winnowed out. Paley also dealt with contemporary hypotheses about the generation of organisms and their features. The lack of naturalistic explanations for organisms (and their features) stumped philosophers. Immanuel Kant stated that

> we may boldly state that it is absurd for human beings even to attempt it, or to hope that perhaps someday another Newton might arise who would explain to us, in terms of natural laws unordered by any intention, how even a mere blade of grass is produced. (Kant [1790] 1987: §400, 282–283)

Yet early scientists sought to provide a naturalistic explanation for blades of grass and other living things without invoking designer gods. For example, in 1750 Benoît de Maillet proposed that all life forms evolved from more primitive marine organisms; in 1781 Johann Blumenbach hypothesized the *Bildungstrieb*, a Newtonian (i.e., law-like) principle of growth that allows that wounds heal, polyps regenerate, and embryos grow (for a brief overview, see De Smedt and De Cruz 2020, 13; De Cruz and De Smedt 2015, 75–76).

In this intellectual milieu we can situate Paley's rejection of naturalistic explanations of the existence of species and their features:

> I am unwilling to give to it the name of an atheistic scheme ... because, so far as I am able to understand it, the original propensities and the numberless varieties of [species] ... are, in the plan itself, attributed to the ordination and appointment of an intelligent and designing Creator. (Paley [1802] 2006, 224–225)

Paley was also responding to David Hume's critique of the design argument. When we infer that watches are designed and houses are built, our inference is partly driven by our knowledge that there are watchmakers and builders. According to Hume, without this knowledge we are unjustified in claiming that an organism bears a striking semblance to a watch/house, and that we can with certainty infer that it was designed:

> If we see a house, Cleanthes, we conclude, with the greatest certainty, that it had an architect or builder; because this is precisely that species of effect which we have experienced to proceed from that species of cause. But surely you will not affirm, that

> the universe bears such a resemblance to a house, that we can with the same certainty infer a similar cause, or that the analogy is here entire and perfect. The dissimilitude is so striking, that the utmost you can here pretend to is a guess, a conjecture, a presumption concerning a familiar cause. (Hume 1779, 51)

Paley was aware of this objection. To properly evaluate the philosophical significance of *Natural Theology*, one needs to keep in mind that the book is not merely a fanciful analogy from watches to organisms. Rather, it is an argument to the best explanation: Paley acknowledged alternative explanations to a designing God but found these lacking—divine design was a better explanation for the existence of organisms and their features than naturalistic hypotheses. However, Paley did not adequately defend his design argument against these explanations and dismissed them too easily, failing to realize that the retention of beneficial random changes in an organism's body or behavior might over time lead to a new species.

Discussion Questions

1. Paley formulated his watch analogy as an argument against atheism, by claiming that the best explanation for the complexity and purposiveness of biological organisms was divine design. Contemporary scientific explanations for biological complexity are better than those in the eighteenth century. Does the watch analogy still hold today? Why, or why not?
2. There are many contemporary versions of the design argument. One of them, the fine-tuning argument, goes as follows: The universe has laws and cosmological constants; if these were just a little bit different, galaxies, stars, and life as we know it would not exist. For example, gravity is a weak force; if it had just been a bit stronger, atoms would not have existed. According to proponents of the fine-tuning argument, the best explanation for why gravity has exactly the strength it has is that God designed the universe. Atheists would either have to posit that laws of physics and cosmological constants are the way they are by an astonishing coincidence, or they would have to posit a multiverse. Do you find this argument compelling?
3. Theistic evolution is the view that evolutionary theory describes how organisms originate and change over time, and that God is responsible for natural selection. But evolution through natural selection involves a lot of suffering, as animals and plants evolve as a result of pressures such as disease and predation. How might a theistic evolutionist respond to this objection?

Further Reading

De Cruz, Helen, and Johan De Smedt. 2015. *A natural history of natural theology: The cognitive science of theology and philosophy of religion*. Cambridge, MA: MIT Press.

De Smedt, Johan, and Helen De Cruz. 2020. *The challenge of evolution to religion*. Cambridge: Cambridge University Press.

Hume, David. 1779. *Dialogues concerning natural religion*. 2nd ed. London.

Kant, Immanuel. (1790) 1987. *Critique of judgment*. Translated by Werner S. Pluhar. Indianapolis: Hackett.

Schupbach, Jonah N. 2005. "Paley's inductive inference to design: A response to Graham Oppy." *Philosophia Christi* 7, no. 2: 491–502.

· CHAPTER 39 ·

The Invisible Gardener, by John Wisdom

The Thought Experiment

Imagine that two gardeners return to their plot after a period of neglect to find that the plants are surprisingly vigorous. One of them exclaims, "Someone must be tending this plot!" The other disagrees and cites the presence of weeds as counterevidence: "Surely, a gardener would have taken care of those." Furthermore, they discover, upon inquiry, that nobody in the neighborhood has seen anyone tending the plot. Perhaps in normal circumstances this would be enough to settle the question. But imagine that the former person, "the believer," doubles down and insists that there is a gardener, but that the gardener is invisible and, generally, not detectable by human experience. In this case, then, the believer and the nonbeliever could agree on all the evidence and yet disagree about whether the evidence supports the gardener hypothesis.

Source of the thought experiment:

Wisdom, John. 1944/1945. "Gods." *Proceedings of the Aristotelian Society* 45: 185–206.

Reflection by Kelli D. Potter, Utah Valley University

This thought experiment was introduced by John Wisdom in an essay entitled "Gods" (Wisdom 1944/1945, 191–192). Wisdom tackles the question of whether belief in God is a hypothesis that can be confirmed or disconfirmed by experiment. He argues that, although beliefs in gods began as hypotheses to explain experience, such beliefs have been transformed over time. He uses the story of the invisible gardener to show how this transformation could occur. The gardener in Wisdom's story is intended to be analogous with God. At first, belief in the gardener is an ordinary belief for which evidence is relevant. But as the believer doubles down in the face of counterevidence, the nature of the belief changes. It is no longer a hypothesis that can be confirmed or disconfirmed. So, too, with belief in God. The gods of ancient Greece appeared and behaved like human beings, with the added characteristics of having great power and being immortal. Like the gardener hypothesis, one could rightly expect that such beliefs would have empirical consequences. But with the development of monotheism, the concept of God became more and more abstract and less and less relevant to experience. God is not a being among beings: God is the ground of all being—that is, being itself. What difference would belief in such a being have for our expectations about future experience?

Of course, many philosophers have treated the question about belief in God as if it *were* a hypothesis. For example, some theists have argued that living organisms reveal order and purpose and that this is evidence for an intelligent designer [see 38, *The watch on the heath*]. To the extent that we can explain the appearance of order and purpose by theories such as Darwin's theory of natural selection, it is not evidence for the existence of God after all. Other nontheistic philosophers have treated the question of God as an evidential matter by arguing that the existence of a great deal of evil in the world makes God's existence less likely. Theists offer explanations of why God would allow evil; but these explanations then make belief in God less like a hypothesis. In effect, such explanations change what we mean by the word "God." One gets the sense that theists in these discussions are moving the goal posts in a process that mirrors the transformation of the believer's commitment that there is a gardener tending the plot. We might call this process "evidence avoidance." Wisdom's invisible gardener is taken up in a modified form by Anthony Flew, who employs it to argue that religious belief has no cognitive meaning whatsoever––that is, that there is no right or wrong answer to the question of God's existence. In order to get this conclusion, he assumes that if nothing counts as evidence against an apparent assertion, then it is not an assertion after all. This is called "the falsification principle" (Flew, Hare, and Mitchell 1995, 96–99). By contrast, Wisdom claims that the fact that belief in God is no longer a hypothesis doesn't preclude a right or wrong answer to the question of God. He uses the analogy that in some criminal court cases the defense will accept the facts as presented by the prosecution, but then go on to argue that this doesn't constitute a violation of the relevant law by pointing to patterns in the evidence ignored by the prosecution. For example, the prosecution and defense might both agree that Jones killed Smith, but they might disagree about whether this act of killing constitutes self-defense. In such a case, the prosecution and the defense don't disagree about the facts but about whether the law applies in the case in question. And, presumably, there are right and wrong answers in such a case (Wisdom 1944/1945, 193–194).

Discussion Questions

1. Are the believer in the invisible gardener and the religious believer really analogous, as Wisdom claims? In what ways are they analogous? What are some of the relevant differences, if any? Is the analogy strong enough to support Wisdom's argument?
2. How does one determine that there is an intelligent being behind some pattern we find in nature? What must we assume about such a being's nature? What kind of patterns in the world would suggest the existence of a God and why? What does this tell you about the concept of God?
3. If belief in God is not a hypothesis that can be confirmed or disconfirmed, then what is it? Is it just meaningless nonsense? Is it an expression of an attitude, perhaps? Or is it possible for there to be matters of fact that cannot be settled by experience? Is there a right or wrong answer to the question about God's existence?

Further Reading

Flew, Anthony, R. M. Hare, and Basil Mitchell. 1963. "Theology and falsification." In *New essays in philosophical theology*, edited by Anthony Flew and Alasdair MacIntyre, 96–99. London: SCM Press.

Scott, Michael. 2013. *Religious language*. London: Palgrave Macmillan.

Wisdom, John. 1944/1945. "Gods." *Proceedings of the Aristotelian Society* 45: 185–206.

· CHAPTER 40 ·

The Fawn in the Forest, by William Rowe

The Thought Experiment

Lightning strikes a tree in a forest far away from human sight. The result is a devastating forest fire. A fawn is trapped, entangled in the bushes, and dies an agonizing slow death. As far as we can see, there is no greater good served by its death. Even a theist should recognize that an omnipotent and omnibenevolent God could have easily relieved its suffering. Yet God didn't do so. From this, what should we conclude about God's existence?

Source of the thought experiment:

Rowe, William. 1979. "The problem of evil and some varieties of atheism." *American Philosophical Quarterly* 16, no. 4: 335–341.

Reflection by Beth Seacord, College of Southern Nevada

In 2019 and 2020, back-to-back brush fires ravaged two continents. Extreme heat and severe drought converged to fuel massive brush fires across Australia that burned for 210 days and consumed an area approximately the size of England and Scotland combined. In South America, fires raged for eight months, devastating thousands of miles of ecologically vital Amazon rainforest. Journalists brought the devastation home to us as they captured photographs of blackened earth punctuated by the charred and twisted bodies of sloth, koalas, and kangaroos consumed in various stages of attempted escape.

Volunteers poured in from all over the world to rescue and rehabilitate those creatures that could be saved. Many went to great lengths to save the displaced animals from terrible pain and their untimely deaths. But why should they do so? Were these volunteers being irrationally sentimental? Most would answer obviously not! There is good reason to think that the lives and experiences of other animals matter. We have the reasonable intuition that pain is no less painful whether the one that suffers is human or not. No matter one's species, we know that suffering is intrinsically bad. This gives us reason to act such that we ought to help relieve the pain and suffering of others (a) when we can do so without sacrificing some other important good (e.g. our own health, safety or livelihood) and (b) when the suffering does not plausibly contribute to some overriding good (e.g., a life-saving surgery).

While morally imperfect human volunteers arrived en masse, the morally perfect, all-powerful God of Western tradition seemed strangely absent. If God exists, then it is puzzling that God would stand by and do nothing while innocents suffer. In fact, we may wonder why any innocent being should suffer. Atheists have an easy answer to this puzzle: In an atheistic universe, nature cares not for the individual; evolution by natural selection is neither merciful nor kind, killing off the weak making room for fitter genes. Thus, gratuitous pain and suffering are not surprising in atheism. In contrast, adherents to Judeo-Christian-Islamic traditions face a much more difficult challenge: If an all-good, all-powerful, and all-knowing God "runs the show," it is very surprising that there should be pointless, meaningless suffering, especially of innocent creatures. This is a central problem for Western theistic religious traditions called "the problem of evil."

Theists often reply that God has good reasons, unknown to us, for everything he allows whether murder, war, rape, torture, or the destruction of a billion animals by fire. Perhaps, a wholly good, omniscient deity may understand that the only way to achieve some greater good (or to avoid some worse evil) is to allow some terrible evil. William Rowe points out that any explanation that invokes a greater good for the sole benefit of humankind will not adequately account for the fact that the vast majority of animal suffering goes unnoticed—either because wild animals suffer far from view or because the vast majority of all sentient life lived and died before *Homo sapiens* walked the earth. To this end, Rowe asks us to imagine that in some far-away forest lightning strikes a dead tree. The tree ignites and starts a raging forest fire. In the fire, "a fawn is trapped, horribly burned, and lies in terrible agony for several days before death relieves its suffering" (Rowe 1979, 337). Unlike the koalas, sloth, and kangaroo whose broken and mangled bodies were recorded on film and published around the globe, the suffering and death of the fawn goes unnoticed. What greater good might God possibly have in mind for that fawn itself or for the world at large? The fawn's suffering is hidden such that the world cannot benefit from its death. What about the fawn itself? Might the fawn's suffering contribute to its own good—a good that outweighs its own terrible suffering? Some might argue that God's permission of the fawn's suffering is morally justified because God will compensate the fawn with an eternally blissful afterlife. But this doesn't really answer the original question of why God allowed the fawn to suffer in the first place. After all, an almighty God could have granted the fawn a place in paradise without it ever having to suffer. If that is the case, then the fawn's suffering is not necessary for any greater good and is, therefore, gratuitous.

Rowe argues that there are many instances of meaningless, horrendous suffering in the world which an omnipotent and wholly good God would prevent if God exists. Rowe concludes that because God does not prevent horrendous gratuitous evils, it is, therefore, extremely unlikely that an all-knowing, all-powerful, wholly good God exists.

Discussion Questions

1. If you noticed that an animal or young child was allowed to suffer while the caretakers stood by and did nothing, what would you conclude about the moral character of the caretakers? Are human caretakers relevantly different than a divine "caretaker?" Why or why not?
2. Can you imagine a greater good that would outweigh the fawn's suffering? Should the fawn benefit from its own suffering? Why or why not?
3. We live in a world with predictable laws of nature. For instance, we know that fires are started under certain predictable conditions. Some theists argue that the cost of living in a world where cause and effect can be anticipated is that some innocent beings will suffer, but living in a knowable universe is such a great good that it outweighs all the pain and suffering that the laws of nature themselves inflict. Do you think this is true? Do you think it is possible that God could have created a world with less pain and suffering? Why or why not?

Further Reading

Alston, William. 1991. "The inductive argument from evil and the human cognitive condition." *Philosophical Perspectives* 5: 311–332.

Draper, Paul. 2012. "Darwin's argument from evil." In *Scientific approaches to philosophy of religion*, edited by Yujin Nagasawa, 49–80. New York: Palgrave-Macmillan.

Linzey, Andrew. 2009. *Creatures of the same God: Explorations in animal theology.* New York: Lantern Books.

· CHAPTER 41 ·

The Rope-Snake Analogy, by Asaṅga

The Thought Experiment

You are walking down a dark street when you think you see a dangerous snake lurking in the shadows. You start to explore the possible dangers you face, and you begin to make up a story about what will happen when the snake notices you. But a second look confirms that it is not a snake! It is a rope that you mistakenly took to be a snake and then filled in a bunch of details to make that label intelligible. As soon as you see that it's a rope, your fear evaporates.

Source of the thought experiment:

Asaṅga. 2019. Mahāyānasaṁgraha III.7. In *A compendium of the Mahāyāna: Asaṅga's Mahāyānasaṃgraha and its Indian and Tibetan commentaries*, vol. 1 of 3, translated by Karl Brunnholzl. Boulder, CO: Snow Lion.

Reflection by Bryce Huebner, Georgetown University

Learning that there are dangerous snakes on a hiking trail will increase the likelihood that you will see any snake that you happen to come across. But it may also lead you to mistake a partially observed stick or a rattling sound in the brush for a snake. Likewise, if you live where dangerous snakes are common, you might expect to find them hiding in dark rooms, and you might occasionally mistake coiled ropes for coiled snakes. For Asaṅga, this was an example of a broader human tendency to mistake illusory experiences for reality—an idea that was central to the Yogācāra tradition of Buddhist philosophy that Asaṅga helped to found in the fourth century CE, in the ancient kingdom of Gandhāra.

We can begin to see why he thought this by considering the way that successful horror movies build on our tendencies to experience fear, dread, or discomfort, in response to even illusory threats. As Asaṅga suggests, such feelings are diminished when we remind ourselves that the events on the screen are unreal. But just as importantly, such feelings will persist so long as we assume that they tell us something important about the world. So we often worry about unseen threats as we walk home from the theater or attempt to go to sleep. And in many cases, the only way to get rid of such feelings is to actively redirect our thoughts, in ways that make the illusory threats feel unreal.

Of course, Asaṅga wasn't just concerned with illusory threats. He used this thought experiment to suggest that the world we experience is illusory, and that our use of words like "snake" and "rope" to refer to complex perceptual experiences leads us to assume that there is stability where there is only change. He would not have seen this radical claim as obvious; but he believed that we can learn to reflect upon the illusory aspects of everyday experience, and that doing so can help us to overcome the habits of thought that sustain our confused understanding of the world. I'm not certain what the world is really like, but I do think that there is something deeply right about this kind of claim.

For example, many of us construct stable and persisting illusions about the people we interact with. We expect some of them to be more distant or hostile than they actually are, and this often leads us to interact with them in ways that evoke further discomfort. We expect other people to be more friendly or helpful than they actually are; and where people violate these expectations, we often feel let down or ignored. Once we have formed these kinds of expectations, it takes a great deal of time and effort to retrain our habitual ways of thinking; but we can dispel these kinds of social illusions by cultivating a richer awareness of our own expectations, and by softening our tendency to assume that people possess stable and persisting character traits (Barrett and Dunne 2018). But as with experiences of illusory snakes or horror films, these illusions will persist until we change our expectations.

Importantly, the more feedback we receive in support of our expectations, the harder it will be to change them. And this has troubling implications. Watching films and visiting websites that portray threats in ways that are tied to racial, cultural, or religious identities, class standing, or immigration status can yield the expectations that these social categories are indicators of threats. This can lead people to internalize embodied tendencies to treat innocuous items like wallets and cell phones as guns, when they are held by people whom we perceive as threats (Tsakiris 2017). More generally, it can produce distorted expectations that will perpetuate exclusionary attitudes as well as problematic power structures. Just as importantly, it can lead to the sense that our way of encountering the world provides us with a good sense of who is likely to be threatening and who is likely to be safe. From inside the resulting worldview, it will be difficult to know which of our experiences merely reflect social illusions and which of them reflect genuine facts about the world. And like any other illusion, these ones will only dissipate if we come to understand how they are produced and why they feel as real as they do.

Asaṅga used rational arguments to diagnose the source of our illusory experiences; and he claimed that meditative practices could be used to combat their pernicious effects. I think this is roughly right: by cultivating a richer awareness of our expectations, and softening our tendency to assume that people possess stable and persisting character traits, we can begin to see through the socially structured distortions that we impose on the world; we can also use meditative practices to cultivate richer desires to pursue compassionate ways of living. This requires a commitment to reshaping emotionally structured expectations. As many Buddhist philosophers have claimed, our ways of categorizing the world call the social categories that we experience into existence; and like these philosophers, I believe that we can develop skills that will help us to build a better world. This will be hard, and it will require confronting pervasive forms of ignorance and dismantling "the false beliefs and misunderstandings that inform our everyday sense of reality" (McRae 2019, 44). But doing so will minimize both the suffering we experience and the suffering that we create in the world.

Discussion Questions

1. Think about a time when you had some expectations that influenced the way you interacted with someone. Or think about a time where someone else had negative expectations about you, which made it difficult to interact with them. Is there anything that you can do "in the moment" to prevent your expectations from influencing your interactions with someone? What does that tell you about the malleability of social expectations?
2. We often assume that we see the world as it really is. But if Asaṅga, and the other South Asian philosophers who used the rope-snake analogy are right, then many of our experiences are likely to be illusory. Is it possible to tell the difference between an illusory

experience and an experience that accurately represents the world? These philosophers argued that we could use logical reasoning and meditative practices to do so. Are they right? Why or why not?

3. Do you think that it's possible to change expectations that are socially entrenched and sustained by feedback from your social world? If so, what would it take to change them?

Further Reading

Barrett, Lisa Feldman, and John Dunne. 2018. "Buddhists in love." *Aeon*, June 4. https://aeon.co/essays/does-buddhist-detachment-allow-for-a-healthier-togetherness

McRae, Emily. 2019. "White delusion and Avidyā: A Buddhist approach to understanding and deconstructing white ignorance." In *Buddhism and whiteness: Critical reflections*, edited by George Yancy and Emily McRae, 43–59. New York: Rowman & Littlefield.

Tsakiris, Manos. 2017. "The brain-heart dialogue shows how racism hijacks perception." *Aeon*, April 14. https://aeon.co/ideas/the-brain-heart-dialogue-shows-racism-hijacks-perception

· PART IX ·

A Thought Experiment in Aesthetics

· CHAPTER 42 ·

Red Square, by Arthur Danto

The Thought Experiment

What makes a work of art that particular work of art, rather than some other work? You might think it's the way that it appears to us, its aesthetic properties. On this view, Mona Lisa's smile, pose, and the sfumato technique are what make the painting the *Mona Lisa*. However, this way of thinking doesn't always work. Consider a work of art entitled *Israelites Crossing the Red Sea*, which is a square piece of canvas, coated with a red layer of paint. Next to it, in the same museum, is an identical-looking red canvas, entitled *Kierkegaard's Mood*. As you walk further down the hallways, you see the next painting, a Russian landscape entitled *Red Square*. You might even see some red primer on canvas, not a work of art at all, but just a beginning that was supposed to become a work entitled *Conversazione Sacra* by Giorgione. As you wander through this museum, you see the painting *Nirvana*, also a red square, as is the painting *Red Table Cloth*, and so on. Now clearly, these works are very different, though they all appear to you exactly the same—a piece of square canvas, framed, and painted red.

Source of the thought experiment:

Danto, Arthur C. 1981. *The transfiguration of the commonplace*. Cambridge, MA: Harvard University Press.

Reflection by Alex King, Simon Fraser University

Stroll through any contemporary art museum and you're bound to hear skeptical onlookers voicing their lack of faith in the art institution. "Come on, my kid could paint that." "That's just a plain white canvas!" "I hope somebody donated this painting; it's barely worth the cost of its materials."

You might think that these incredulous museum-goers make a good point. Really, what is the difference between *Red Square* and the identical but unfinished red canvas from Giorgione's studio? They're visually indiscernible, so how could one be art and the other not? And how could one be such good art that it's in a fancy art museum, while something identical by someone's kid isn't even impressive enough to get hung up on the refrigerator?

Danto's thought experiment raises a number of provocative questions, questions that take him an entire book to answer. He is primarily concerned with the great conundrum of twentieth-century philosophy of art: What *is* art?

For him, it's obvious that the primed Giorgione canvas is not art, but that the other red squares he describes are art. The contrast here is between art and what he tantalizingly calls "mere real things." It's not that artworks aren't real things; they are. But there's something special about art objects. They have a different sort of status in addition to being real things.

For example, we know what to do with beds. If we see our own bed, we get in and sleep or read or scroll on our phones at will. We tidy it up, or we don't. If we find ourselves in a room with someone else's bed, we know that we shouldn't do any of those things without their permission because it's a private space and it's theirs. However, imagine encountering Tracey Emin's famous installation artwork *My Bed* (1998). If you did, you would see her actual unmade, rumpled bed with all of its mess and smell and private bodily debris (dirty tissues, empty alcohol bottles, spent ketchup packets, even used condoms). You might not be quite sure what to do with it. Can you walk up to it, even touch it? It's confusing.

The uncertainty about what to do with *My Bed* arises from the fact that Emin's bed is art, while other beds we encounter are mere real things. They are real things in the way that tables or trees are mere real things. They don't have any special status or dictate special rules for observation, attention, and interaction. Art, however, does all of these things. We are meant to ponder it, to interrogate it, to try to find meaning within it.

So what makes something art? Why is Emin's bed art while yours isn't? Danto's first and most memorable lesson is that, because all of the red squares are visually identical, an object's visible features alone cannot make it art (or not). The explanation has to be more complicated.

This opens a Pandora's box of philosophical possibilities. Maybe the artist's *intention* is what matters. Maybe we have the power to make something into art just by calling it art. Or maybe it's *expression* that's key. In that case, it's because Giorgione's canvas doesn't express anything that it isn't art. Or maybe it's not just expression but the *communication* of that expression to others. Or maybe it's that the object has a certain kind of relationship to those art historical *institutions* decried by skeptics.

There is a secondary lesson, too. It's about what happens once we restrict our attention to those red squares we call artworks. Some of these paintings might be better than others. Maybe *Israelites Crossing the Red Sea* is better than *Kierkegaard's Mood*. But because they are visually identical, it can't be an artwork's visually detectable features alone that make it better or worse than other artworks.

We might look to any of the features listed here, such as the artist's intention, or we might look elsewhere to their differing art historical features, such as originality, or to their differing social and historical context. The Russian landscape *Red Square* might be a reference to the geographical place in Moscow or a commentary on Russian communism. It has, potentially, a very different meaning from *Israelites Crossing the Red Sea*.

We have, then, two different questions: What makes something art? And what makes something *good* art?

That these questions are different is itself an important final lesson. When protestors object to Emin's bed or minimalist art like Danto's imagined red squares (or very real pieces like Kazimir Malevich's *Black Square* (1915) or Ellsworth Kelly's *Dark Blue Panel* (1982)), they might be trying to say one of two very different things. First, they might be accusing these pieces of literally not being art. For Danto, this is a nonstarter. You might disagree, but for Danto, *Israelites Crossing the Red Sea* clearly is art. Alternatively, they might be accusing these pieces of being *bad art*, of not being worthy of our attention and consideration, of not being worth their often sky-high prices. This is a very different sort of criticism. It threatens the authority of art institutions in one way: it accuses them of trying to trick gullible audiences into thinking bad art is good and to scam them into buying expensive museum admissions tickets. But it does not threaten the authority of art institutions to legitimate something *as art*. After all, for something to be bad art, it has to be art in the first place.

Discussion Questions

1. Do you think you could just go home and call your bed art, and that would make it so? Do you think that your intention for something to be art is even necessary for its being art?
2. Danto focuses on paintings, but think about different artistic media. If two short stories are *exactly* identical in their wording and formatting, do you think one could be art and the other not? Do you think one could be good and the other bad? What about pieces of music? Movies?
3. Danto draws a firm and important line separating works of art from mere real things. What do you think he might say about architecture, industrial and graphic design, cuisine, or fashion? Does every object have to be one or the other, or is there some gray in between?

Further Reading

Abell, Catharine. 2012. "Art: What it is and why it matters." *Philosophy and Phenomenological Research* 85, no. 3: 671–691.

Dickie, George. 1974. *Art and the aesthetic: An institutional analysis.* Ithaca, NY: Cornell University Press.

Levinson, Jerrold. 1979. "Defining art historically." *British Journal of Aesthetics* 19, no. 3: 232–250.

Glossary

Alief An *alief* is an innate or habitual propensity to respond to an apparent stimulus in a particular way. In contrast to a belief, which is a reason-based assessment of a situation, an alief is an automatic response to the situation's salient features. In most cases, our aliefs and our beliefs coincide; in certain cases, our aliefs pull us in one direction, while our beliefs pull us in another.

Anatta (Sanskrit *anatman*) The doctrine of "no-self" or "non-self." This is a rejection of the Brahmanist idea, popular at the time of the development of Buddhism, that there exists a substantive, changeless, and persisting self that grounds and is identifiable with the subject of conscious experience.

Atheism Atheists endorse the metaphysical claim that God does not exist (in reality).

Benevolence The virtue of appropriately perceiving, feeling, thinking, and acting in response to the suffering and joy of others; commonly associated with emotions such as sympathy, empathy, and compassion.

Chance An interpretation of the mathematical theory of probability as a measure of the objective randomness of physically indeterministic events. If coins are truly random, then before a coin is flipped, its chance of coming up heads is 50 percent, but after it has been flipped, the chance is strictly speaking either 0 or 100 percent, even if you don't know how it came up. Some philosophers claim that the world is deterministic, so that strictly speaking all chances are either 0 or 100 percent, and our talks about coins and weather and even quantum mechanics are just reports of our subjective confidence rather than objective chance. (See also *Probability*.)

Coherentism The claim that each of our beliefs is justified to the extent to which it fits or coheres with our overall system of beliefs. Coherentism denies the foundationalist assumptions that our beliefs are ultimately derivable from certain or indubitable basic beliefs (See also *Foundationalism*).

Conciliationism The position in epistemology that says that if you are confronted with disagreement from someone you deem an epistemic peer, then you should typically revise your opinion, either by doubting your own view or by moving it toward the view of the person you disagree with. (See also *Epistemic Peer, Steadfastness*.)

Confidence A measure of how strongly someone believes something. It is often said to govern how people make decisions in the face of uncertainty—if you are highly confident that it won't rain, you may leave the umbrella at home, but if your confidence is somewhat lower, you may bring your umbrella. When it is made mathematically precise as an interpretation of probability, it is often called "credence." (See also *Chance, Credence, Probability*.)

Contingently true A statement that is contingently true is one that could be true or false, but happens to be true. It is true in the actual world, but it could be false in other possible worlds. An example is "grass is green." (See also *Necessarily true*.)

Credence Mathematically precise measurement of a person's confidence in line with the mathematical theory of probability. (See also *Probability*.)

Daoism A loose group of thinkers who emerged in ancient China, one of the most famous being Zhuangzi. Daoists criticized "artificiality," from moral rules to philosophical theorizing, which they thought tended to damage our natural tendencies to spontaneity and compassion. They thought that natural places and creatures were better models of how to live a good life.

Descriptivism In the philosophy of language, descriptivism is the theory according to which a speaker who uses a name refers to the thing that satisfies a description she associates with the name.

Eidos An eternal and unchanging "form" or "idea," or an object of pure thought or reason, in contrast to things in space and time that can be perceived with the senses.

Epicurean physics The theories of the natural world system associated with the Epicurean school, founded by Epicurus (341–270 BCE). In particular, Epicurean physics included atomism, the view that bodies are ultimately made up of tiny, invisible, indivisible bits. These atoms move around in space and interact according to fixed rules.

Epistemic peer Someone who is your rough equal in those characteristics (e.g. intelligence, thoughtfulness, freedom from bias, and familiarity with the evidence) that are responsible for forming accurate beliefs about a certain matter. (See also *Conciliationism, Steadfastness.*)

Evil Bad or undesirable states of affairs. "Evil" can refer to moral wrongdoing (e.g., murder, rape, etc.) as well as physical and psychological suffering (e.g., depression, anxiety, trauma, and various mental illnesses).

Falsification principle This principle was formulated by Karl Popper, who used it as a criterion for science. For Popper, a scientific hypothesis must be falsifiable. By contrast, Anthony Flew applied this to religious discourse in his argument that religious discourse is meaningless. Flew's version of the principle is as follows: a statement is an assertion only if it is falsifiable. Flew also claimed that an assertion is falsifiable only if there exists evidence that would count against or be incompatible with the truth of the assertion.

Foundationalism The claim that our beliefs are justified to the extent that they are in turn justified by more basic beliefs. Foundationalists differ in whether they take the basic beliefs that ground all other beliefs to be the product of logical reasoning alone (rationalism) or the deliverances of our sense perception (empiricism).

Friendship A distinctive kind of personal relationship, involving sorts of interest and concern that mark out a friend as enjoying a special place in one's life. Features of friendships include shared interests, mutual concern and affection, and special degrees of openness and intimacy. Friendships are often tied into family, professional, and romantic relationships.

General will The intention in a group and the individuals composing it to act in accordance with their joint and collective interest, perhaps as decided by common deliberation and joint decision.

Inference to the best explanation Choosing one hypothesis among a number of competing hypotheses that best explains the data or situation one is confronted with, using criteria including greater precision, comprehensiveness, simplicity, and unifying power of phenomena that before were seemingly disparate.

Intentionality This is also sometimes called "aboutness." Our mental states have the power to be about something; for example, if you imagine the Eiffel Tower (which you may have seen in pictures, or maybe even in reality), then that thought is "about" the Eiffel Tower. In philosophy of mind, a big question is how mental states acquire this property. What is it about my belief about the Eiffel Tower that makes it about the Eiffel Tower, rather than the Golden Gate Bridge, for example?

Justice as fairness This describes principles that are not only legitimate but are the most just for arranging political and social institutions in a democratic society of free and equal individuals. Because, for John Rawls, citizens are fundamentally equal and differences between them are morally arbitrary, these principles begin with the assumption that social goods should be distributed equally and that any inequalities that are introduced must improve the position of the least well off.

Language-game Ludwig Wittgenstein uses the term "language-game" (*Sprachspiel*) to highlight the fact that, much like games, languages are governed by constitutive rules (of grammar). He argues that it is these rules for using words that typically determine their meaning, and not some object they stand for. A language-game is thus understood to be a system of communication "by means of which children learn their native language" (*PI* §7). Confusingly, Wittgenstein uses the term to refer to both (i) the whole overall system "consisting of language and the actions into which it is woven" (ibid.) and (ii) specified fragments of linguistic practice. The latter may either constitute a complete primitive language-game in themselves or form part of "the whole language-game" (which he sometimes refers to as "the human language-game" and "our language-game").

Natural kind term A word that purports to pick out a set of things that "cuts nature at the joints" because the members are grouped together independently of human interests or reactions. Thus, "water," "electron," and "alligator" are natural kind terms, while "boat" and "cool" are not.

Natural theology Called "natural" because it took its evidence either from direct observation of the natural world or from observations made by the nascent sciences branching off natural philosophy, and "theology" because it interpreted these observations in a Christian framework. Of course, observations can also be interpreted within other religious frameworks, such as Jewish or Hindu natural theology.

Necessarily true A statement that is necessarily true can't be false or is true in all possible worlds. Common examples include mathematical truths like "2 + 2 = 4." (See also *Contingently true.*)

Paideia Education or cultivation aiming not just at the acquisition of knowledge but a general kind of enlightenment and coherence of character.

Personal identity In philosophy, personal identity refers to a series of puzzles that arise about us as persons, particularly on how our identity remains the same, or changes, over time. For example, to what extent is forty-two-year-old me (a philosophy professor, a mother, among other things) the same as fifteen-year-old me (a high schooler, living with her parents). What makes our identity the same? Is there some self that persists over time, or is it an illusion?

Phenomenal character The phenomenal character of an experience is what it is like to undergo the experience for the subject. For example, the phenomenal character of a red experience is the distinctive way of what it is like to see (or hallucinate) something red.

Physicalism This is the philosophical thesis that everything is physical or ultimately supervenes on the physical. This is even the case for things that don't appear to be physical at first, such as emotions, or beliefs. The physicalist would argue that an emotion supervenes on our brain states; that is, there are physical states of our brain, of neurons firing and neurotransmitters being involved, such that they cause an emotion such as anger to arise in you.

Prisoner's dilemma A thought experiment in the form of a dilemma faced by two prisoners who have been arrested for robbing a bank. They are separately held and questioned. The prosecutor offers them a choice: if you confess, while your accomplice remains silent, I'll let you go free, and he will spend twenty years in prison. If he confesses while you stay silent, you'll spend twenty years in prison and he'll go free. If you both confess, you get five years each. If you both stay silent, I'll charge you with two years each. The dilemma is that—since you cannot know what your accomplice will do—your best choice is to confess, though overall this means you'll end up in a worse situation than if you both stayed silent.

Probability A mathematical theory assigning numbers between 0 and 1 (or between 0 and 100 percent) to sentences based on how certain they are. When it represents objective physical uncertainty (as some say occurs with coin flips, dice rolls, or perhaps quantum events), it is called "chance." When it represents subjective mental uncertainty (like when a detective or a scientist is considering multiple hypotheses about some objective truth), it is called "confidence" or "credence." (See also *Chance, Confidence,* and *Credence.*)

Problem of evil A puzzle for the coherence of theism; if God is all-good, all-powerful, and all-knowing, why is there terrible moral and natural "evil"? (See also *Evil*)

Reference (according to Gottlob Frege) Reference means the aspect of meaning that denotes what objects or properties our expressions pick out. The reference of expressions is what determines the truth-value of sentences they appear in, and the referent of a sentence is simply its truth-value. More generally in the philosophy of language, "reference" is the relation between words and things that allows us to talk about them. (See also *Sense.*)

Relativism A set of doctrines that say our judgments—like true or false, or right or wrong—are partly rooted in different contexts or frameworks. If so, those judgments do not enjoy the special authority we often think they do. Seeing certain practices as "morally wrong" may be relative to a certain culture. Relativism is often misunderstood as saying "anything goes," when actually it does nothing of the sort.

Sense (in Frege) The aspect of meaning that describes the way the referent is presented. (See also *Reference.*)

Sinthomosexual A term coined by Lee Edelman, drawing on Jacques Lacan's term, *sinthome*, which is the knot of desire unique to an individual. Edelman's term stands for a cultural fantasy that puts the homosexual in the place of the *sinthome*. The sinthomosexual is seen as a threat to heteronormative investment in reproductive futurism. Where social orders associate queerness with death, the queer response should be to claim the future in a different way.

Skepticism Our word *skepticism* comes from a Greek verb that means "to consider" or "to inquire into." In the Hellenistic period, the Academic skeptics allegedly claimed that we know that we know nothing. The rival Pyrrhonists taught that, while it might turn out that in the future we will know something, presently, for any proposition we entertain, there seem to be equally weighty reasons to believe and to not believe that it is true. In later periods "skepticism" was the name given to any view that claimed that we don't know or, more forcefully, that we cannot know. One can be a skeptic about certain kinds of things (say, about moral claims) while remaining "dogmatic" about others (such as claims about physics). If someone claims that we don't know anything at all, that person is a "global" skeptic.

Standing beliefs (also known as *dispositional beliefs*) Things that you count as believing even while you are not consciously rehearsing the belief. For example, you probably know what month this is, and you counted that as having knowledge (that standing belief) *even before* being asked the question.

Steadfastness In epistemology, the view that it is often permissible not to change your opinion when you disagree with someone you deem your epistemic peer. (See also *Conciliationism, Epistemic Peer.*)

Subjective values Experientially grounded values attaching to lived experiences: values that attach to the contentful features of "what it's like" to have rich, developed experiences as embedded in a range of mental states such as beliefs, emotions, and desires.

Testimony An act of communication, either verbal or nonverbal, offered by a speaker with the intention to convey information.

Theism Theists endorse the metaphysical claim that there is a god that exists (in reality). Many theists also believe that God is a "maximally great" personal agent that is all-powerful, all-knowing, and all-good.

Transformative experience An experience that is both epistemically and personally transformative, it changes your knowledge and abilities and who you are. It brings about a profound epistemic shift that changes a person's core personal preferences.

Truth-value The truth-value of a sentence is the answer to the question of whether the sentence is true or false.

Well-being (also known as *welfare* or *quality of life*) How well or badly things are going for someone. The better things are going for someone, the higher they are in well-being.

What's the Best Kids Trivia Book?

1,700 Questions in 7 Categories

David Fickes

Printed in the United States of America

First Printing: 2019

Introduction

By nature, I tend to collect trivia without trying. Until relatively recently, I had never sought out trivia; however, after creating a holiday trivia presentation for a community party and then showing it at one of our fitness studio spinning classes, I found myself creating weekly trivia. The cycling clients enjoyed the diversion of answering questions while they exercised, so I continued.

I have tried to ensure that the information is as accurate as possible, and to retain its accuracy, I have also tried to avoid questions whose answers can quickly change with time. Since the simple answer is often not all you want to know, the answers also frequently include additional details to put them in context and provide further information.

There are 1,700 questions in 7 categories – Animals, History, Miscellaneous, Science and Nature, U.S. Geography, U.S. Presidents, and World Geography. The categories are selected to be most appropriate for kids both in terms of interest and educational value, but the questions themselves haven't been altered from the adult versions since I don't see any reason to make the questions easier. To make it quick and easy to test yourself or others without initially seeing the answers, each category is divided into short quizzes with 10 questions followed by their answers.

This is book 6 of my *What's the Best Trivia?* series; I hope you enjoy it, and if you do, look for other books in the series covering a variety of trivia topics.

Contents

Animals

Quiz 1

1) What is the offspring of a cob and a pen?
2) What is a monotreme?
3) What is a bird's vocal organ called?
4) What is the largest venomous snake?
5) How many toes does a rhinoceros have on each foot?
6) What order of mammals has the most species?
7) The Komodo dragon is native to what country?
8) What was the first animal placed on the endangered species list?
9) What two islands are the natural habitat of the orangutan?
10) How many eyelids do camels have?

Quiz 1 Answers

1) Swan
2) Egg laying mammal
3) Syrinx
4) King cobra – up to 18 feet long
5) Three
6) Rodents
7) Indonesia
8) Peregrine falcon - 1973
9) Borneo and Sumatra
10) Three – for sand protection

Quiz 2

1) What color is octopus blood?
2) What is the fastest swimming fish?
3) Only one species of bear is almost exclusively carnivorous, and only one species is almost exclusively herbivorous; what are these two species?
4) What male fish species give birth?
5) Ribbon worms will do what if they can't find food?
6) What bird has the largest wingspan?
7) How many pairs of legs does a shrimp have?

8) What two animals are on the Australian coat of arms?
9) Alligators are naturally found in the United States and what other country?
10) What is the only female animal that has antlers?

Quiz 2 Answers

1) Blue – A copper rich protein carries oxygen instead of the iron rich protein in other animals.
2) Sailfish – 68 mph
3) Polar bear and giant panda
4) Seahorse and pipefish
5) Eat themselves; they can eat a substantial portion of their own body and still survive.
6) Albatross – up to over 11 feet
7) Five
8) Emu and kangaroo
9) China
10) Caribou or reindeer

Quiz 3

1) What fish's name is thought to derive from the Latin meaning "to leap"?
2) What is the largest species of deer?
3) What lives in a formicary?
4) What did ancient Egyptians do to mourn the deaths of their cats?
5) What is a rhinoceros horn made of?
6) What animal has the world's longest distance migration?
7) What animal lives in a drey?
8) Along with some species of sharks, what common ocean fish needs to swim continuously to breathe?
9) What is the heaviest snake?
10) What is the only snake that builds a nest?

Quiz 3 Answers

1) Salmon
2) Moose – up to 7 feet tall and 1,500 pounds
3) Ants
4) They shaved off their own eyebrows.

5) Hair
6) Sooty shearwater – It is one of the most common seabirds in the world and has been tracked electronically migrating 40,000 miles.
7) Squirrel
8) Tuna – They can't pump water through their gills without swimming.
9) Anaconda – up to 550 pounds
10) King cobra – It lays up to 40 eggs at once and builds a nest from vegetation to help keep the eggs safe.

Quiz 4

1) Fireflies are what kind of insect?
2) What fish is known as poor man's lobster?
3) What breed of dog can't bark?
4) What type of creature lives in a sett?
5) What kind of animal does cashmere come from?
6) What do insects do with their spiracles?
7) Other than elephants, what is the heaviest land animal?
8) What is the only insect that can turn its head?
9) What kind of whale is Moby Dick?
10) What is the only land mammal native to New Zealand?

Quiz 4 Answers

1) Beetle
2) Monk fish
3) Basenji
4) Badger
5) Goat
6) Breathe
7) Rhinoceros – up to 5,100 pounds
8) Praying mantis
9) Sperm whale
10) Bat

Quiz 5

1) What animal has the most taste buds?
2) Of all the animal species scientists have studied, what is the only one that shows no outward signs of conciliatory behavior?

3) What breed of dog, known for its thick white coat, is named for the nomadic people of Siberia who bred it?
4) What creature can be Indian, White, or Broad Lipped?
5) What mammal has the shortest known gestation period with an average of just 12 days?
6) What is the largest land predator?
7) What is the more common name of the chaparral cock?
8) Owls have how many eyelids?
9) What species of animal has sub-species including Masai, Reticulated, and Rothschild's?
10) Armadillos are good swimmers, but what other method do they use to cross bodies of water?

Quiz 5 Answers

1) Catfish – It has over 100,000 taste buds both in its mouth and all over its body, about 10 times more than humans.
2) Domestic cat
3) Samoyed
4) Rhinoceros
5) Opossum
6) Polar bear – up to 11 feet long and 1,700 pounds
7) Roadrunner
8) Three – They have one for blinking, one for sleeping, and one for keeping their eyes clean.
9) Giraffe
10) They walk underwater; they can hold their breath for six to eight minutes.

Quiz 6

1) Oysters can change what about themselves based on environmental conditions?
2) What animal's name translates from Arabic as "fast walker"?
3) What is the largest invertebrate (animal without a backbone) species?
4) What animal has the longest known lifespan of all vertebrate (animals with a backbone) species?
5) An elephant is a pachyderm; what does pachyderm literally mean?
6) What is unique about a crocodile's tongue?
7) A female cat is called a molly; after she has become a mother, what

is she called?
8) What is the heaviest bird capable of flight?
9) What is unusual about a cat's jaw?
10) Besides elephants and rhinoceroses, what other animals are considered pachyderms?

Quiz 6 Answers

1) Gender – It can change back and forth based on conditions.
2) Giraffe
3) Colossal squid – up to 46 feet long and 1,650 pounds
4) Greenland shark – 400 years
5) Thick skinned
6) They can't stick it out; it is attached to the roof of their mouth; their tongue helps keep their throat closed underwater, so they can open their mouth to hunt prey.
7) A queen
8) Kori bustard – It is from Africa and weighs about 40 pounds.
9) It can't move sideways, so they can't chew large chunks.
10) Hippopotamuses

Quiz 7

1) What is the name for a group of elk?
2) Adult domestic cats meow for what purpose?
3) At what age does a filly become a mare?
4) What is a group of rhinoceros called?
5) Humans have seven neck vertebrae; how many do giraffes have?
6) Birds don't have what basic body function of most animals?
7) Horses can't do what normal body function through their mouths?
8) What is the only animal that naturally has an odd number of whiskers?
9) Why are bald eagles called bald when they aren't?
10) How many legs do butterflies have?

Quiz 7 Answers

1) Gang
2) To communicate with humans - They don't meow to each other.
3) Five
4) Crash

5) Seven
6) They don't urinate. Birds convert excess nitrogen to uric acid instead of urea; it is less toxic and doesn't need to be diluted as much. It goes out with their other waste and saves water, so they don't have to drink as much.
7) Breathe – A soft palate blocks off the pharynx from the mouth except when swallowing.
8) Catfish
9) Bald comes from the old English word piebald which means white headed.
10) Six

Quiz 8

1) Including hunting dives, what is the fastest bird in the world?
2) Where is the only place in the world that alligators and crocodiles exist together naturally in the wild?
3) What is the largest lizard?
4) What is the national animal of Scotland?
5) What country has the largest population of poisonous snakes?
6) What is the most common group of insects?
7) Iguanas have three of something that most animals have two; what is it?
8) Lemurs are native to what island nation?
9) What animal has the longest tongue relative to its size?
10) What is the sleepiest animal in the world?

Quiz 8 Answers

1) Peregrine falcon – 242 mph
2) Southern Florida
3) Komodo dragon – up to 10 feet long and 250 pounds
4) Unicorn
5) Australia
6) Beetles – followed by flies
7) Eyes – A third parietal eye on top of their head can just distinguish light and dark.
8) Madagascar
9) Chameleon – Its tongue is about twice the length of its body.
10) Koala – It sleeps 22 hours per day.

Quiz 9

1) What shark is thought to be the largest to have ever lived on Earth?
2) What is the world's largest reptile?
3) What animal can survive temperatures from -458 to 300 degrees Fahrenheit, 1,000 atmospheres of pressure, radiation hundreds of times higher than the lethal dose for humans, the vacuum of space, and can live for 30 years without food or water?
4) What kind of animal lives in a holt?
5) What is the world's largest rodent?
6) What is the fastest moving land snake?
7) What animal has the world's largest egg?
8) What color is a polar bear's skin?
9) What happens to a bear's urine when they hibernate?
10) What is the largest animal ever known to have lived on Earth?

Quiz 9 Answers

1) Megalodon – It became extinct about 2.6 million years ago and was up to 59 feet long and 65 tons.
2) Saltwater crocodile – up to 20 feet long and 3,000 pounds
3) Tardigrade – They are water dwelling, eight-legged micro (about 0.02 inches long) animals that were discovered in 1773 and are found everywhere from mountain tops to the deep sea and from tropical rainforests to the Antarctic.
4) Otter
5) Capybara – up to 150 pounds
6) Black mamba – 12 mph
7) Whale shark – The ostrich has the largest laid egg.
8) Black
9) They don't urinate in hibernation; their body converts the urine into protein, and they use it as food.
10) Blue whale – up to 100 feet long and 200 tons

Quiz 10

1) What is the largest current day shark?
2) What animal has the largest brain?
3) What bird species is the highest flying ever recorded?
4) Why is a giraffe's tongue black or purple?
5) What animal has the most legs?

6) A flamboyance is a group of what animals?
7) What do sea otters do while they are sleeping, so they don't drift apart?
8) In terms of the senses, what do most birds lack?
9) What is the fastest two-legged animal?
10) If cats are feline, what are sheep?

Quiz 10 Answers

1) Whale shark – up to 41 feet long and 47,000 pounds
2) Sperm whale – 17 pounds
3) Ruppell's griffon vulture – It has been spotted at 37,000 feet; they have special hemoglobin that makes their oxygen intake more effective.
4) To prevent sunburn - It is exposed a lot of the time while they eat.
5) Millipede – up to 750
6) Flamingos
7) Hold hands
8) Sense of smell
9) Ostrich – over 40 mph
10) Ovine

Quiz 11

1) The U.S. has the most dogs of any country in the world; what country has the second most?
2) The U.S. has the most domestic cats of any country in the world; what country has the second most?
3) What land animal has the longest tail?
4) What part of their bodies do butterflies taste with?
5) What is the V-shaped formation of a flock of geese called?
6) What is nidification?
7) You can tell the age of a whale by counting the rings in its what?
8) What animal produces the loudest sound?
9) The okapi belongs to what family of animals?
10) Dalmatian dogs originated in what country?

Quiz 11 Answers

1) Brazil
2) China

3) Giraffe – up to eight feet long
4) Feet
5) Skein
6) Nest building
7) Earwax
8) Sperm whale – 230 decibels
9) Giraffe
10) Croatia – Dalmatia region

Quiz 12

1) Killer whales aren't whales; what are they?
2) What percent of kangaroos are lefthanded?
3) During WWI, the British army tried to train what animal to battle submarines?
4) When a woodpecker's beak hits a tree, how many times the force of gravity does it experience?
5) What animal has the greatest bite force?
6) What is the only insect considered kosher?
7) How many species of insect are native to Antarctica?
8) How old was the world's oldest dog?
9) How many blood types do dogs have?
10) What are the only two animal species known to seek visual clues from another animal's eyes?

Quiz 12 Answers

1) Dolphins – The similarities with dolphins include teeth, streamlined bodies, rounded head, beak, echolocation, living in pods, and group hunting.
2) Almost 100%
3) Seagulls – They were supposed to poop on periscopes.
4) 1,000 times
5) Nile crocodile – 5,000 psi
6) Locust
7) One – Antarctic midge
8) 29 years
9) 13
10) Humans and dogs – Dogs only do it with humans.

Quiz 13

1) Humans need 16 to 20 images per second to perceive something as a moving picture rather than a flickering image; how may images per second do dogs need?
2) On average, how many people do sharks kill per year?
3) What happens as soon as sand tiger shark embryos develop teeth while still in the womb?
4) Why don't sharks get cavities?
5) What country has the world's largest feral camel herd?
6) What country has all 10 of the deadliest snakes in the world?
7) How many species of bear are alive today?
8) What is a group of bears called?
9) Scientists believe that herrings use what unusual method to communicate?
10) What was the penalty in ancient Egypt for killing a cat even accidentally?

Quiz 13 Answers

1) 70 – Older televisions could only produce 50 images per second, so dogs would only see flickering images; modern televisions are fast enough to appear as moving pictures to dogs.
2) 12
3) The largest of the embryos in each of the two uteruses attacks and eats its siblings leaving just two pups to be born.
4) The outside of their teeth is made of fluoride.
5) Australia – There were as many as 1 million camels at one time; they were imported in the 19th century and many were later set free as the automobile took over. They roam freely with no natural predators.
6) Australia
7) Eight – sun, sloth, spectacled, American black, Asian black, brown, polar, giant panda
8) A sloth
9) Farts – Herrings have excellent hearing and their farts produce a high-pitched sound; the farts aren't from flatulence but from gulping air at the surface and storing it in their swim bladder.
10) Death

Quiz 14

1) Based on oxygen usage, what animal is the most efficient swimmer?
2) Which of the basic tastes can't cats taste?
3) How many eyes do bees have?
4) Why is horseshoe crab blood worth $14,000 per quart?
5) What mammal needs the least sleep?
6) What blood type do mosquitoes like most?
7) What species of animal (not microscopic) has the largest size difference between males and females?
8) Excluding man, what animal species has the longest tested memory?
9) Research has shown that most mammals on average live for about the same number of heartbeats; how many?
10) Silkworms live on a diet of leaves from only what plant?

Quiz 14 Answers

1) Jellyfish – It uses 48% less oxygen than any other known animal; they never stop moving.
2) Sweet – They don't have taste receptors for sweet; this applies to all cats domestic and wild.
3) Five
4) Its unique chemical properties make it very valuable in the health care industry for bacterial testing. It can coagulate around as little as one part in a trillion of bacterial contamination, and the reaction only takes forty-five minutes instead of two days with mammalian blood.
5) Giraffes – They only sleep 30 minutes a day on average just a few minutes at a time.
6) Type O
7) Blanket octopus – Females are 10,000 to 40,000 times larger than males; females may be 6.5 feet in length; males are 1 inch.
8) Dolphins – Bottlenose dolphins have unique whistles like names; studies have shown that they remember the whistle of other dolphins they have lived with even after 20 years of separation.
9) 1.5 billion – Larger animals have slower heartbeats, so they live longer; humans used to fit the pattern prior to health and medical improvements.
10) Mulberry

Quiz 15

1) What land mammal has the most teeth?
2) What land animal has the most teeth?
3) Some snakes, Komodo dragons, sharks, and turkeys are all capable of what biblical feat?
4) What female mammal can literally die if she doesn't mate?
5) What is a group of owls called?
6) What was the first domesticated animal?
7) Humans only have 1, but leeches have 32 what?
8) What is a group of cats called?
9) What bird can only eat when its head is upside down?
10) What is the only creature that can turn its stomach inside out?

Quiz 15 Answers

1) Opossum – 50
2) Giant armadillo – up to 100
3) Virgin births
4) Ferret – The female stays in heat until she mates; if she doesn't, very high levels of estrogen remain in her blood for a long time and can cause aplastic anemia and death. She doesn't have to get pregnant, but she must mate.
5) Parliament
6) Dog – at least 14,000 years ago and possibly as much as 40,000 years ago
7) Brains – Each controls a different segment of their body.
8) Clowder
9) Flamingo
10) Starfish

Quiz 16

1) What animal has the largest eye?
2) An elephant has 40,000 what in its trunk?
3) What animal produces its own sunscreen?
4) In ancient China, what dog breed was restricted to the aristocracy?
5) What insect may be the most efficient predator and possibly has the best vision of any animal?
6) What animal always gives birth to four identical offspring?

7) The nine-banded armadillo and humans have what in common?
8) The minnow is the smallest member of what fish family?
9) Based on AKC registrations, what are the three most popular purebred dog breeds in the U.S.?
10) What land mammal has the best sense of smell?

Quiz 16 Answers

1) Giant and colossal squid - up to 11-inch diameter
2) Muscles – Humans only have about 650 muscles in their entire body.
3) Hippopotamus – They produce a mucus like secretion that keeps them cool and acts as a powerful sunscreen.
4) Pekingese
5) Dragonfly - Humans have three light sensitive proteins in the eye for red, blue, and green (tri-chromatic vision); dragonflies have up to 33. Their bulbous eyes have 30,000 facets and can see in all directions at once. Studies have also shown that they catch as much as 95% of their intended prey.
6) Armadillo - A single embryo splits into four as part of their normal reproduction.
7) Leprosy – They are the only animals known to be infected.
8) Carp or cyprinid
9) Labrador Retrievers, German Shepherds, Golden Retrievers
10) Bear – Black bears have been observed to travel 18 miles in a straight line to a food source; grizzlies can find an elk carcass underwater, and polar bears can smell a seal through 3 feet of ice.

Quiz 17

1) A horse's height is measured from the ground to what part?
2) What would happen to you if you ate a polar bear's liver?
3) A newborn Bactrian camel has how many humps?
4) What biological aspect of a mouse is bigger than an elephant's?
5) What animal has the highest blood pressure?
6) What is the only native North American marsupial?
7) The ostrich is the largest bird in the world; what is the second largest?
8) How many compartments does a cow's stomach have?
9) What is the longest living land mammal after man?
10) What is the longest living land animal of any kind?

Quiz 17 Answers

1) Withers - base of the neck above the shoulders
2) You would get vitamin A poisoning and could die. Polar bears have 50-60 times normal human levels of vitamin A in their liver, and it is about 3 times the tolerable level that a human can intake.
3) None - Baby camels don't get their humps until they start eating solid food.
4) Sperm - Large animals tend to have high numbers of smaller sperm.
5) Giraffe – about 300 over 200
6) Opossum
7) Southern cassowary – It lives in the tropical rainforests of Indonesia, New Guinea, and the islands of northern Australia and averages about 100 pounds compared to 230 pounds for the ostrich.
8) Four
9) Elephant – up to 86 years
10) Tortoise – up to 250 years

Quiz 18

1) What is a newly hatched swan called?
2) How many rows of whiskers does a cat have?
3) What resin used in varnish is a secretion of an insect?
4) What is the largest cat in the Americas?
5) What fish's skin was once used commercially as sandpaper?
6) Which leg of a chicken is more tender, left or right leg?
7) What can't rats do that makes them particularly vulnerable to poison?
8) What does the horned toad squirt from its eyes when attacked?
9) The cheetah is the fastest land animal; what is the second fastest?
10) What is the closest living relative to the Tyrannosaurus Rex?

Quiz 18 Answers

1) Cygnet
2) Four
3) Shellac – lac insect
4) Jaguar – It is the third largest cat after the tiger and lion.
5) Shark

6) Left leg – Chickens scratch with their right leg building up more muscle in that leg and making it tougher than the left.
7) Vomit
8) Blood
9) Pronghorn antelope – 55 mph
10) Chicken

Quiz 19

1) What bird has the biggest brain relative to its body size?
2) What was the first bird domesticated by man?
3) For animals, what is the summer equivalent to hibernation?
4) How many claws does a normal house cat have?
5) What is the only known animal to regularly prey on adult bears?
6) How many hearts does an octopus have?
7) What is the only dog breed specifically mentioned in the Bible?
8) What color is a polar bear's fur?
9) Napoleon's life was saved by what breed of dog?
10) A cat is feline; what kind of animal is leporine?

Quiz 19 Answers

1) Hummingbird – over 4% of its body weight
2) Goose – 5,000 years ago
3) Estivation – Animals slow their activity for the hot, dry summer months.
4) 18 – five on each front paw and four on each back paw
5) Tiger
6) Three
7) Greyhound
8) It has no color; it is transparent and appears white only because it reflects visible light.
9) Newfoundland – It saved him from drowning.
10) Rabbit

Quiz 20

1) What land vertebrate animal has the largest relative size difference between males and females?
2) What is a group of butterflies called?
3) What animal kills the most people annually worldwide?

4) What is the largest mollusk in the world?
5) What is the world's loudest insect?
6) What is the longest living insect?
7) What is the smallest known mammal by weight?
8) Why can't giraffes cough?
9) What animal has the densest fur?
10) What is the largest snake ever known to have ever existed on Earth?

Quiz 20 Answers

1) Anaconda snake - Female anacondas are on average 4.7 times larger than males.
2) Kaleidoscope
3) Mosquito – Mosquitos are by far the deadliest animal in the world killing over 700,000 people worldwide annually primarily from malaria. Snakes are the second most deadly animal killing about 50,000 people; dogs are third at about 25,000 people annually mainly through rabies. Crocodiles are the biggest killer of the large animals at about 1,000 people worldwide; the hippopotamus is the world's deadliest large land mammal, killing an estimated 500 people per year.
4) Giant clam - They can reach 4 feet in length and weigh more than 500 pounds. They live in the warm waters of the South Pacific and Indian Oceans and can live more than 100 years.
5) Cicada – They can produce sounds as loud as about 120 decibels which is equivalent to sitting in the front row of a loud rock concert.
6) Termite queen - They have been known to live for at least 50 years, and some scientists believe they may live to 100.
7) Etruscan shrew – They weigh about 0.06 ounces on average. They have a very fast metabolism and eat 1.5–2 times their own body weight per day. They also have the fastest heartbeat of any mammal at 1,500 beats per minute.
8) Their necks are so long that their lungs are too far away from their epiglottis, and coughing is a combination movement of the lungs and epiglottis.
9) Sea otters - They have up to 1 million hairs per square inch on the densest parts of their bodies.
10) Titanoboa - It lived about 60 million years ago and was up to 42 feet long and weighed up to 2,500 pounds.

History

Quiz 1

1) Alexander the Great was king of what country?
2) What year did Ferdinand Magellan complete the first circumnavigation of the world?
3) In what country were Arabic numerals first used?
4) Who made the first solo round the world flight?
5) What U.S. founding father was carried to the Constitutional Convention in a sedan chair carried by prisoners?
6) Who succeeded Adolf Hitler in 1945 as leader of Germany?
7) Who was the first honorary U.S. citizen?
8) Who was Temujin better known as?
9) Who was *Time* magazine's 1938 man of the year?
10) What queen married two of her brothers?

Quiz 1 Answers

1) Macedonia
2) 1522
3) India
4) Wiley Post – 1933
5) Benjamin Franklin
6) Admiral Karl Donitz
7) Winston Churchill
8) Genghis Khan
9) Adolf Hitler
10) Cleopatra

Quiz 2

1) Good King Wenceslas was king of what country?
2) The spire on the Empire State building was meant to be used for what?
3) What year did the Berlin wall fall?
4) Who was the first African American in space?
5) Who was the first man to set foot on all the continents other than Antarctica?

6) During the War of 1812, British troops invaded and burned what U.S. landmark?
7) What year was the first telephone call made?
8) What year did the Volkswagen Beetle make its first appearance?
9) Who was the first British monarch to visit America?
10) Who taught Alexander the Great?

Quiz 2 Answers

1) Bohemia - current Czech Republic
2) Airship dock
3) 1989
4) Guion Bluford - 1983
5) Captain James Cook
6) White House
7) 1876
8) 1938
9) George VI - 1939
10) Aristotle

Quiz 3

1) What year was the first U.S. minimum wage instituted?
2) What year did India gain independence from British colonial rule?
3) What book was given to all officers in the Confederate army during the U.S. Civil War?
4) What civilization first domesticated guinea pigs and used them for food, sacrifices, and household pets?
5) Through what town did Lady Godiva ride naked?
6) Who was outlaw Harry Longabaugh better known as?
7) What country did Abel Tasman discover in 1642?
8) By what name is Princess Sophia of Anhalt-Zerbst better known?
9) What country invented the crossbow?
10) Who ordered the Russian nobility to become more European by shaving off their beards?

Quiz 3 Answers

1) 1938 – 25 cents per hour
2) 1947
3) Les Misérables – Robert E. Lee believed the book symbolized their

cause.

4) Incas
5) Coventry, England
6) Sundance Kid
7) New Zealand
8) Catherine the Great
9) China – about 700 BC
10) Peter the Great

Quiz 4

1) What nationality was the first person in space who wasn't American or Russian?
2) What was the name of Alexander the Great's horse?
3) Who was Abraham Lincoln's first choice to lead the Union army?
4) Where was the first U.S. federal penitentiary?
5) British King Edward VIII abdicated his throne to marry who?
6) Who discovered the source of the Nile River?
7) What Roman killed himself after his defeat at Actium?
8) How many years were there between the first female in space and the first American female in space?
9) What country was the first to allow women to vote in 1893?
10) How many manned *Apollo* flights preceded the Moon landing?

Quiz 4 Answers

1) Czech – Vladimir Remek in 1978
2) Bucephalus
3) Robert E. Lee
4) Leavenworth, Kansas - 1895
5) Wallis Simpson
6) John Hanning Speke - 1858
7) Mark Antony
8) 20 years – A Soviet woman was the first in 1963.
9) New Zealand
10) Four

Quiz 5

1) The saying “Don’t give up the ship!” comes from the last words of

Captain James Lawrence in what war?

2) What is widely considered "The Gun that Won the West"?
3) What explorer visited Australia and New Zealand and surveyed the Pacific coast of North America?
4) What did the Romans call the tenth part of a legion?
5) Why was the Eiffel Tower built?
6) What year did U.S. prohibition come to an end?
7) What explorer's last words were "I have not told half of what I saw"?
8) What year was NASA founded?
9) What famous battle took place July 1 to July 3, 1863?
10) What Spanish soldier of fortune led the expedition that discovered the Pacific Ocean?

Quiz 5 Answers

1) War of 1812
2) Winchester Model 1873 rifle
3) Captain George Vancouver
4) Cohort - 300 to 600 men
5) Celebrate the 100th anniversary of the French Revolution
6) 1933
7) Marco Polo
8) 1958
9) Gettysburg
10) Vasco Balboa

Quiz 6

1) Who is known as the father of modern economics?
2) How long was Nelson Mandela in prison?
3) Who was King of Mycenae and commander of the Greek forces in the Trojan War?
4) What did Albert Einstein call "the hardest thing in the world to understand"?
5) Who was the first American born child of English settlers?
6) Who is known as the father of medicine?
7) Introduced in 1888, the first vending machine in the U.S. dispensed what item?
8) The U.S. icon Uncle Sam is based on Samuel Wilson who did what

during the War of 1812?
9) Who is the youngest American astronaut to travel in space?
10) What country did the Romans call Hibernia?

Quiz 6 Answers

1) Adam Smith
2) 27 years
3) Agamemnon
4) Income taxes
5) Virginia Dare
6) Hippocrates
7) Gum
8) Meat packer – He supplied barrels of beef to the army stamped with "U.S." for United States, but soldiers started referring to it as Uncle Sam's.
9) Sally Ride – 32
10) Ireland

Quiz 7

1) What religion was Adolf Hitler?
2) What was the family name of the French brothers who were pioneers in hot air ballooning and conducted the first untethered flights?
3) What year did the U.S. celebrate its sesquicentennial?
4) Who did Adolf Hitler dictate *Mein Kampf* to while in prison?
5) Who was the first Christian emperor of Rome?
6) Who first suggested the idea of daylight saving time in an essay he wrote in 1784?
7) What happened July 15, 1815 on the *HMS Bellerophon*?
8) Who was the first person to circumnavigate Antarctica?
9) What was the name of Charles Darwin's survey ship?
10) What car brand was named for the founder of Detroit, Michigan?

Quiz 7 Answers

1) Roman Catholic
2) Montgolfier
3) 1926 – 150-year anniversary
4) Rudolf Hess

5) Constantine the Great - emperor from 306 to 337
6) Benjamin Franklin
7) Napoleon surrendered
8) James Cook – 1773
9) Beagle
10) Cadillac – French explorer Antoine de la Mothe Cadillac founded Detroit in 1701.

Quiz 8

1) On December 1, 1917, who opened Boys Town, a farm village for wayward boys, near Omaha, Nebraska?
2) Who assassinated John Lennon?
3) Where did Churchill, Roosevelt and Stalin meet in 1945?
4) Who was known as the father of the atomic bomb?
5) *Sputnik* 2 was launched into space in 1957; what was the name of the dog that was on board?
6) At the battle of Actium, who defeated Mark Antony and Cleopatra?
7) What country's troops sustained the greatest number of deaths in WWII?
8) In the 15th century, what was the war between the houses of Lancaster and York?
9) *The Ladies' Mercury* in 1693 was the world's first what?
10) What river is Pocahontas buried along?

Quiz 8 Answers

1) Father Edward Flanagan
2) Mark David Chapman
3) Yalta
4) Robert Oppenheimer
5) Laika
6) Octavian or Emperor Augustus
7) Soviet Union
8) War of the Roses
9) Periodical designed and published for women
10) Thames in England

Quiz 9

1) What was the first lighthouse?

2) Who made the first phone call to the Moon?
3) What battle was fought at Senlac Hill?
4) In 1917, Janette Rankin become the first woman in the U.S. to do what?
5) What is the oldest college in the U.S.?
6) Who was the last English king to die on the battlefield?
7) What is the most powerful explosion on Earth ever witnessed by humans?
8) What was the name of Robert E. Lee's horse?
9) What disease is believed to have killed more people than any other throughout history?
10) What year did the *Titanic* sink?

Quiz 9 Answers

1) Pharos of Alexandria – 280 BC
2) Richard Nixon
3) Battle of Hastings - 1066
4) Elected to the U.S. Congress
5) Harvard – 1636
6) Richard III - 1485
7) Mount Tambora volcanic eruption in 1815 in Indonesia – The explosion was equivalent to 800 megatons of TNT, 14 times larger than the largest man-made explosion.
8) Traveller
9) Malaria – Over 1 million people still die from malaria annually.
10) 1912

Quiz 10

1) Who was the first American astronaut who wasn't in the military when they went into space?
2) What political cartoonist popularized the use of the elephant and donkey as symbols of the two main U.S. political parties?
3) What was the first U.S. state to secede from the Union on December 20, 1860?
4) The Statue of Liberty originally also served what functional role?
5) In honor of whose death in 1931 were all non-essential lights in the U.S. turned off for one minute?
6) What American statesman wrote the collection of essays *Fart Proudly*?

7) Who was the first person to enter space (100 km above the Earth) twice?
8) How many states joined the Confederate States of America?
9) Who was married to Adolf Hitler for one day?
10) What was the name of the B-29 that dropped the bomb on Hiroshima?

Quiz 10 Answers

1) Neil Armstrong - He had been a Navy fighter pilot but was a civilian when he joined NASA.
2) Thomas Nast – He also helped create the modern image of Santa Claus.
3) South Carolina
4) Lighthouse
5) Thomas Edison
6) Benjamin Franklin
7) Joseph A. Walker – X-15 rocket aircraft in 1963
8) 11
9) Eva Braun
10) *Enola Gay*

Quiz 11

1) Opened in 1852, what infamous prison was off the coast of French Guiana?
2) What war did Joan of Arc's inspirational leadership help end?
3) What year did the first manned space flight occur?
4) The New Testament was originally written in what language?
5) What did Russian Valentina Tereshkova become the first woman to do in 1963?
6) In what war did jet fighter planes first battle each other?
7) According to legend, what historical figure died of a nosebleed on his wedding night?
8) The island of Krakatoa was almost entirely destroyed by a volcanic eruption in what year?
9) What city became the U.S. national capital in 1789?
10) Who was America's first public enemy number one?

Quiz 11 Answers

1) Devil's Island
2) The Hundred Years War – 1337 to 1453
3) 1961
4) Greek
5) Travel in space
6) Korean War
7) Attila the Hun
8) 1883
9) New York
10) John Dillinger

Quiz 12

1) What famous priest ministered to the Molokai lepers from 1873 until his death?
2) What was the date for D-Day?
3) What was the last Chinese dynasty?
4) What was the predecessor to the United Nations?
5) How many witches were burned at the stake during the Salem witch trials?
6) Who was the first person to reach the South Pole in 1911?
7) What was discovered at Qumran in 1947?
8) What was the first ship to reach the *Titanic* after it sank?
9) The only woman ever awarded the U.S. Medal of Honor received it for her service in what war?
10) What ship collided with the Swedish liner *Stockholm* on July 26, 1956?

Quiz 12 Answers

1) Father Damien
2) June 6, 1944
3) Manchu
4) League of Nations
5) None - Twenty were executed, but most were hung, and none were burned.
6) Roald Amundsen
7) Dead Sea Scrolls

8) *Carpathia*
9) Civil War – Mary Edwards Walker was a surgeon at a temporary Washington, D.C. hospital and was captured and arrested as a spy after crossing enemy lines to treat wounded civilians.
10) *Andrea Doria*

Quiz 13

1) What year did Canada become a country?
2) Who was the first person to sail around the Cape of Good Hope?
3) Who was named *Time* magazine's Man of the Century in 1999?
4) How many states are needed to ratify an amendment to the U.S. Constitution?
5) Where was the tallest tsunami wave ever recorded?
6) Who assassinated Robert Kennedy?
7) Who was the first queen of England?
8) What is the only nation that created nuclear weapons and then voluntarily eliminated them?
9) Who was the oldest person to sign the Declaration of Independence?
10) Who is the longest reigning British monarch?

Quiz 13 Answers

1) 1867
2) Vasco da Gama - 1498
3) Albert Einstein
4) 38 – 75% of the states
5) Lituya Bay, Alaska in 1958 - An 8.0 earthquake dropped 40 to 50 million cubic yards of rock and ice 3,000 feet down into the bay creating a 1,720-foot wave.
6) Sirhan Sirhan
7) Mary I or Mary Tudor - 1553
8) South Africa
9) Benjamin Franklin – 70 at the time
10) Queen Elizabeth II – She surpassed her great-great-grandmother Victoria's reign in 2015.

Quiz 14

1) Less than a year before Abraham Lincoln was assassinated, who

saved Lincoln's oldest son Robert from being hit by a train?
2) Tenochtitlan was the capital of what empire?
3) What U.S. Constitutional amendment granted women the right to vote?
4) What year was the Pledge of Allegiance written?
5) In what city did Rosa Parks refuse to give up her seat?
6) Where was the world's first underwater tunnel?
7) What was the first U.S. department store?
8) Who organized the Boston Tea Party?
9) Who is the only person to win two unshared Nobel Prizes?
10) What did Robert Heft design in 1958 as a part of a junior high history class project?

Quiz 14 Answers

1) Edwin Booth – brother of John Wilkes Booth
2) Aztec
3) 19th
4) 1892
5) Montgomery, Alabama
6) Thames River, London – 1843
7) Macy's – 1858
8) Samuel Adams
9) Linus Pauling
10) Current 50-star United States flag

Quiz 15

1) What was the nickname for the *Hughes H-4 Hercules* aircraft that made a single flight in 1947?
2) What year did Switzerland last go to war with another country?
3) What country landed the first man-made object on the Moon?
4) What empire lasted from 1324 to 1922?
5) What country did Adolf Hitler describe as a pimple on the face of Europe?
6) The final link of the first U.S. transcontinental railway was completed in what state?
7) What country has the oldest parliament in the world?
8) Who was the first *Time* magazine man of the year?
9) Israel was founded in what year?

10) How did Socrates commit suicide?

Quiz 15 Answers

1) *Spruce Goose*
2) 1515
3) Soviet Union – *Luna* 2 in 1959
4) Ottoman or Turkish Empire
5) Switzerland – Hitler hated Switzerland and thought it had no right to exist; he had a planned invasion but never initiated it.
6) Utah - 1869
7) Iceland - 930
8) Charles Lindbergh – 1927
9) 1948
10) Drank poison hemlock

Quiz 16

1) What year did the gunfight at the O.K. Corral take place?
2) What year was the U.S. Constitution written?
3) What year was the last public execution in the U.S.?
4) What was the first Confederate state to be readmitted to the Union after the Civil War?
5) What was suffragette Susan B. Anthony talking about when she said, "I think it has done more to emancipate women than anything else in the world. It gives women a feeling of freedom and self-reliance"?
6) How many people have died outside the Earth's atmosphere?
7) What newspaper mistakenly ran the infamous "Dewey Defeats Truman" headline?
8) How many people have walked on the Moon?
9) Who was the last man to walk on the Moon?
10) What country was known to Europeans as Cathay from the 11th to the 16th century?

Quiz 16 Answers

1) 1881
2) 1787
3) 1936 – Kentucky
4) Tennessee

5) Bicycle
6) Three – *Soyuz 11* in 1971
7) *Chicago Daily Tribune*
8) 12
9) Eugene Cernan - 1972
10) China

Quiz 17

1) What year did the U.S. complete the Louisiana Purchase?
2) The end of the Pony Express line was in what western city?
3) What state was the first to elect a woman to the U.S. Congress?
4) What is the bloodiest single day of battle in U.S. history?
5) What was the first nation to have a female prime minister?
6) Who was the first woman to win a Nobel Prize?
7) Who is the only person to win *Time* magazine's person of the year three times?
8) In what city was Archduke Ferdinand killed precipitating WWI?
9) What Spanish explorer is credited with discovering the Mississippi River?
10) Who inherited the throne of Scotland at the age of six days?

Quiz 17 Answers

1) 1803
2) Sacramento, California
3) Montana - 1916
4) Battle of Antietam in the Civil War - 22,000 dead, wounded, or missing
5) Sri Lanka – 1960
6) Marie Curie - 1903
7) Franklin D. Roosevelt
8) Sarajevo, Bosnia and Herzegovina - 1914
9) Hernando de Soto - 1541
10) Mary, Queen of Scots or Mary I

Quiz 18

1) What country first tried unsuccessfully to build the Panama Canal?
2) Who was the pilot in the first fatal airplane crash?

3) What African country was settled by Americans?
4) Before devoting his life to philosophy, what was Socrates' profession?
5) What is the world's oldest snack food?
6) What was the first U.S. college to confer degrees on women?
7) Who was the first female candidate for U.S. vice president on a major party ticket?
8) What was the first city to reach a population of 1 million people?
9) What famous general was attacked by rabbits and had to retreat?
10) Who was the first woman appointed to the U.S. Supreme Court?

Quiz 18 Answers

1) France
2) Orville Wright
3) Liberia
4) Mason or stone cutter
5) Pretzels – 6th century
6) Oberlin College – 1841
7) Geraldine Ferraro – 1984
8) Rome – 5 BC
9) Napoleon – In 1807, Napoleon had just signed the Treaty of Tilsit ending his war with Russia; to celebrate, he went on a rabbit hunt. Hundreds of rabbits had been gathered for the hunt in cages, but when they were released, they swarmed toward Napoleon and his men rather than running away. They swarmed Napoleon's legs and started climbing up; he was forced to retreat to his coach and depart. Instead of wild rabbits, they had bought tame rabbits that weren't afraid of people and probably thought it was feeding time.
10) Sandra Day O'Connor – 1981

Quiz 19

1) Who was Germany's first female chancellor?
2) What was the first major war campaign fought entirely by air forces?
3) Who was the first American casualty of the Revolutionary War?
4) What U.S. Constitutional amendment ended slavery?
5) What country gained its independence from Denmark in 1944?
6) Kim Campbell was the first female prime minister of what country?
7) In what century did Cleopatra rule Egypt?

8) What was the first man made object to break the sound barrier?
9) Who is the Danish explorer who gave his name to a strait, sea, island, glacier, and land bridge?
10) Who was accused in The Trial of the Century which opened January 1, 1935?

Quiz 19 Answers

1) Angela Merkel - 2005
2) Battle of Britain - 1940
3) Crispus Attucks
4) 13th
5) Iceland
6) Canada – June 25 to November 4, 1993
7) 1st century BC
8) Whip
9) Vitus Bering
10) Bruno Richard Hauptmann – Lindbergh kidnapping

Quiz 20

1) Who was the first female U.S. Attorney General?
2) Who is the head of state of New Zealand?
3) What world leader had the nickname "The Great Asparagus"?
4) Who reached the summit of Mount Everest with Edmund Hilary in 1953?
5) Who was the first man to hit a golf ball on the Moon?
6) On taking power in 1959, Fidel Castro banned what board game and ordered all sets destroyed?
7) The 1964 Nobel Peace Prize was awarded to its youngest recipient up to that point; who was it?
8) The Statue of Liberty was originally intended for what country?
9) What year did London get back to its pre-WWII population?
10) Who headed the Gestapo?

Quiz 20 Answers

1) Janet Reno - 1993
2) Queen Elizabeth II
3) Charles de Gaulle – He got the name in military school because of his looks.

4) Tenzing Norgay – Sherpa
5) Alan Shepard - 1971
6) Monopoly – He viewed it as the embodiment of capitalism.
7) Martin Luther King Jr. – 35
8) Egypt – They rejected it.
9) 2015
10) Heinrich Himmler

Quiz 21

1) What is the longest war in U.S. history?
2) What is the loudest sound in recorded history?
3) The Egyptian pyramids were built by what kind of workers?
4) Who had the largest volunteer army in world history?
5) How many times in history has a submerged submarine deliberately sunk a submerged submarine?
6) Elena Cornaro Piscopia was the first woman in the world to receive a PhD degree in what year?
7) Roman gladiator fights started as a part of what ceremony?
8) From the middle ages until 1809, Finland was part of what country?
9) What are the five permanent members of the United Nations Security Council?
10) What two countries did Hadrian's wall separate?

Quiz 21 Answers

1) Afghan War – started 2001
2) Eruption of Krakatoa in 1883 – It ruptured people's eardrums 40 miles away and was clearly heard 3,000 miles away.
3) Paid laborers – not slaves
4) India – 2.5 million during WWII
5) Once - 1945
6) 1678 – Italy
7) Funerals – When wealthy nobles died, they would have bouts at the graveside.
8) Sweden
9) United States, United Kingdom, France, Russia, China
10) England and Scotland – The wall was built by the Romans from 122-128 AD.

Quiz 22

1) What year was the first magazine ever launched?
2) In 1917, Germany invited what country to join WWI by attacking the U.S. to recover lost territories?
3) What was the first country to implement daylight saving time?
4) How long did it take Berlin to get back to its pre-WWII population?
5) What makes Graca Machel unique among first ladies of the world?
6) Who was the first Hispanic to serve on the U.S. Supreme Court?
7) What year was Antarctica first sighted?
8) Sheep grazed in New York's Central Park until what year?
9) How many Americans were killed in the Hiroshima atomic blast?
10) Of all the countries that celebrate an independence day, the largest number gained independence from what country?

Quiz 22 Answers

1) 1663 – German philosophy and literature magazine
2) Mexico
3) Germany – in 1916 to save energy in WWI
4) It still hasn't.
5) First lady of two separate countries – widow of Nelson Mandela (South Africa president) and Samora Machel (Mozambique president)
6) Sonia Sotomayor - 2009
7) 1820
8) 1934 – They were moved during the Great Depression for fear they would be eaten.
9) 12 – prisoners of war
10) Great Britain (58) - followed by France (26), Russia (21), Spain (21)

Quiz 23

1) Where were the remains of England's King Richard III found?
2) What is the world's oldest currency still in use?
3) What was the only independent South American country to send troops to fight in WWII?
4) The Eiffel Tower wasn't intended to be permanent; it was scheduled for demolition in 1909 but was saved to be used as what?
5) Prior to the 20th century in North America, what now popular and expensive food was considered a mark of poverty, used for

fertilizer, and fed to slaves?

6) Why are there 60 seconds in a minute and 360 degrees in a circle?
7) Mississippi was the last state to officially ratify the 13th amendment abolishing slavery in what year?
8) Who was the last pharaoh of Egypt?
9) How many sides does the Great Pyramid of Giza have?
10) What year was the last man on the Moon?

Quiz 23 Answers

1) Buried under a parking lot in Leicester England in 2013. He died on the battlefield in 1485.
2) British pound – 1,200 years
3) Brazil
4) Radio tower
5) Lobster – Its reputation changed when modern transportation allowed shipping live lobsters to urban centers.
6) The ancient Babylonians did math in base 60 instead of base 10 and developed the concepts.
7) 2013 – Mississippi ratified the amendment in 1995 but didn't notify the U.S. archivist and didn't officially complete the process until 2013.
8) Cleopatra
9) Eight – Each of the four sides are split from base to tip by slight concave indentations.
10) 1972

Quiz 24

1) When the Persians were at war with the Egyptians, they rounded up and released as many of what animal as they could on the battlefield?
2) What two countries still haven't officially signed a peace treaty between them ending WWII?
3) Queen Elizabeth II served in what capacity in WWII?
4) Tsutomu Yamaguchi is the only recognized person in the world to survive what?
5) What country lost the greatest percentage of its population in WWII?
6) What was the only U.S. soil Japan occupied during WWII?
7) Why did so many U.S. police departments adopt navy blue

uniforms?

8) In what year was the first African American elected to serve in the U.S. Congress?
9) Louis Bonaparte, Napoleon's brother, was called the "King of Rabbits"; why?
10) What was the third country to develop an atomic bomb?

Quiz 24 Answers

1) Cats – Knowing the Egyptians reverence for cats, they knew they would not want to do anything to hurt the cats; the Persians won.
2) Japan and Russia – dispute over the Kuril Islands
3) Mechanic and driver
4) Both Hiroshima and Nagasaki atomic blasts – He was in Hiroshima on business for the first bomb and then returned home to Nagasaki.
5) Poland – 20%
6) Aleutian Islands – two remote islands
7) They were surplus army uniforms from the Civil War.
8) 1870 – a senator from Mississippi and a representative from South Carolina
9) He mispronounced the Dutch phrase "I am your King," and instead said "I am your rabbit," when he took over rule of the Netherlands in 1806.
10) Great Britain - 1952

Quiz 25

1) Who is credited as being the first person to put wheels on an office chair?
2) Notre Dame Cathedral was almost demolished in the 19th century; what saved it?
3) How long did the Spanish Inquisition last?
4) Alexander the Great, Julius Caesar, Genghis Khan, Napoleon, Mussolini and Hitler all suffered from ailurophobia; what is it?
5) Of the seven wonders of the ancient world, only the Great Pyramid of Giza still exists; which of the other seven wonders disappeared most recently?
6) Who was Europe's only Muslim king?
7) Who was the first person to fly across the English Channel?
8) In what war was "The Charge of the Light Brigade"?

9) Who did Winston Churchill succeed as British prime minister at the outbreak of WWII?
10) How many people were executed for Abraham Lincoln's assassination?

Quiz 25 Answers

1) Charles Darwin – 1840
2) Victor Hugo wrote *The Hunchback of Notre Dame* partially to save the cathedral from demolition.
3) 356 years – 1479 to 1834
4) Fear of cats
5) Lighthouse at Alexandria – It was toppled by earthquakes in the early 14th century, and its ruined stones were carried off by the late 15th century.
6) King Zog of Albania – coronated in 1928
7) Louis Bleriot - 1909
8) Crimean War – British forces against Russia in 1854
9) Neville Chamberlain
10) Four

Quiz 26

1) In what country were the Guns of Navarone installed during WWII?
2) What was discovered in 1922 by Howard Carter?
3) Who sailed in the *Golden Hind*?
4) Where did the mutineers of the *Bounty* settle?
5) In 1911, Hiram Bingham discovered what?
6) As a result of WWII, what Norwegian politician's name became synonymous with traitor?
7) In 1763, Great Britain traded Havana, Cuba to Spain for what?
8) Who did the U.S. buy the Virgin Islands from?
9) Who taught the theory of evolution in 1925 contrary to Tennessee law?
10) What two European countries entered the American Revolutionary War on the side of the Americans?

Quiz 26 Answers

1) Turkey
2) Tutankhamun's tomb

3) Sir Francis Drake
4) Pitcairn Islands
5) Lost city of Machu Picchu
6) Vidkun Quisling
7) Florida
8) Denmark - 1917
9) John T. Scopes – Scopes Monkey Trial
10) France and Spain

Quiz 27

1) What country was the first to introduce old age pensions?
2) What country originated the concentration camp?
3) Other than the war itself, what killed an estimated 43,000 U.S. servicemen mobilized for WWI?
4) Who ran the first marathon upon which all others are based?
5) What is the oldest known name for the island of Great Britain?
6) In what month did the Russian October Revolution take place?
7) What country was the first to abolish capital punishment for all crimes?
8) What did Lucien B. Smith invent in 1867 that had a great impact on the American west?
9) Who was the first U.S. Postmaster General?
10) Who was the second man on the Moon?

Quiz 27 Answers

1) Germany – 1889
2) Great Britain – during the Boer War from 1900-1902
3) Influenza – about half of all U.S. military deaths in Europe
4) Pheidippides - He ran 140 miles round trip from Athens to Sparta over mountainous terrain to ask for military aid; marched 26 miles from Athens to Marathon; fought all morning, and then ran 26 miles to Athens with the victory news and died of exhaustion.
5) Albion
6) November - It was October in the old Julian calendar.
7) Venezuela - by constitution in 1863
8) Barbed wire
9) Benjamin Franklin
10) Buzz Aldrin

Quiz 28

1) Who was offered the presidency of Israel in 1952 and turned it down?
2) In 1861, *The Times* newspaper of London carried the world's first what?
3) Edward Teach became famous as who?
4) What pet did Florence Nightingale carry with her?
5) Who is known as the father of history?
6) What did the ancient Greeks use instead of soap to clean themselves?
7) What country invented french fried potatoes?
8) What city was the first U.S. national capital?
9) Who was the first elected head of a nation to give birth in office?
10) During WWII when Hitler visited Paris, what did the French do to the Eiffel Tower?

Quiz 28 Answers

1) Albert Einstein
2) Weather forecast
3) Blackbeard the pirate
4) Owl – She carried it in her pocket.
5) Herodotus
6) Olive oil – They rubbed it into their skin and then scraped it off along with dirt and dead skin.
7) Belgium - late 17th century
8) Philadelphia, Pennsylvania
9) Benazir Bhutto – Pakistan in 1990
10) They cut the lift cables, so Hitler would have to climb the steps if he wanted to go to the top.

Quiz 29

1) What was Mahatma Gandhi's profession?
2) What nationality was Cleopatra?
3) How tall was Napoleon?
4) What date was V.E. Day?
5) What British prime minister's mother was born in Brooklyn, New York?

6) What two mountain ranges did Hannibal and his elephants march through in 218 BC?
7) What was the D-Day invasion password?
8) Which side did Britain support in the U.S. Civil War?
9) What year followed 1 BC?
10) What country declared war on both Germany and the Allies in WWII?

Quiz 29 Answers

1) Lawyer
2) Greek
3) 5 feet 7 inches - The average adult French male of his time was 5 feet 5 inches, so he was taller than average; some of the confusion is the units his height was reported in and that his personal guards who he was usually seen with were required to be quite tall.
4) May 8, 1945
5) Winston Churchill
6) Pyrenees and Alps
7) Mickey Mouse
8) Confederacy
9) 1 AD
10) Italy – One month after surrendering to the allies, Italy declared war on Germany, its former ally.

Quiz 30

1) What country contains the Waterloo battlefield?
2) The rallying cry "Remember the Maine!" came from what war?
3) What was Al Capone finally imprisoned for in 1931?
4) Who reached the South Pole in January 1912 only to find that Amundsen had gotten there first?
5) What ancient marvel did Nebuchadnezzar build?
6) Who invented the automobile in 1885?
7) What war did Florence Nightingale tend troops in?
8) What caused 20 million deaths in 1918?
9) Who was the Iron Chancellor of Germany?
10) What was American folk hero John Chapman's nickname?

Quiz 30 Answers

1) Belgium
2) Spanish-American War
3) Income tax evasion
4) Captain Robert Scott
5) Hanging Gardens of Babylon
6) Karl Benz
7) Crimean – 1853 to 1856
8) Influenza
9) Otto von Bismarck – He was chancellor from 1871-1890.
10) Johnny Appleseed

Quiz 31

1) How many stars were on the U.S flag in 1913?
2) Who founded the De Beers mining company?
3) Who was the first president of independent Texas?
4) What were the original seven wonders of the ancient world?
5) What fighting unit is headquartered in Corsica?
6) What war caused the most American deaths?
7) What was the first railroad to cross the U.S.?
8) Who was the first American in space?
9) Who was Helen Keller's teacher?
10) What date was Hiroshima bombed?

Quiz 31 Answers

1) 48 – Alaska and Hawaii weren't states yet.
2) Cecil Rhodes – creator of the Rhodes Scholarships
3) Sam Houston
4) Great Pyramid of Giza, Colossus of Rhodes, Lighthouse of Alexandria, Mausoleum at Halicarnassus, Temple of Artemis at Ephesus, Statue of Zeus at Olympia, Hanging Gardens of Babylon
5) French Foreign Legion
6) Civil War – about 620,000 deaths, almost half of all U.S. deaths in all wars combined
7) Union Pacific - 1869
8) Alan Shepard Jr. - 1961
9) Anne Sullivan

10) August 6, 1945

Miscellaneous

Quiz 1

1) How did the term "piggy bank" originate?
2) What does the word karaoke literally mean?
3) In 1892, Juan Vucetich was the first person to solve a crime using what?
4) Who was the first pilot to fly faster than the speed of sound?
5) The hard piece at the end of a shoelace is called what?
6) What is the only number spelled out in English that has the same number of letters as its value?
7) The U.S. $10,000 bill was last printed in 1945 and is the largest denomination ever in public circulation; whose portrait appeared on it?
8) What articles of clothing are tokens in the game Monopoly?
9) What word is in 1,200 different languages without changing?
10) How long after tin cans were invented was the can opener invented?

Quiz 1 Answers

1) Pygg clay – An orange clay called pygg was used to make dishes and jars that were sometimes used to hold spare change. At some point, people decided to use pygg clay to make pig-shaped banks.
2) Empty orchestra
3) Fingerprints
4) Chuck Yeager
5) Aglet
6) Four
7) Salmon P. Chase – Secretary of the Treasury
8) Shoe and top hat
9) Amen
10) 45 years

Quiz 2

1) According to the Bible, how long did Methuselah live?
2) What is the name of the dog on the Cracker Jack box?

3) What vegetable did Mark Twain describe as "cabbage with a college education"?
4) What country eats the most chocolate per capita?
5) What is the longest railway line in the world?
6) In what country were fortune cookies invented?
7) What country has the highest per capita consumption of turkey?
8) Who was the first person other than royalty to appear on a British stamp?
9) What is the most commonly used word in the world?
10) From what common condition would you be suffering if you had podobromhidosis?

Quiz 2 Answers

1) 969 years
2) Bingo
3) Cauliflower
4) Switzerland
5) Trans-Siberian Railway – 5,772 miles
6) United States
7) Israel
8) William Shakespeare
9) OK
10) Smelly feet

Quiz 3

1) What is the only number spelled out in English that has letters in alphabetical order?
2) What game has the most books written about it?
3) The feeling from hitting your funny bone is due to hitting what?
4) What is the most popular crop in U.S. home gardens?
5) Frank Lloyd Wright's son John invented what after watching workers move timber?
6) What kind of condition is protanopia?
7) What was the first type of product sold in aerosol spray cans?
8) Before 1938, toothbrushes were made using hairs from what?
9) What two birds did Noah send out from the ark?
10) What ancient measure is the distance from the elbow to the tip of the middle finger?

Quiz 3 Answers

1) Forty
2) Chess
3) Ulnar nerve
4) Tomatoes
5) Lincoln Logs
6) Color blindness
7) Insecticide
8) Boar
9) Dove and raven
10) Cubit

Quiz 4

1) What familiar word is derived from a Latin word that means "place where three roads meet"?
2) What globally successful product was created by Dr. John Pemberton?
3) What are the rings or spots of light you see when you rub your eyes called?
4) What was the name of the apostle who replaced Judas Iscariot?
5) Gail Borden invented what food item?
6) Since pigs don't sweat much, where does the expression "sweat like a pig" come from?
7) What color is an aircraft's black box flight recorder?
8) How many colored squares are there on a Rubik's Cube?
9) What Hebrew word means "so be it"?
10) What was the first U.S. consumer product sold in the former Soviet Union?

Quiz 4 Answers

1) Trivia
2) Coca-Cola
3) Phosphenes
4) Matthias
5) Condensed milk
6) It comes from the iron smelting process. Iron ore was smelted into pig iron which got its name because the mold the iron was poured

into had ingots at right angles to a center channel and resembled a litter of piglets suckling on their mother. They knew the pig iron was cool enough to transport when it started to sweat from condensation as it cooled which originated the term "sweat like a pig."

7) Orange
8) 54
9) Amen
10) Pepsi

Quiz 5

1) What year was the first automatically sliced commercial bread produced?
2) What does a month beginning on a Sunday always have?
3) What carbonated beverage started out in the 1890s as Brad's Drink?
4) A standard barrel of crude oil holds roughly how many gallons?
5) Who was the first member of the British royal family to graduate from a university?
6) In what country did chocolate originate?
7) What IQ level is the beginning of genius?
8) What is the last word of the Bible?
9) What number can't be represented in Roman numerals?
10) In terms of pounds consumed, what is the most popular vegetable in the U.S.?

Quiz 5 Answers

1) 1928 - Missouri
2) Friday the 13th
3) Pepsi
4) 42
5) Prince Charles
6) Mexico
7) 140
8) Amen
9) Zero
10) Potato

Quiz 6

1) According to the Bible, how tall is Goliath?
2) What was the first product to have a barcode?
3) The dot over the letter "i" is called what?
4) "Fidelity, Bravery, and Integrity" is which U.S. organization's motto?
5) A gross is equal to 144 units; how many units are in a great gross?
6) What toy was originally called the Pluto Platter?
7) What country invented cheesecake?
8) In terms of production volume, what is the most popular fruit in the world?
9) According to the Bible, how many wise men were there?
10) What letter begins the fewest words in the English language?

Quiz 6 Answers

1) Six cubits - about nine feet
2) Wrigley's gum
3) Tittle
4) FBI
5) 1728 – 12 gross
6) Frisbee
7) Greece
8) Tomato – The tomato is technically a fruit.
9) It doesn't say. It says wise men and mentions the gifts; there is no indication of how many wise men.
10) X

Quiz 7

1) Who is the largest toy distributor in the world?
2) Who or what are taikonauts?
3) What is the cultivation of grapes known as?
4) What is the world's best-selling candy bar?
5) The practice of performing in public places for tips and gratuities is known as what?
6) What country consumes the most Coca-Cola per capita?
7) What causes a jumping bean to jump?
8) What is the middle day of a non-leap year?

9) What foreign country is visited most by Americans?
10) What city is home to the Mayo Clinic?

Quiz 7 Answers

1) McDonald's – About 20% of its meals are Happy Meals with a toy.
2) Chinese astronauts
3) Viticulture
4) Snickers
5) Busking
6) Mexico
7) Moth grub moving inside the bean
8) July 2
9) Mexico
10) Rochester, Minnesota

Quiz 8

1) What does UNICEF stand for?
2) What country consumes the most meat per capita?
3) What continent has the largest number of Roman Catholics?
4) What dog has a statue erected in Edinburgh, Scotland?
5) Before taking its current name, what company was originally called Backrub?
6) Why did pirates wear earrings?
7) What is the only miracle mentioned in all four Bible gospels?
8) What language has the most words?
9) How many people have won two Nobel Prizes?
10) What is AM an abbreviation for in time designations?

Quiz 8 Answers

1) United Nations International Children's Emergency Fund
2) Australia
3) South America
4) Greyfriars Bobby
5) Google
6) To improve their eyesight – They believed the precious metal in an earring had healing powers.
7) The feeding of the 5,000

8) English
9) Four – Marie Curie, Linus Pauling, John Bardeen, Frederick Sanger
10) Ante meridiem – meaning before noon in Latin

Quiz 9

1) What mode of transport was invented in 1959 by the Armand Bombardier?
2) What is the name of the strong, heavy grating lowered to block the entrance to a castle?
3) What is Barbie the doll's full name?
4) What species of bird's nest is used to make bird's nest soup?
5) What modern word comes from a knight who was free for hire?
6) How many people took refuge on Noah's ark?
7) How many times is a Roman numeral's value increased if it has a line over it?
8) What was the first Lifesaver flavor?
9) What is the largest library in the world?
10) What soft drink first appeared in the Old Corner Drug store in Waco, Texas in 1885?

Quiz 9 Answers

1) Snowmobile
2) Portcullis
3) Barbara Millicent Roberts
4) Swift – The nest is saliva that has dried and hardened.
5) Freelance
6) Eight – Noah and his wife and his three sons and their wives
7) 1,000 times
8) Peppermint
9) Library of Congress, Washington, DC
10) Dr. Pepper

Quiz 10

1) In what country was Greenpeace founded in 1971?
2) What year did Disneyland open?
3) What is unique about the word detartrated?
4) What is the most frequently sold item at Walmart?
5) Alfred Carlton Gilbert, a 1908 Olympic gold medal pole vaulter,

invented what popular toy?

6) What is the most commonly used noun in the English language?
7) What country consumes the most fish per capita?
8) Before 1687, clocks didn't have what?
9) What person has the most statues in their honor in the U.S.?
10) What is the singular of graffiti?

Quiz 10 Answers

1) Canada
2) 1955
3) Longest palindrome word in English – same forwards and backwards
4) Bananas
5) Erector Set
6) Time
7) Iceland
8) Minute hands
9) Sacagawea
10) Graffito

Quiz 11

1) In what game would you use a squidger?
2) What two cities represent letters in the phonetic alphabet?
3) As referenced in the Bible, what is myrrh?
4) What is the largest inhabited castle in the world?
5) What is the oldest authenticated age ever for a human?
6) Who was the first person to speak to Jesus after he had risen from the dead?
7) What is the most widely played card game in the world?
8) What is the name of the piece flipped into the cup in tiddlywinks?
9) What is the most commonly used punctuation mark?
10) What is the most common surname in the world?

Quiz 11 Answers

1) Tiddlywinks – Squidgers are the larger discs used to shoot the winks.
2) Lima and Quebec

3) A gum resin from trees
4) Windsor Castle – 590,000 square feet
5) 122
6) Mary Magdalene
7) Solitaire
8) Wink
9) Comma
10) Chang

Quiz 12

1) What did the ancient Romans throw at weddings?
2) Which of the five senses is less sharp after you eat too much?
3) What is the lowest rank of British nobility?
4) A pirate who is yelling, "Avast, ye mateys" is telling his mates to do what?
5) What country eats the most donuts per capita?
6) What country has the most vending machines per capita?
7) What did Simon of Cyrene do in the Bible?
8) In Scrabble, what two letters are worth 10 points?
9) On a pencil, what do the initials HB stand for?
10) What is the first color mentioned in the Bible?

Quiz 12 Answers

1) Walnuts – They signified hoped for fertility of bride.
2) Hearing
3) Baron
4) Stop or cease
5) Canada – The presence of 3,000 Tim Hortons restaurants is a major factor.
6) Japan – one for every 23 people
7) Carried Christ's cross
8) Q and Z
9) Hard black
10) Green

Quiz 13

1) Hotfoot Teddy was the original name of what American icon?

2) What language (not dialect) has the most characters in its alphabet?
3) What is the Decalogue more commonly known as?
4) What country has the most emigrants (people living in other countries)?
5) What is the study of word origins called?
6) Characters such as those in Chinese where a word is represented by a picture are called what?
7) What body of water is referenced in the Bible as the Great Sea?
8) In psychology, the tendency for people to believe they are above average is an effect named after what fictional town?
9) What U.S. state's constitution is the longest in the world?
10) What is a chef's hat called?

Quiz 13 Answers

1) Smokey the Bear
2) Cambodian (Khmer) – 74
3) Ten Commandments
4) Mexico
5) Etymology
6) Ideograms
7) Mediterranean Sea
8) Lake Wobegon – from Garrison Keillor's *A Prairie Home Companion*
9) Alabama – 310,000 words
10) Toque

Quiz 14

1) Who is credited with suggesting the word hello be used when answering a telephone?
2) What country has the world's oldest operating amusement park?
3) What is the button on the top of a baseball cap called?
4) For what purpose was the mouthwash Listerine originally created for?
5) What country has four of the five highest circulation newspapers in the world?
6) What is coulrophobia?
7) What is the most expensive man-made object ever built?
8) What was the first car model to sell 20 million units?

9) How many possible ways are there to make change for a dollar?
10) What was the first ready to eat breakfast cereal?

Quiz 14 Answers

1) Thomas Edison – Alexander Graham Bell thought ahoy was better.
2) Denmark – 1583
3) Squatchee
4) Surgical disinfectant
5) Japan
6) Fear of clowns
7) International Space Station - $160 billion
8) Volkswagen Beetle
9) 293
10) Shredded wheat

Quiz 15

1) John Montagu is credited with inventing what food item?
2) How many acres in a square mile?
3) What year did the first enclosed climate-controlled mall open in the U.S.?
4) What was Play-Doh originally created for?
5) How did the terms uppercase and lowercase originate regarding letters?
6) What year was the first automobile speeding ticket issued?
7) How many eyes are there in a deck of 52 cards?
8) What is the pleasant odor after a rain called?
9) What are the four railways in the game Monopoly?
10) What is a dactylogram?

Quiz 15 Answers

1) Sandwich – He was the fourth Earl of Sandwich.
2) 640
3) 1956 – Edina, Minnesota
4) Wallpaper cleaning putty to remove coal dust in the 1930s
5) In early print shops, individual pieces of metal type were kept in boxes called cases; the smaller, more frequently used letters were kept in a lower case that was easier to reach; the less used capital letters were kept in the upper case.

6) 1896 in England - The car was going 8 mph; the speed limit for cars was 2 mph. You could go over 2 mph if you had someone walk in front of the car waving a red flag to alert people.
7) 42 – The jack of hearts, jack of spades, and king of diamonds are in profile with only one eye showing.
8) Petrichor
9) Reading, Pennsylvania, B&O, Short Line
10) Fingerprint

Quiz 16

1) What are the dots on dice called?
2) What U.S. state has only two escalators in the entire state?
3) What is the most used letter in the English alphabet?
4) What are the only three countries that don't use the metric system?
5) What was the original flavor of the Twinkie filling?
6) How many dots are used in each letter in the Braille system?
7) What was the first U.S. military academy to admit women?
8) What fast food franchise has the most locations worldwide?
9) What are the six murder weapons in the game Clue?
10) What is the world's busiest airport based on passenger traffic?

Quiz 16 Answers

1) Pips
2) Wyoming
3) E
4) United States, Liberia, Myanmar
5) Banana cream
6) Six
7) Coast Guard
8) Subway
9) Lead pipe, revolver, rope, knife, wrench, candlestick
10) Atlanta, Georgia

Quiz 17

1) What year was the first published use of the word hello?
2) What is the least used letter in the English alphabet?
3) The material that became Kleenex originally was used for what?

4) What do you call a group of unicorns?
5) What did the famous Hollywood sign in Los Angeles originally say?
6) How did the Snickers candy bar get its name?
7) What is the opposite of the Orient?
8) In what country did spinach originate?
9) What does ZIP stand for in ZIP code?
10) What food was invented in a sanitarium in 1894?

Quiz 17 Answers

1) 1827 – Hello is a relatively recent word and was initially used to attract attention or express surprise; it didn't get its current meaning until the telephone arrived.
2) Q
3) Gas mask filters in WWI
4) A blessing
5) Hollywoodland
6) Named after the creator's horse
7) The Occident
8) Iran – ancient Persia
9) Zone Improvement Plan
10) Kellogg's Corn Flakes

Quiz 18

1) What is the U.S. national tree?
2) Inspired by burrs, George de Mestral invented what product in the 1940s?
3) Up until 1954, what color were U.S. traffic stop signs?
4) What country has the longest constitution in the world?
5) What is the most common time to wake up in the middle of the night?
6) The U.S. has more airports than any other country; what country has the second most?
7) In 1829, Walter Hunt invented what common fastening item?
8) What Roman measurement is 1,500 paces?
9) Who gave the United Nations the land to build their New York headquarters?
10) What is the world's oldest monotheistic religion?

Quiz 18 Answers

1) Oak
2) Velcro
3) Yellow
4) India – 146,000 words
5) 3:44 AM
6) Brazil - about one-third as many as the U.S.
7) Safety pin
8) League
9) John D. Rockefeller
10) Judaism

Quiz 19

1) How did the duffel bag get its name?
2) Based on enrollment, what is the largest university in the U.S.?
3) Who was the first U.S. citizen to be canonized as a saint?
4) What is a pangram?
5) Where was the highest surface wind speed ever recorded on Earth?
6) What are the monkeys Mizaru, Kikazaru, and Iwazaru better known as?
7) Until the 1770s, what was used to erase lead pencil marks?
8) The U.S. has the most Nobel Prize winners in history; what country is second?
9) What was first published in the *New York World* newspaper on December 21, 1913?
10) In what country did checkers originate?

Quiz 19 Answers

1) Duffel, Belgium – The thick cloth used to make the bag originated there.
2) University of Central Florida
3) Mother Frances Xavier Cabrini – 1946
4) Sentence or verse that contains all letters in the alphabet at least once
5) Mount Washington, New Hampshire - 231 mph
6) See No Evil, Hear No Evil, Speak No Evil
7) Bread – decrusted, moistened and balled up

8) United Kingdom
9) Crossword puzzle
10) Egypt – as early as 200 BC

Quiz 20

1) The U.S. has the most billionaires; what country has the second most?
2) The headquarters of Greenpeace are in what city?
3) What is the international distress signal one level less serious than Mayday?
4) In the Bible, who is Noah's grandfather?
5) What is the name for the part of a sundial that casts the shadow?
6) What is the name of the seat for riding on an elephant?
7) On a QWERTY keyboard, what two letters have raised marks to assist with touch typing?
8) In 1969, what category was added to the Nobel Prizes?
9) What European country's orchestra is bigger than its army?
10) Churches in Malta have two of what item to confuse the devil?

Quiz 20 Answers

1) China
2) Amsterdam
3) Pan-Pan
4) Methuselah – He fathered Noah's father at age 187.
5) Gnomon – from Greek meaning indicator
6) Howdah
7) F and J
8) Economics
9) Monaco
10) Clocks - one with the right time and one with the wrong time

Quiz 21

1) According to the Bible, what are Adam and Eve's three named children?
2) "March of the Volunteers" is what country's national anthem?
3) What year was the game of Monopoly released in the U.S.?
4) What Italian tractor maker first tried making cars in the 1960s?
5) What two people appeared separately on the first U.S. postage

stamps issued in 1847?

6) What is the most widely used (most countries and dishes) vegetable in the world?
7) What male human feature was taxed in Elizabethan times?
8) What English word has the most definitions?
9) What name is mentioned most in the Bible?
10) What is the world's most popular first name?

Quiz 21 Answers

1) Cain, Abel, Seth
2) China
3) 1935
4) Ferruccio Lamborghini
5) George Washington and Benjamin Franklin
6) Onion
7) Beards
8) Set – 464 definitions in the Oxford English dictionary
9) David – followed by Jesus
10) Mohammed and its variations

Quiz 22

1) Who manages Sweden's official Twitter account?
2) Chinese checkers originated in what country?
3) There is a cognitive bias called the cheerleader effect; what is it?
4) What is hippopotomonstrosesquippedaliophobia?
5) In ancient Greece, throwing an apple at someone was a declaration of what?
6) Jesus' name translated directly from Hebrew to English would be what?
7) What is the only country that is exempt from the international rule that a country's name must appear on its postage stamps?
8) What is the most searched tutorial on YouTube?
9) If you suffer from epistaxis, what is wrong?
10) In 1891, Whitcomb Judson invented what for fastening shoes?

Quiz 22 Answers

1) A random citizen is chosen each week to manage the account.
2) Germany – 1892

3) Bias that causes people to think that individuals are more attractive when they are in a group likely due to the averaging out of unattractive idiosyncrasies.
4) Fear of long words
5) Love
6) Joshua – Jesus comes from translating Hebrew to Greek to Latin to English.
7) Great Britain – They were the first country with postage stamps and had no name on them and were exempted when the rule was made.
8) How to kiss
9) Nosebleed
10) Zipper

Quiz 23

1) What year was the company Nintendo founded?
2) Petroleum is the most valuable traded commodity; what is the second most valuable commodity?
3) King Nebuchadnezzar who built the Hanging Gardens of Babylon is the best-known historical sufferer of the psychological disorder boanthropy; what is boanthropy?
4) If you have a case of pronoia; what is it?
5) In 1997, Pope John Paul II nominated Saint Isidore of Seville to be the patron saint of what?
6) What is the only country in the world where more than 50% of adults have college degrees?
7) What is the world's largest gold depository?
8) Where did rock paper scissors originate?
9) What is Captain Crunch's full name?
10) What is Minnie Mouse's full first name?

Quiz 23 Answers

1) 1889 – It originally produced handmade playing cards.
2) Coffee - followed by natural gas, gold, wheat
3) The sufferer believes they are a cow or ox.
4) Opposite of paranoia – feeling that a conspiracy exists to help you
5) Internet
6) Canada – 51%
7) Manhattan Federal Reserve Bank – about 6,700 tons

8) China – about 2,000 years ago
9) Captain Horatio Magellan Crunch
10) Minerva

Quiz 24

1) What country eats the most macaroni and cheese per capita?
2) All the gold ever mined would fit in how many Olympic size swimming pools?
3) What defines a blue moon?
4) Of the 12 men who walked on the Moon, 11 were what as children?
5) In what country did *Apollo* astronauts train because they felt it most resembled the surface of the Moon?
6) What single word is the opposite of extinct?
7) How many people in modern recorded history have been struck dead by a meteorite?
8) If you have caries, what do you have?
9) What are the three most commonly used nouns in English?
10) The word muscle comes from the Latin musculus which means what?

Quiz 24 Answers

1) Canada
2) Four
3) The second full moon in a calendar month – It happens about every three years; thus, the expression "once in a blue moon" for something that doesn't occur very often.
4) Boy Scouts
5) Iceland
6) Extant
7) One – In 2016 in India, a 40-year-old man was relaxing outside on the grounds of a small engineering college when there was the sound of an explosion; he was found next to a two-foot crater and later succumbed to injuries sustained.
8) Tooth decay
9) Time, person, year
10) Little mouse – A flexed muscle was thought to resemble a mouse.

Quiz 25

1) Where did German chocolate cake originate?
2) The word goodbye is a contraction of what phrase?
3) What was the earliest chocolate treat?
4) At what hour of the night are the most Americans sleeping?
5) At what hour of the day are the most Americans awake?
6) What letter starts the most words in the English language?
7) How many letters is the longest English word with one syllable?
8) Until the 19th century, the word hypocrites referred to what profession?
9) What is the shortest complete English sentence?
10) What does ambisinistrous mean?

Quiz 25 Answers

1) United States – It is named after American baker Samuel German.
2) God be with ye.
3) Hot chocolate – Aztecs
4) 3:00 AM – 95.1%
5) 6:00 PM – 97.5%
6) S
7) Nine letters – including words such as scratched, screeched, stretched, straights, strengths
8) Actors
9) Go.
10) No good with either hand - opposite of ambidextrous

Science and Nature

Quiz 1

1) What is extracted from the ore cinnabar?
2) Who is the Bluetooth wireless technology named after?
3) What medical condition is detected using the Ishihara test?
4) What condition is singultus?
5) In computing, what is half of a byte called?
6) What sense is most closely linked to memory?
7) What are the only two elements that are liquid at room temperature?
8) What is the only rock that floats in water?
9) Hansen's disease is more commonly known as what?
10) What is the second hardest gem after diamond?

Quiz 1 Answers

1) Mercury
2) King Harald “Bluetooth” Gormsson – He ruled Denmark in the 10th century.
3) Color blindness
4) Hiccups
5) Nibble
6) Smell
7) Mercury and bromine
8) Pumice
9) Leprosy
10) Sapphire

Quiz 2

1) What scale is used to measure wind speed?
2) What planet is often called the Earth’s twin because it is nearly the same size and mass and has similar composition?
3) A positive number that equals the sum of its divisors excluding itself is called what?
4) What is saffron made from?
5) What is the second largest planet in our solar system?

6) The heat of chili peppers is measured in what?
7) The density of what is measured on the Ringelmann Scale?
8) What two planets in our solar system don't have moons?
9) What is the lightest known solid element?
10) The Fields Medal is awarded for achievement in what field?

Quiz 2 Answers

1) Beaufort
2) Venus
3) Perfect number
4) Crocus flowers – Only the stigma part of the flower is used; it takes 70,000 to 250,000 flowers to make one pound of saffron.
5) Saturn
6) Scoville Heat Units
7) Smoke
8) Mercury and Venus
9) Lithium
10) Mathematics

Quiz 3

1) What number on the Richter scale does an earthquake have to reach to be considered major?
2) What scale is used to measure the hardness of minerals?
3) On what planet, other than Earth, did a man-made object first land?
4) What color has the longest wavelength in the visible spectrum?
5) Where in the human body is the labyrinth?
6) What is the largest nerve in the human body?
7) What does the human lacrimal gland produce?
8) The Fahrenheit and Celsius temperature scales are the same at what temperature?
9) What device converts alternating current into direct current?
10) The small intestine is made up of the jejunum, ileum, and what?

Quiz 3 Answers

1) Seven
2) Mohs scale
3) Mars

4) Red
5) Ear
6) Sciatic
7) Tears
8) 40 degrees below zero
9) Rectifier
10) Duodenum

Quiz 4

1) Who invented carbonated soda water?
2) What is the male part of a flower called?
3) What are the four types of adult human teeth?
4) Where does Earth rank in size among the planets in our solar system?
5) Syncope is the medical name for what condition?
6) What element has the lowest boiling point?
7) What is the heaviest naturally occurring element?
8) During hot or dry periods, what is the equivalent of hibernation?
9) The process where food browns during cooking is known as what?
10) What was the very first animal to go into space?

Quiz 4 Answers

1) Joseph Priestley – also discovered oxygen
2) Stamen
3) Incisors, canines, premolars, molars
4) Fifth
5) Fainting
6) Helium – negative 452.1 degrees Fahrenheit
7) Uranium
8) Estivation
9) Maillard reaction
10) Fruit flies – They were sent up in 1947 in a captured V2 rocket and were recovered alive.

Quiz 5

1) Where on the human body are the most sweat glands?
2) The chemical formula H_2O_2 refers to what?

3) What is the point in the Moon's orbit that is farthest from the Earth called?
4) After nitrogen and oxygen, what is the third most abundant gas in the atmosphere?
5) What species is the oldest living individual tree?
6) What metal is the best conductor of electricity?
7) Who discovered X-rays?
8) What is the only part of the human body that cannot repair itself?
9) Thomas Edison was involved in a rivalry over which form of electricity would be commercialized; Edison supported direct current; who was his rival that supported alternating current?
10) The Big Dipper is part of what constellation?

Quiz 5 Answers

1) Bottom of the feet
2) Hydrogen peroxide
3) Apogee
4) Argon
5) Bristlecone pine - 5,000 years
6) Silver – It is slightly more conductive than copper but much more expensive.
7) Wilhelm Roentgen
8) Teeth
9) Nikola Tesla
10) Ursa Major or Great Bear

Quiz 6

1) After calcium, what is the second most abundant mineral in the human body?
2) What are the Magellanic Clouds?
3) Lateral epicondylitis is the medical name for what common medical condition?
4) From what plant is the poison ricin obtained?
5) What is an apparatus that converts molecules into ions and separates the ions according to their mass-to-charge ratio called?
6) What is rayon made from?
7) On the periodic table, what is the first element alphabetically?
8) What does AM stand for on radios?

9) How much longer is a day on Mars than a day on Earth?
10) Who is the oldest person ever to go into space?

Quiz 6 Answers

1) Phosphorus
2) Galaxies
3) Tennis elbow
4) Castor oil plant
5) Mass spectrometer
6) Wood pulp
7) Actinium
8) Amplitude modulation
9) 40 minutes
10) John Glenn – 77

Quiz 7

1) What is the most abundant element in the universe?
2) What is the opposite of nocturnal?
3) Stonehenge is made of what two main types of rock?
4) The Saffir-Simpson scale measures the intensity of what?
5) How long is an eon?
6) What is the name for the point in a planet's orbit when it is nearest the Sun?
7) What is the name of the process where plants lose water into the atmosphere?
8) What part of the human body is the axilla?
9) In the electromagnetic spectrum, what comes between X-rays and visible light?
10) What planet circles the Sun every 84 years?

Quiz 7 Answers

1) Hydrogen – about 75% of the universe's mass
2) Diurnal
3) Bluestone and sandstone
4) Hurricanes
5) 1 billion years
6) Perihelion

7) Transpiration
8) Armpit
9) Ultraviolet light
10) Uranus

Quiz 8

1) What standard international unit of power is equal to 1.341 horsepower?
2) Where will you find the Malpighi's pyramids?
3) What is the number 10 to the power of 100 called?
4) What element is named after the Greek word for green?
5) What name is given to the socket in the human skull that holds the eye?
6) How many vertebrae in the human spine?
7) The atomic mass in the periodic table is stated relative to the weight of what element?
8) What is the standard international unit of force?
9) From what plant is the heart drug digitalis obtained?
10) The phenomenon where hot water may freeze faster than cold is known as what?

Quiz 8 Answers

1) Kilowatt
2) Kidneys – cone shaped tissues
3) Googol
4) Chlorine
5) Orbit
6) 33
7) Carbon – more specifically carbon-12
8) Newton – One newton equals the force needed to accelerate one kilogram of mass at the rate of one meter per second squared.
9) Foxglove
10) Mpemba Effect

Quiz 9

1) Most of the world's supply of cork comes from what type of tree?
2) Due to its unique chemical qualities, what natural food can remain in an edible form for centuries?

3) What is the smallest named time interval?
4) What is the effect of the Earth's rotation on the wind called?
5) What is the most abundant metal in the Earth's crust?
6) What name is given to a chemical reaction that takes in heat?
7) Who formulated the laws which first explained the movements of the planets properly?
8) What color is at the top of a rainbow?
9) What gives onions their distinctive smell?
10) What is the brightest star in the night sky?

Quiz 9 Answers

1) Oak – cork oak trees predominantly in Portugal and Spain
2) Honey – Three-thousand-year-old edible honey has been found in tombs.
3) Planck time – 5.39×10^{-44} seconds
4) Coriolis
5) Aluminum
6) Endothermic
7) Johannes Kepler
8) Red – Violet is at the bottom.
9) Sulfur – When cut or crushed, a chemical reaction changes an amino acid to a sulfur compound.
10) Sirius – Dog Star

Quiz 10

1) What planet in our solar system has the longest day?
2) What are metals not considered precious called?
3) What is the only planet in our solar system less dense than water?
4) An astronomical unit is defined by what distance?
5) Located near the root of human hair follicles, the arrector pili muscles are responsible for what phenomenon?
6) What figure has four sides all the same length but no right angles?
7) What was the name of the first electronic general-purpose computer?
8) What blood type qualifies as a universal donor?
9) What year was the first email sent?
10) What is the only tree that grows in saltwater?

Quiz 10 Answers

1) Venus – 243 Earth days
2) Base metals
3) Saturn
4) Earth to the Sun – 93 million miles
5) Goosebumps
6) Rhombus
7) ENIAC – 1946
8) O negative
9) 1971
10) Mangrove

Quiz 11

1) What are the four states of matter observable in everyday life?
2) What is the largest two-digit prime number?
3) Marble is formed by the metamorphosis of what rock?
4) What is the densest naturally occurring element?
5) In its natural form, aspirin comes from the bark of what tree?
6) What metal has the highest melting point?
7) How many times does the Moon revolve around the Earth in a year?
8) What is the smallest organ in the human body?
9) What is the largest 3-digit prime number?
10) Who was the first person to explain why the sky is blue?

Quiz 11 Answers

1) Solid, liquid, gas, plasma
2) 97
3) Limestone
4) Osmium – about 25 times denser than water
5) White willow tree
6) Tungsten – 6,192 degrees Fahrenheit
7) 13
8) Pineal gland – in the center of the brain
9) 997
10) Leonardo da Vinci

Quiz 12

1) What is the study of fungi called?
2) Pascal is a measure of what?
3) What is the best-selling personal computer model of all time?
4) What is the longest muscle in the human body?
5) How many orbits has the Sun made around the center of the Milky Way Galaxy in its life?
6) Who first proposed the concept of contact lenses?
7) What planet in our solar system has the shortest day?
8) What is the equivalent megapixels of the human eye?
9) Approximately 2% of all people have what eye color?
10) How many constellations are in the night sky?

Quiz 12 Answers

1) Mycology
2) Pressure
3) Commodore 64 – 17 million units with a 1 MHz processor and 64KB RAM
4) Sartorius – from the pelvis to just below the inside of the knee
5) About 20 – It takes about 230 million years for one orbit.
6) Leonardo da Vinci
7) Jupiter – 10 hours
8) 576 megapixels
9) Green – Brown is 55%; hazel and blue are 8% each.
10) 88

Quiz 13

1) What is the tallest mountain in the known universe?
2) What are the four lobes of the human brain?
3) How many planets in our solar system have moons?
4) What planet in our solar system has the most moons?
5) What is the densest planet in our solar system?
6) What is the most malleable naturally occurring metal?
7) What year was the first Apple computer released?
8) What human organ has the highest percentage of fat?
9) What is the only part of the human body without a blood supply?
10) What is the more common name for an Einstein Rosen Bridge?

Quiz 13 Answers

1) Olympus Mons on Mars – 69,459 feet
2) Frontal, occipital, parietal, temporal
3) Six – Earth, Mars, Jupiter, Saturn, Uranus, Neptune
4) Jupiter – 63
5) Earth
6) Gold
7) 1976
8) Brain – up to 60% fat
9) Cornea
10) Wormhole

Quiz 14

1) What year was the first cell phone call made?
2) What is the fastest healing part of the human body?
3) What two planets in our solar system rotate clockwise?
4) What is the name for the dark gray color the eyes see in perfect darkness because of optic nerve signals?
5) What is the smallest muscle in the human body?
6) How many bones do human babies have?
7) The first web site was launched by CERN in what year?
8) What is the hottest planet in our solar system?
9) What is the closest galaxy to our own Milky Way?
10) Where are the Islands of Langerhans?

Quiz 14 Answers

1) 1973
2) Tongue
3) Venus and Uranus
4) Eigengrau
5) Stapedius – in the middle ear
6) 300 – Some fuse together to form the 206 bones in adults.
7) 1991
8) Venus – 864 degrees Fahrenheit
9) Andromeda – 2.5 million light-years
10) Human pancreas – produce insulin

Quiz 15

1) In what year will Halley's Comet next appear?
2) If you hear thunder about 15 seconds after seeing lightning, how far away was the lightning?
3) What is the largest moon in our solar system?
4) What year was the first internet domain name registered?
5) Sphenopalatine ganglioneuralgia is the medical term for what?
6) How many zeroes in a sextillion?
7) Who invented the electric battery in 1800?
8) In the human body, the hallux is more commonly known as what?
9) In 1997, what was the first mammal to be cloned from an adult cell?
10) The average lightning bolt is about five miles long and how wide?

Quiz 15 Answers

1) 2061 – last seen in 1986
2) About three miles - Sound travels about one mile in five seconds.
3) Ganymede – moon of Jupiter, about 41% of the size of Earth
4) 1985
5) Brain freeze – ice cream headache
6) 21
7) Alessandro Volta
8) Big toe
9) Dolly the sheep
10) One inch

Quiz 16

1) What is the name for a three-dimensional object that has only one surface and has no orientation?
2) What name is given to atoms with the same number of protons but different numbers of neutrons?
3) A sequence of numbers where each number is the sum of the two prior numbers is called what?
4) How long can a human live unprotected in space?
5) In space, what color would the Sun appear to be?
6) What was the first man made object in space?
7) Astronauts in space are trained to go to the bathroom every two

hours; why?

8) While alone in the *Apollo 15* command module orbiting the Moon in 1971, astronaut Al Worden set what world record?
9) Why do Russian astronauts take guns into space?
10) Neil Armstrong didn't say, "That's one small step for man, one giant leap for mankind," when he set foot on the Moon; what did he say?

Quiz 16 Answers

1) Mobius strip – such as a strip of paper with a half twist joined at the ends
2) Isotopes
3) Fibonacci sequence
4) About 30 seconds – if they don't hold their breath
5) White
6) German V2 rocket – 1942
7) You can't tell if your bladder is full in space.
8) Most isolated human ever – He was 2,235 miles from the nearest human.
9) To protect themselves from bears if they land off course
10) "That's one small step for a man, one giant leap for mankind" – That is what Armstrong insisted he said; the word "a" before man wasn't heard clearly.

Quiz 17

1) What year was the word scientist first used?
2) What was the occupation of the first person to propose the big bang origin of the universe?
3) What planet in our solar system has a longer day than its year?
4) Who is the only person to win Nobel Prizes in two different areas of science?
5) What is the world's most visited website?
6) What is the first part of the human body to form in the womb?
7) What is the speed in miles per hour of the Earth's orbit around the Sun?
8) In 1991, the world's first webcam was created to do what?
9) How do the Moon and Sun fit together so perfectly in a solar eclipse?
10) Who first proposed that the Sun was the center around which the

planets orbit?

Quiz 17 Answers

1) 1833
2) Priest – Georges Lemaitre
3) Venus – 243 days for one rotation (1 day), 225 days for one orbit around the Sun (1 year)
4) Marie Curie – physics and chemistry
5) Google
6) Asshole – Every human starts out as an asshole.
7) 66,600 mph
8) Check the status of a coffee pot at Cambridge University
9) By chance, the Sun is about 400 times larger than the Moon, and it is also about 400 times further away from the Earth, so the two appear to be the same size in the sky.
10) Aristarchus of Samos in the 3rd century BC - Copernicus developed a fully predictive model in the 16th century but wasn't the first to propose the concept.

Quiz 18

1) What is a galactic or cosmic year?
2) The Catholic church made Galileo recant his theory that the Earth revolves around the Sun; how many years later did the church declare Galileo was right?
3) The most perfectly round natural object known in the universe is star 5,000 light-years away; prior to that discovery, what was the most perfectly round natural object known?
4) How many people do you need in a group to have a 50% chance that two will have the same birthday?
5) What does Wi-Fi stand for?
6) What is the layer of the atmosphere closest to the Earth's surface called?
7) What is extirpation?
8) The human eye can differentiate more shades of what color than any other?
9) In the human body, what is a limbal dermoid?
10) The busiest muscles in the human body are found where?

Quiz 18 Answers

1) The amount of time it takes the Sun to orbit once around the center of the Milky Way Galaxy – about 230 million years
2) 359 years – in 1992
3) Sun
4) 23 – It is known as the Birthday Paradox; the probability goes up to 99.9% with just 70 people.
5) Nothing – It doesn't mean wireless fidelity or anything else; it is just a branding name picked by a company hired for the purpose.
6) Troposphere
7) Local extinction – Species is extinct locally but still exists elsewhere.
8) Green – That is why night vision goggles are green.
9) A cyst in the eye formed in the womb when skin cells get misplaced in the eye. The cyst can grow hair, cartilage, sweat glands, even teeth just like skin can.
10) Eyes – They move 100,000 times a day.

Quiz 19

1) Water doesn't conduct electricity well, so why is electricity so dangerous with water?
2) Walnuts, almonds, pecans, and cashews aren't technically nuts; what are they?
3) When you die, what sense is the last to go?
4) Apples, peaches, and raspberries belong to what plant family?
5) In total darkness, most people naturally adjust to how long of a cycle instead of 24 hours?
6) What parts of the human body never stop growing?
7) In terms of how long it takes to process input, what is the fastest human sense?
8) What planet has the strongest winds in our solar system?
9) On average, what is the coldest planet in our solar system?
10) Mohs hardness scale's hardest substance is diamond; what is the softest?

Quiz 19 Answers

1) The impurities in water make it a good conductor.
2) Drupes – also include peaches, plums and cherries. Drupes are a

type of fruit where an outer fleshy part surrounds a shell or pit with a seed inside.

3) Hearing
4) Roses
5) 48 hours – 36 hours of activity and 12 hours of sleep
6) Ears and nose – parts composed of cartilage
7) Hearing – as little as 0.05 seconds
8) Neptune – more than 1,200 mph
9) Neptune – minus 353 degrees Fahrenheit
10) Talc

Quiz 20

1) What is the only bone in the human body that isn't attached to any other bone?
2) What is mainly extracted from pitchblende?
3) Alphabetically, what is the last element in the periodic table?
4) Ageusia is the loss of what sense?
5) Who performed the first heart transplant?
6) What calculation device was invented by William Oughtred in 1662?
7) In 1971, what U.S. space probe was the first to orbit another planet?
8) The camellia sinensis evergreen shrub produces what?
9) What do you use your zygomaticus muscle for?
10) What is the white trail behind a jet plane comprised of?

Quiz 20 Answers

1) Hyoid bone – in the throat
2) Uranium
3) Zirconium
4) Taste
5) Dr. Christian Barnard
6) Slide rule
7) *Mariner 9*
8) Tea
9) Smiling
10) Ice crystals

Quiz 21

1) What is the world's tallest grass?
2) An alloy of iron, chromium, and nickel makes what?
3) What country grew the first orange?
4) What French philosopher created analytical geometry?
5) What are the world's smallest natural trees?
6) What is the most common infectious disease in the world?
7) Where on the human body is the thinnest skin?
8) The Easter lily is a native plant of what country?
9) Who first noticed that the Sun had spots?
10) What color are sunsets on Mars?

Quiz 21 Answers

1) Bamboo
2) Stainless steel
3) China
4) Rene Descartes
5) Dwarf willows – They grow in Greenland and are only about two inches high.
6) Hepatitis B – More than one-quarter of the world's population is infected.
7) Eyelid - 0.05 mm thick
8) Japan
9) Galileo
10) Blue

Quiz 22

1) What compound puts the heat in chili peppers?
2) What is the hardest bone in the human body?
3) Who is known as the father of geometry?
4) What wheel did Blaise Pascal invent in search of perpetual motion?
5) Who established the science of genetics in 1866?
6) How many prime numbers are there that are less than 20?
7) How long does it take the Moon to revolve around the Earth to the nearest day?
8) What are the four major human blood types?
9) What is the common name for the fruit Citrus grandis?

10) What makes Mars red?

Quiz 22 Answers

1) Capsaicin
2) Jawbone
3) Euclid
4) Roulette wheel
5) Gregor Mendel
6) Eight numbers - 2, 3, 5, 7, 11, 13, 17, 19
7) 27 days
8) A, B, AB, O
9) Grapefruit
10) It is covered in iron oxide (rust).

Quiz 23

1) Atoms stop moving at what temperature?
2) What Polish astronomer demonstrated in 1512 that the Sun is the center of the solar system?
3) What is the largest gland in the human body?
4) What five tastes can a human distinguish?
5) What is a googolplexian?
6) What planet in our solar system has the shortest year?
7) What is the end cause of every human death?
8) What is the fastest growing plant?
9) What month is the Earth closest to the Sun?
10) The word laser is an acronym for what?

Quiz 23 Answers

1) Zero degrees Kelvin or absolute zero - equivalent to minus 459.67 degrees Fahrenheit
2) Nicholas Copernicus
3) Liver
4) Sweet, sour, bitter, salty, umami
5) The largest named number - A googol is 1 followed by 100 zeroes; a googolplex is 1 followed by a googol of zeroes; a googolplexian is 1 followed by a googolplex of zeroes.
6) Mercury – 88 Earth days
7) Cerebral hypoxia – Lack of oxygen to the brain is the final cause of

death regardless what initiates it.

8) Bamboo – Some species can grow three feet in a day.
9) January
10) Light amplification by stimulated emission of radiation

Quiz 24

1) What is the largest muscle in the human body?
2) What is the longest bone in the human body?
3) What is the simplest gem in chemical composition?
4) Who discovered Saturn's rings?
5) What part of the eye continues to grow throughout a person's life?
6) What is the most frequently broken bone in the human body?
7) What are the three major classifications for rocks?
8) What plant does natural vanilla flavoring come from?
9) What tiny vessel connects an artery with a vein?
10) In math, what does a "lemniscate" shape mean?

Quiz 24 Answers

1) Gluteus maximus
2) Femur
3) Diamond – composed only of carbon
4) Galileo
5) Lens
6) Clavicle or collar bone
7) Igneous, metamorphic, sedimentary
8) Orchid
9) Capillary
10) Infinity - Lemniscate is a shape with two loops meeting at a central point.

Quiz 25

1) What is the oldest known vegetable?
2) What is the clotting protein in blood called?
3) What metal is the major constituent of rubies?
4) What is the hardest substance in the human body?
5) What do astronomers call a giant cloud of gas and dust?
6) About 2,400 years ago, what did Hippocrates describe as "man's

best medicine"?

7) What is the process of wave like muscle contractions that moves food in the digestive tract starting in the esophagus called?
8) What was the first man-made object to leave the solar system?
9) Which isotope of carbon is used for radiocarbon dating?
10) What is the first prime number after 1,000,000?

Quiz 25 Answers

1) Pea
2) Fibrin
3) Aluminum
4) Tooth enamel
5) Nebula
6) Walking
7) Peristalsis
8) *Pioneer 10*
9) Carbon-14
10) 1,000,003

U.S. Geography

Quiz 1

1) What is the largest city on the Mississippi River?
2) What is the oldest city in the U.S.?
3) What is the name of the island between the two waterfalls at Niagara Falls?
4) What is the highest waterfall in the U.S.?
5) What is the least populous state capital?
6) What major city is named after a U.S. vice president of the 1840s?
7) What state has the largest area of inland water?
8) Which of the 48 contiguous states extends farthest north?
9) What state's three most populous cities all have names beginning with the letter C?
10) What is the least accessible state capital?

Quiz 1 Answers

1) Memphis, Tennessee
2) St. Augustine, Florida – 1565
3) Goat Island
4) Yosemite Falls – 2,425 feet
5) Montpelier, Vermont
6) Dallas – George Mifflin Dallas was vice president for James K. Polk.
7) Alaska
8) Minnesota
9) Ohio – Columbus, Cleveland, Cincinnati
10) Juneau Alaska – fly or take a boat

Quiz 2

1) The Statue of Liberty stands on what island?
2) What is the largest island in the contiguous 48 states?
3) How many miles separate the U.S. and Cuba?
4) What state has a Union Jack on its flag?
5) What is the only borough of New York City that is not mainly on an island?
6) What state capital is named after a famous German statesman?

7) What state is the geographic center of North America?
8) What state is closest to Bermuda?
9) In the 48 contiguous states, what is the largest city based on land area?
10) What is the second largest wine producing state?

Quiz 2 Answers

1) Liberty Island
2) Long Island
3) 90
4) Hawaii
5) Bronx
6) Bismarck, North Dakota – after Otto von Bismarck
7) North Dakota
8) North Carolina
9) Jacksonville, Florida – 758 square miles
10) Washington

Quiz 3

1) What national park has the nickname "Crown of the Continent"?
2) What is the only state with a one syllable name?
3) By area, what is the third largest state?
4) What is the only state with the same name as a country?
5) How many state capitals are named after presidents?
6) What state capital has the largest population?
7) What is the highest peak east of the Mississippi River?
8) What two state capitals include the name of the state?
9) What is the only state flag that has an image of a president?
10) What is the most densely populated state?

Quiz 3 Answers

1) Glacier National Park
2) Maine
3) California
4) Georgia
5) Four – Lincoln, Jefferson City, Jackson, Madison
6) Phoenix, Arizona

7) Mount Mitchell – 6,684 feet in North Carolina
8) Oklahoma City and Indianapolis
9) Washington
10) New Jersey

Quiz 4

1) In the 48 contiguous states, what is the most northern state capital?
2) What is the deepest gorge in the U.S.?
3) How many states border the Gulf of Mexico?
4) What are the five boroughs of New York City?
5) What state has the most counties?
6) What is the tallest volcano in the contiguous 48 states?
7) What is the only non-rectangular state flag?
8) How many states border the Atlantic Ocean (excluding the Gulf of Mexico)?
9) What is the oldest city west of the Rocky Mountains?
10) What state has the fewest counties?

Quiz 4 Answers

1) Olympia, Washington
2) Hells Canyon – 7,993 feet deep on the Snake River on the Oregon and Idaho border
3) Five – Florida, Alabama, Mississippi, Louisiana, Texas
4) Bronx, Queens, Staten Island, Manhattan, Brooklyn
5) Texas – 254
6) Mount Rainier – 14,411 feet in Washington
7) Ohio – swallowtail design
8) 14 – Maine, New Hampshire, Massachusetts, Rhode Island, Connecticut, New York, New Jersey, Delaware, Maryland, Virginia, North Carolina, South Carolina, Georgia, Florida
9) Astoria, Oregon - 1811
10) Delaware – three

Quiz 5

1) What is the most visited U.S. national park?
2) What state is the geographic center of the 48 contiguous states?
3) What is the only state that ends with a "K"?

4) By area, what is the largest U.S. city?
5) What is the highest elevation state capital?
6) Fort Knox is in what state?
7) What is the only state that borders just one other state?
8) What two state capitals are named for royalty?
9) What is the only two-sided state flag (different designs on each side)?
10) How many states share a land or water border with Canada?

Quiz 5 Answers

1) Great Smoky Mountains
2) Kansas
3) New York
4) Sitka, Alaska – 2,870 square miles
5) Santa Fe, New Mexico – 7,000 feet
6) Kentucky
7) Maine
8) Annapolis, Maryland and Albany, New York – They were named for Princess Anne of Denmark and Norway who became Queen of England and for the Duke of York and Albany who became King James II of England.
9) Oregon
10) 13 - Alaska, Washington, Idaho, Montana, North Dakota, Minnesota, Michigan, Ohio, Pennsylvania, New York, Vermont, New Hampshire, Maine

Quiz 6

1) How many states don't border either the ocean or one of the Great Lakes?
2) What three rivers meet in Pittsburgh?
3) What is the flattest state?
4) What is the only two-word state capital in a two-word state?
5) The Mississippi river runs through or along how many states?
6) What two state capitals sit on the borders of other states?
7) What is the only state name that doesn't share any letters with its capital city?
8) What is the only state capital without a McDonald's?
9) What two state capitals are located on the Mississippi River?

10) In the 48 contiguous states, what is the most southern state capital?

Quiz 6 Answers

1) 20 - Arizona, Arkansas, Colorado, Idaho, Iowa, Kansas, Kentucky, Missouri, Montana, Nebraska, Nevada, New Mexico, North Dakota, Oklahoma, South Dakota, Tennessee, Utah, Vermont, West Virginia, Wyoming
2) Allegheny, Monongahela, Ohio
3) Florida – 345 feet between its highest and lowest points
4) Santa Fe, New Mexico
5) 10 – Arkansas, Illinois, Iowa, Kentucky, Louisiana, Minnesota, Mississippi, Missouri, Tennessee, Wisconsin
6) Carson City, Nevada (California border) and Trenton, New Jersey (Pennsylvania border)
7) South Dakota – Pierre
8) Montpelier, Vermont
9) St. Paul and Baton Rouge
10) Austin, Texas

Quiz 7

1) What is the only state name that can be typed on one row of a standard keyboard?
2) What is the largest island in the U.S.?
3) What is the most visited U.S. city?
4) What is the only state on the east coast to fall partly in the central time zone?
5) What state has the highest per capita income?
6) What state has the highest percentage foreign born population?
7) What state has the lowest median age?
8) What state has the highest median age?
9) What state has the largest number of active volcanoes?
10) What is the westernmost state?

Quiz 7 Answers

1) Alaska
2) Hawaii
3) Orlando, Florida - New York City is second.

4) Florida
5) Connecticut
6) California
7) Utah
8) Maine
9) Alaska – 130 out of the 169 active volcanoes in the U.S.
10) Alaska

Quiz 8

1) What state has the most miles of rivers?
2) What state has the most national parks?
3) What state has the highest percentage of federal land?
4) What two states share the longest border?
5) How many states refer to themselves as commonwealths in their names?
6) What state capital was once the national capital?
7) What U.S. state is closest to Africa?
8) What is the only letter that doesn't appear in any state name?
9) What is the longest state from north to south?
10) At its closest point, what is the distance between the U.S. and Russia?

Quiz 8 Answers

1) Nebraska – major rivers include Platte, Niobrara, Missouri, Republican
2) California – nine
3) Nevada – 81%
4) Texas and Oklahoma – 700 miles
5) Four – Kentucky, Massachusetts, Pennsylvania, Virginia - There is no legal distinction just a naming difference from earlier times.
6) Annapolis, Maryland
7) Maine – Quoddy Head peninsula is 3,154 miles from Morocco.
8) Q
9) Alaska – 1,479 miles
10) 2.4 miles

Quiz 9

Quiz 9 Answers

1) 11 – Alaska, Texas, California, Montana, New Mexico, Arizona, Nevada, Colorado, Oregon, Wyoming, Michigan
2) 11 – Alabama, Arizona, California, Florida, Georgia, Hawaii, Louisiana, Mississippi, New Mexico, South Carolina, Texas
3) A small part of eastern Oregon is in the mountain time zone, and a small part of western Florida is in the central time zone. When the change from daylight saving time to standard time is made, these two areas share the same time for one hour after the central time zone has fallen back to standard time and before the mountain time zone has.
4) There isn't one.
5) Bedloe's Island
6) 39
7) Miami – Julia Tuttle
8) 27 – Alaska, California, Connecticut, Idaho, Illinois, Indiana, Iowa, Maine, Massachusetts, Michigan, Minnesota, Montana, Nebraska, Nevada, New Hampshire, New York, North Dakota, Ohio, Oregon, Pennsylvania, Rhode Island, South Dakota, Utah, Vermont, Washington, Wisconsin, Wyoming
9) Kodiak Island, Alaska – 3,672 square miles
10) Ontario – borders Minnesota, Michigan, Ohio, Pennsylvania, New York

Quiz 10

1) In the 48 contiguous states, what is the most western state capital?
2) How many states does the Canadian province of Alberta border?
3) What state has the highest lowest elevation point?
4) By area, what is the largest lake entirely within the U.S.?
5) By area, what is the largest lake entirely within one state?
6) What state has the lowest highest elevation point?
7) What two states have a lowest elevation point below sea level?
8) By area, what is the fourth largest state?
9) Which of the contiguous 48 states has the longest border with Canada?
10) What were the last four states to join the U.S.?

Quiz 10 Answers

1) Olympia, Washington
2) One – Montana
3) Colorado – 3,315 feet
4) Lake Michigan
5) Great Salt Lake
6) Florida – 345 feet
7) California and Louisiana
8) Montana
9) Michigan
10) New Mexico, Arizona, Alaska, Hawaii

Quiz 11

1) What is the most commonly occurring place name in the U.S.?
2) By area, what is the largest state east of the Mississippi River?
3) What is the source of the Mississippi River?
4) What New Mexico resort town was named after a radio game show?
5) By area, what is the smallest state?
6) How many states border the Great Lakes?
7) What is the highest mountain in the U.S.?
8) What is the highest mountain in the contiguous 48 states?
9) What state capital is 10 miles from Princeton University?
10) What is the only state name that ends in three vowels?

Quiz 11 Answers

1) Washington
2) Georgia
3) Lake Itasca, Minnesota
4) Truth or Consequences
5) Rhode Island
6) Eight - Illinois, Indiana, Michigan, Minnesota, New York, Ohio, Pennsylvania, Wisconsin
7) Denali or Mount McKinley, Alaska – 20,310 feet
8) Mount Whitney, California – 14,505 feet
9) Trenton, New Jersey
10) Hawaii

Quiz 12

1) What state receives the least sunshine?
2) What is the southernmost state?
3) After Canada and Mexico, what country is closest to the U.S.?
4) How many states border California?
5) What two states share the most borders with other states?
6) What state has the lowest average elevation?
7) How many states are at least partially north of the southernmost part of Canada and at least partially south of the northernmost point of Mexico?
8) What state has the longest border with Canada?
9) How many states border the Pacific Ocean?
10) What was the first state with a woman governor?

Quiz 12 Answers

1) Alaska
2) Hawaii
3) Russia – 2.4 miles
4) Three – Oregon, Nevada, Arizona
5) Missouri and Tennessee – eight states border each
6) Delaware – 60 feet average elevation
7) One – California
8) Alaska
9) Five – Washington, Oregon, California, Alaska, Hawaii
10) Wyoming – 1925

Quiz 13

1) What state has the least rainfall?
2) What landmark became 1,313 feet shorter in 1980?
3) What is the only state that borders a Canadian territory?
4) How many states border Mexico?
5) What state has the second longest coastline?
6) What four states have active volcanoes?
7) What city has the only royal palace in the U.S.?
8) What state has the most rainfall?
9) What is the easternmost state capital?
10) What is the easternmost state?

Quiz 13 Answers

1) Nevada – 9.5 inches mean annual precipitation
2) Mount St. Helens
3) Alaska
4) Four – California, Arizona, New Mexico, and Texas
5) Florida
6) Alaska, California, Hawaii, Washington
7) Honolulu, Hawaii
8) Hawaii – 63.7 inches mean annual precipitation
9) Augusta, Maine
10) Alaska – stretches into the Eastern Hemisphere

Quiz 14

1) What state capital has the largest land area?
2) What state capital has more than 30 Buddhist temples?
3) What state has the highest average elevation?
4) What state has the smallest population?
5) What is the largest U.S. city on the Great Lakes?
6) What is the only state that ends with three consonants?
7) What state has the most tornadoes on average?
8) Where is the lowest elevation land point in the U.S.?
9) What is the deepest lake in the U.S.?
10) By area, what is the smallest state west of the Mississippi River?

Quiz 14 Answers

1) Juneau, Alaska
2) Honolulu, Hawaii
3) Colorado – 6,800 feet average
4) Wyoming
5) Chicago
6) Massachusetts
7) Texas
8) Death Valley, California – 279 feet below sea level
9) Crater Lake – 1,949 feet
10) Hawaii

Quiz 15

1) What Is the most popular street name in the U.S.?
2) By volume, what is the largest lake entirely within the U.S.?
3) Of the 10 tallest mountains in the U.S., how many are in Alaska?
4) By volume, what is the largest lake entirely within one state?
5) What state has the highest percent of its area that is water?
6) What state has the lowest percent of its area that is water?
7) How many states are entirely north of the southernmost point of Canada?
8) By area, what state has the largest county?
9) By population, what state has the largest county?
10) What state had the first commercial oil well in the U.S.?

Quiz 15 Answers

1) Park
2) Lake Michigan
3) 10 – Mt. Whitney, the highest peak in the contiguous 48 states, is the 11th highest in the U.S.
4) Lake Iliamna, Alaska
5) Michigan – followed by Hawaii and Rhode Island
6) New Mexico – followed by Arizona and Colorado
7) 13 - Alaska, Washington, Oregon, Idaho, Montana, North Dakota, South Dakota, Minnesota, Wisconsin, Michigan, Vermont, New Hampshire, Maine
8) California – San Bernardino county is 20,105 square miles.
9) California – Los Angeles county
10) Pennsylvania

Quiz 16

1) At the start of the 20th century, how many U.S. states were there?
2) What was the first U.S. state?
3) What was the first U.S. national monument?
4) What is the oldest U.S. state capital?
5) What two states donated land to create Washington, D.C.?
6) What is the highest peak between the Rocky Mountains and the Appalachian Mountains?
7) The border between what two states is partially formed by the

Continental Divide?
8) What state's southern border is formed by a river of the same name?
9) What two Canadian provinces only border one state?
10) What is the longest interstate highway?

Quiz 16 Answers

1) 45 – Oklahoma, New Mexico, Arizona, Alaska, and Hawaii weren't states yet.
2) Delaware – December 7, 1787
3) Devils Tower, Wyoming – 1906
4) Santa Fe, New Mexico – founded in 1609
5) Maryland and Virginia
6) Mount Magazine – 2,753 feet in the Ouachita Mountains in Arkansas
7) Idaho and Montana
8) Ohio
9) Alberta and New Brunswick
10) I-90 from Boston to Seattle – 3,111 miles

Quiz 17

1) How many national capital cities were there before Washington, D.C.?
2) What state has the only active diamond mine?
3) By area, what is the second largest lake entirely within the U.S.?
4) What state has the longest coastline?
5) What three states have their eastern and western borders entirely defined by water?
6) What is the widest state from east to west?
7) What four states meet at Four Corners?
8) How many states have never elected a female governor, U.S. senator, or U.S. representative?
9) How many different capital cities has Texas had as a republic and state?
10) What year did New Mexico and Arizona become the 47th and 48th states?

Quiz 17 Answers

1) Eight – Philadelphia, Baltimore, Lancaster, York, Princeton, Annapolis, Trenton, New York City
2) Arkansas
3) Great Salt Lake
4) Alaska
5) Hawaii, Florida, Iowa
6) Alaska – 2,400 miles
7) New Mexico, Arizona, Colorado, Utah
8) Zero – Mississippi was the last remaining state until they elected a female U.S. representative in 2018.
9) 12 – including Galveston, Houston, Austin
10) 1912

U.S. Presidents

Quiz 1

1) Who is the only president to serve two nonconsecutive terms?
2) Who was the first president to attend Monday night football?
3) Who was the last president with facial hair?
4) Who was the first president born in a hospital?
5) What president twice served as an executioner?
6) Who are the only two first ladies born outside the U.S.?
7) Who was the first president to live in the White House?
8) Who is the only president born on the Fourth of July?
9) What first lady refused secret service coverage and was given her own gun?
10) Who was the first president to have been divorced?

Quiz 1 Answers

1) Grover Cleveland - 22nd and 24th president
2) Jimmy Carter
3) William Howard Taft
4) Jimmy Carter
5) Grover Cleveland – in his duty as sheriff
6) Louisa Adams and Melania Trump
7) John Adams
8) Calvin Coolidge
9) Eleanor Roosevelt
10) Ronald Reagan

Quiz 2

1) Who is the youngest ever president?
2) Who was the first president depicted on a circulating U.S. monetary coin?
3) What president's mother had the first name Stanley?
4) What didn't president James Buchanan have that every other president has had?
5) What president's wife saw him elected but died before his inauguration?

6) What two first lady's husbands and sons both served as U.S. president?
7) Who gave Caroline Kennedy her dog Pushinska while her dad was president?
8) What president had the most children?
9) What president had the shortest term?
10) What president was shot at twice at point-blank range but survived because both guns misfired?

Quiz 2 Answers

1) Theodore Roosevelt – 42
2) Abraham Lincoln
3) Barack Obama
4) A wife – He never married.
5) Andrew Jackson
6) Barbara Bush and Abigail Adams
7) Nikita Khrushchev
8) John Tyler – 15 by two wives
9) William Henry Harrison – 31 days - He caught a cold on inauguration day that turned into a fatal case of pneumonia. His grandson Benjamin would later also be president.
10) Andrew Jackson – first presidential assassination attempt

Quiz 3

1) What does the S stand for in Harry S. Truman?
2) Who was the only president to get married at the White House?
3) Who was the heaviest president?
4) What president remarried his wife three years after their wedding because her first divorce wasn't finalized?
5) What is the most common first name of presidents?
6) Who was the tallest president?
7) Who was the shortest president?
8) Who is the only man to have been both Chief Justice of the U.S. Supreme Court and president?
9) What president is commonly credited with inventing the swivel chair?
10) Who was the first president born outside the original 13 states?

Quiz 3 Answers

1) Nothing – The S was in honor of both of his grandfathers but didn't stand for a middle name.
2) Grover Cleveland
3) William Howard Taft – about 340 pounds when he left office
4) Andrew Jackson
5) James – six presidents
6) Abraham Lincoln – 6 feet 4 inches
7) James Madison – 5 feet 4 inches
8) William Howard Taft
9) Thomas Jefferson
10) Abraham Lincoln

Quiz 4

1) At president Andrew Jackson's funeral in 1845, who was removed for swearing?
2) Who was the first president to ride in an automobile while in office?
3) Who was the only president to be held as a prisoner of war?
4) What president was the first to use the Oval Office?
5) Who was the first president to fly on official business?
6) What president enacted the law requiring cigarette manufacturers to put health warnings on their packages?
7) Who are the only two men who have run effectively unopposed for president?
8) What president tried to create the "Great Society"?
9) What president said, "Forgive your enemies, but never forget their names"?
10) What president wrote 37 books?

Quiz 4 Answers

1) His pet parrot
2) Theodore Roosevelt
3) Andrew Jackson – He joined the Revolutionary War at age 13 and was captured by the British.
4) William Howard Taft – He made the West Wing a permanent building and had the Oval Office built.
5) Franklin D. Roosevelt - 1943 secret trip to Casablanca

6) Lyndon B. Johnson
7) George Washington and James Monroe
8) Lyndon B. Johnson – set of domestic programs to eliminate poverty and racial injustice
9) John F. Kennedy
10) Theodore Roosevelt

Quiz 5

1) Who is the only president ever granted a patent?
2) Who was the editor of the magazine *Babies Just Babies* when her husband was elected president?
3) Who was the first president to be photographed at his inauguration?
4) Who was the first vice president to become president upon the death of a president?
5) Three first ladies are tied as the tallest at 5 feet 11 inches; who are they?
6) What two presidents died on July 4, 1826?
7) What president had a raccoon for a pet while in the White House?
8) Who is the oldest person to win a presidential election?
9) Who was the first Roman Catholic vice president?
10) Who is the youngest ever elected president?

Quiz 5 Answers

1) Abraham Lincoln - a device that helped buoy vessels over shoals
2) Eleanor Roosevelt
3) James Buchanan
4) John Tyler – He succeeded William Henry Harrison who died of pneumonia 31 days after inauguration.
5) Melania Trump, Michelle Obama, Eleanor Roosevelt
6) Thomas Jefferson and John Adams
7) Calvin Coolidge – The raccoon was a gift and was supposed to be served for Thanksgiving dinner; Coolidge made it a pet and even walked it on a leash on the White House grounds.
8) Ronald Reagan – 73 at time of his re-election
9) Joseph Biden
10) John F. Kennedy - 43

Quiz 6

1) Who was the first president to win a Nobel Prize?
2) Which president was a Rhodes Scholar?
3) Which first lady was later elected to public office?
4) Who was the only president not elected president or vice president?
5) What is the most common birth state for presidents?
6) What president signed Father's Day into law?
7) Who was the only Eagle Scout president?
8) Who was the first vice president who didn't go on to become president?
9) What president was born as Leslie Lynch King Jr.?
10) Who was the first president to govern over all 50 states?

Quiz 6 Answers

1) Theodore Roosevelt
2) Bill Clinton
3) Hilary Clinton
4) Gerald Ford
5) Virginia – eight
6) Lyndon B. Johnson
7) Gerald Ford
8) Aaron Burr – third vice president
9) Gerald Ford
10) Dwight D. Eisenhower

Quiz 7

1) What president was a head cheerleader in high school?
2) Who was the first president to declare war?
3) Who was the first president to be impeached?
4) Who was vice president when Abraham Lincoln was assassinated?
5) Who was the youngest first lady ever?
6) Who was the first president to leave the U.S. while in office?
7) How many presidents were only children?
8) Who was the only president to win a Pulitzer Prize?
9) How many presidents have won the Nobel Peace Prize?
10) What president imposed the first federal income tax?

Quiz 7 Answers

1) George W. Bush
2) James Madison – War of 1812
3) Andrew Johnson – 1868
4) Andrew Johnson
5) Frances Folsom Cleveland – She was 21 when she married Grover Cleveland in the White House; he was 49.
6) Theodore Roosevelt – He went to Panama to inspect canal construction.
7) Zero
8) John F. Kennedy – for *Profiles in Courage*
9) Four – Theodore Roosevelt, Woodrow Wilson, Jimmy Carter, Barack Obama
10) Abraham Lincoln

Quiz 8

1) Who was the only president with a PhD?
2) Who was the only president to never sign a bill into law?
3) Who was the first republican president?
4) Who was the first president to appear on television?
5) What two presidents were Quakers?
6) Who was the first president paid a salary of $100,000 or more?
7) Who was president when electricity was installed in the White House?
8) Who was president when running water was installed in the White House?
9) What president had a special bathtub big enough to hold four men installed in the White House?
10) How many presidents never attended college?

Quiz 8 Answers

1) Woodrow Wilson – history and political science
2) William Henry Harrison – 31 days as president
3) Abraham Lincoln
4) Franklin D. Roosevelt
5) Herbert Hoover and Richard Nixon
6) Harry S. Truman

7) Benjamin Harrison – 1889
8) Andrew Jackson - 1833
9) William Howard Taft
10) Nine – Washington, Jackson, Van Buren, Taylor, Fillmore, Lincoln, Andrew Johnson, Cleveland, Truman

Quiz 9

1) Who was the first president born outside the contiguous 48 states?
2) How many presidents were born as British subjects?
3) What is the most common religious affiliation for presidents?
4) How many presidents have been left handed?
5) How many presidents served as vice presidents?
6) What president was in office when the term "first lady" was first used?
7) How many presidents were assassinated in office?
8) How many presidents died in office?
9) How many presidential candidates have won the popular vote but lost the election?
10) What president lived the longest?

Quiz 9 Answers

1) Barack Obama
2) Eight – Washington, John Adams, Jefferson, Madison, Monroe, John Quincy Adams, Jackson, William Henry Harrison
3) Episcopalian
4) Eight – Garfield, Hoover, Truman, Ford, Reagan, G.W. Bush, Clinton, Obama
5) 14
6) Rutherford B. Hayes – 1877
7) Four – Lincoln, Garfield, McKinley, Kennedy
8) Eight – Harrison, Taylor, Lincoln, Garfield, McKinley, Harding, Franklin D. Roosevelt, Kennedy
9) Four – Andrew Jackson against John Quincy Adams, Samuel Tilden against Rutherford B. Hayes, Al Gore against George W. Bush, and Hilary Clinton against Donald Trump
10) Gerald Ford – 93; Reagan was also 93 but was 45 days younger.

Quiz 10

1) What president died at the youngest age?
2) What first lady lived the longest?
3) Who was the oldest first lady at time of inauguration?
4) How many first ladies have died while their husband was in office?
5) Who was the only president who had been a union leader?
6) What three presidents have won Grammys for best spoken word album?
7) How many elected vice presidents became president for the first time through election?
8) How many presidents didn't have a wife when they took office?
9) What president worked as a lifeguard?
10) What president sent Lewis and Clark on their expedition?

Quiz 10 Answers

1) John F. Kennedy – 46
2) Bess Truman – 97
3) Barbara Bush – 63
4) Three – Tyler, Harrison, Wilson
5) Ronald Reagan – president of the Screen Actors Guild
6) Clinton, Carter, Obama
7) Two – Martin Van Buren and George H.W. Bush - Originally, the vice president wasn't elected separately.
8) Six – Jefferson, Jackson, Van Buren, and Arthur were all widowers; Cleveland married while in office; Buchanan never married.
9) Ronald Reagan
10) Thomas Jefferson

Quiz 11

1) Who was the first president to visit Alaska?
2) What was George Washington's first occupation?
3) Who was the first U.S. senator to serve as president?
4) Who was the first governor to serve as president?
5) Who won the first presidential election after the 26th amendment gave 18-year-olds the right to vote?
6) What president was known as "The Great Engineer"?
7) What president created the Drug Enforcement Agency?

8) What president was known as "The Trust Buster"?
9) Who was the first sitting president to visit Hiroshima?
10) James Buchanan was morally opposed to slavery but believed it was protected by the constitution, so what did he do?

Quiz 11 Answers

1) Warren Harding – 1923
2) Surveyor
3) James Madison
4) Jimmy Carter
5) Richard Nixon
6) Herbert Hoover – He was a mining engineer who worked around the world and had a large engineering consulting company.
7) Richard Nixon
8) Theodore Roosevelt
9) Barack Obama
10) He bought slaves with his own money and freed them.

Quiz 12

1) When accused of being two-faced, what president said, "If I had two faces, would I be wearing this one?"
2) Franklin D. Roosevelt was the first president to use an armored car; who did the car previously belong to?
3) What religious holiday was Abraham Lincoln assassinated on?
4) Who was the first president born in the U.S.?
5) What was Ronald Reagan's pet name for Nancy?
6) Under the original terms of the U.S. Constitution, the president didn't choose his own vice president; how was it decided?
7) When president Truman visited Disneyland in 1957, why did he refuse to go on the Dumbo ride?
8) What physical trait did George Washington, Thomas Jefferson, Andrew Jackson, Martin Van Buren, and Dwight Eisenhower have in common?
9) Who was the first president born in the 20th century?
10) What president signed the treaty to purchase Alaska from Russia?

Quiz 12 Answers

1) Abraham Lincoln

2) Al Capone
3) Good Friday
4) Martin Van Buren – eighth president
5) Mommy poo pants
6) The candidate with the second most electoral votes was vice president.
7) As a Democrat, he didn't want to be seen riding in the symbol of the Republican party.
8) Redheads
9) John F. Kennedy
10) Andrew Johnson

Quiz 13

1) Walt Whitman's poem "O Captain! My Captain!" was written about what president?
2) How many future presidents signed the Declaration of Independence?
3) Who was the only president who earned an MBA degree?
4) In what city was president McKinley assassinated?
5) What disease did John F. Kennedy contract as a young child?
6) Who was the first president to campaign by telephone?
7) Who was the first president to call the presidential residence the White House?
8) What U.S. president weighed the least?
9) Who was the first president to ride a railroad while in office?
10) What constitutional amendment limits the president to two terms?

Quiz 13 Answers

1) Abraham Lincoln – It was written after Lincoln's assassination.
2) Two – John Adams and Thomas Jefferson
3) George W. Bush
4) Buffalo, New York
5) Scarlet fever
6) William McKinley
7) Theodore Roosevelt
8) James Madison – 100 pounds
9) Andrew Jackson
10) 22nd

Quiz 14

1) Who was the last president who wasn't either a Democrat or Republican?
2) According to his wife, what was Abraham Lincoln's hobby?
3) Who was the first president to run against a woman candidate?
4) Originally, people bowed to the U.S. president; who was the first president to shake hands rather than bowing?
5) Who was the first president to attend a baseball game?
6) George Washington, John Adams, and Thomas Jefferson were all avid collectors and players of what game?
7) Who was the first president to visit all 50 states?
8) Who was the first president to have a beard?
9) What president was once a fashion model?
10) What president collected *Spiderman* and *Conan the Barbarian* comic books?

Quiz 14 Answers

1) Millard Fillmore – 1850
2) Cats – He loved them and could play with them for hours; he once allowed a cat to eat from the table at a formal White House dinner.
3) Ulysses S. Grant – Virginia Woodhull was a nominee of the Equal Rights Party in 1872.
4) Thomas Jefferson
5) Benjamin Harrison – 1892
6) Marbles
7) Richard Nixon
8) Abraham Lincoln
9) Gerald Ford – *Cosmopolitan* and *Look* magazines in the 1940s
10) Barack Obama

Quiz 15

1) Who was the first president who was a Boy Scout?
2) What president served in the U.S. House of Representatives after he served as president?
3) How many presidents regularly wore beards while in office?
4) What president was the first to have a child born in the White House?
5) Who was the first president born west of the Mississippi River?

6) Who was the only president who made his own clothes?
7) Who was the only president to serve in both the Revolutionary War and the War of 1812?
8) What president had the largest feet?
9) What Christmas item did Theodore Roosevelt ban from the White House?
10) Who was the first Navy veteran to become president?

Quiz 15 Answers

1) John F. Kennedy
2) John Quincy Adams
3) Five – Lincoln, Grant, Hayes, Garfield, Benjamin Harrison
4) Grover Cleveland – 1893
5) Herbert Hoover – Iowa
6) Andrew Johnson – He had been a tailor's apprentice and opened his own tailor shop; he made his own clothes most of his life.
7) Andrew Jackson
8) Warren G. Harding – size 14
9) Christmas trees – He had environmental concerns.
10) John F. Kennedy

Quiz 16

1) What five surnames have been shared by more than one president?
2) Who was the only president that never lived in Washington, D.C.?
3) What president was the target of two assassination attempts in 17 days?
4) What president had the largest personal book collection in the U.S. and sold it to become part of the Library of Congress?
5) What play was Abraham Lincoln watching when he was assassinated?
6) Who was the first president inaugurated in Washington, D.C.?
7) Who was the first president with no prior elected political experience?
8) Who was the first president to travel in a car, plane, and submarine?
9) Who was president when the first U.S. national park was created?
10) Who was the first president to hold a televised news conference?

Quiz 16 Answers

1) Adams, Harrison, Johnson, Roosevelt, Bush
2) George Washington
3) Gerald Ford
4) Thomas Jefferson
5) *Our American Cousin*
6) Thomas Jefferson
7) Zachary Taylor – 12th president and Mexican-American War general
8) Theodore Roosevelt
9) Ulysses S. Grant – Yellowstone was the first national park in the world.
10) Dwight D. Eisenhower

World Geography

Quiz 1

1) What country are the Galapagos Islands part of?
2) What is the highest mountain in the Western Hemisphere?
3) What kind of animal are the Canary Islands named after?
4) What country has the longest land border?
5) What is the world's third most populous country?
6) Easter Island is a territory of what country?
7) By area, what is the second largest lake in North America?
8) What is the capital of Mongolia?
9) What South American country has Pacific and Atlantic coastlines?
10) What is the most northern African country?

Quiz 1 Answers

1) Ecuador
2) Aconcagua – 22,841 feet in Argentina
3) Dogs – The name comes from the Latin "canaria" for dog; when the first Europeans arrived, they found large dogs on Gran Canaria.
4) China – 13,743 miles and 14 countries
5) United States
6) Chile
7) Huron – 23,012 square miles
8) Ulaanbaatar
9) Colombia
10) Tunisia

Quiz 2

1) What is the lowest average elevation continent?
2) By area, what is the largest of the Canadian provinces and territories?
3) What country has the world's longest road tunnel?
4) What city has the world's busiest McDonald's restaurant?
5) By area, what is the world's fifth largest country?
6) What is the highest active volcano in the world?
7) By area, what is the largest lake in South America?

8) What is the largest island in the Arctic Ocean?
9) What country has the most volcanoes (active and extinct)?
10) What is the smallest ocean?

Quiz 2 Answers

1) Australia – 984 feet average elevation
2) Nunavut – 808,200 square miles
3) Norway – 15.2 miles
4) Moscow, Russia
5) Brazil
6) Ojos Del Salado – 22,595 feet on the Chile and Argentina border
7) Maracaibo – 5,100 square miles
8) Baffin - 195,928 square miles
9) United States – 173
10) Arctic

Quiz 3

1) What Central American country extends furthest north?
2) What capital city is on the slopes of the volcano Pichincha?
3) How many locks are there on the Suez Canal?
4) What country has the highest average elevation?
5) What two Canadian provinces are landlocked?
6) What two countries have square flags?
7) What is the only river that crosses the equator in both a northerly and southerly direction?
8) What European country has the longest coastline?
9) At over 9,000 miles in length, what country's Highway 1 forms a complete loop along its borders?
10) What is the second largest island in Europe?

Quiz 3 Answers

1) Belize
2) Quito, Ecuador
3) Zero
4) Bhutan – 10,760 feet average elevation
5) Alberta and Saskatchewan
6) Switzerland and Vatican City

7) Congo
8) Norway
9) Australia
10) Iceland – 39,702 square miles

Quiz 4

1) What is the least densely populated country in the world?
2) From what South American country does the Orinoco River flow into the Atlantic Ocean?
3) What country does China have its longest land border with?
4) By area, what is the smallest continent?
5) The Canary Islands are part of what country?
6) What is the second largest city in England?
7) What river is known as China's Sorrow?
8) What is the longest canal in the world?
9) What European country has no single head of state?
10) By area, what is the largest island in Asia?

Quiz 4 Answers

1) Mongolia – Areas like Greenland have even lower density, but they aren't independent countries.
2) Venezuela
3) Mongolia
4) Australia
5) Spain
6) Birmingham
7) Yellow – due to its devastating floods
8) Grand Canal of China – 1,104 miles
9) Switzerland
10) Borneo – 287,000 square miles

Quiz 5

1) What country has the third largest English-speaking population?
2) By area, what is the largest Mediterranean island?
3) What country has the fourth largest population?
4) By volume, what is the largest lake in South America?
5) What country took its name from a line of latitude?

6) What country's phone book is alphabetized by first name?
7) What is the most populous country the equator passes through?
8) What is the highest elevation capital city in Europe?
9) What country issued the first Christmas stamp in 1898?
10) What is the world's most northerly national capital city?

Quiz 5 Answers

1) Pakistan
2) Sicily – 9,927 square miles
3) Indonesia
4) Lake Titicaca
5) Ecuador
6) Iceland – Everyone is referenced by their first name; they don't have surnames in the traditional sense; the surname is their father's first name suffixed with either son or daughter.
7) Indonesia
8) Madrid – 2,188 feet
9) Canada
10) Reykjavik, Iceland – 64 degrees north latitude

Quiz 6

1) What was the last province to become part of Canada?
2) What is the longest river in Asia?
3) What is the world's largest gulf?
4) How many oceans are there and what are their names?
5) What is the world's most southerly national capital?
6) What is the second longest river in North America?
7) What country has the longest coastline?
8) What is the world's highest elevation national capital city?
9) What peninsula does Mexico occupy?
10) Alphabetically, what country comes between Portugal and Romania?

Quiz 6 Answers

1) Newfoundland
2) Yangtze – 3,915 miles
3) Gulf of Mexico – 600,000 square miles

4) Five – Atlantic, Pacific, Indian, Arctic, Southern
5) Wellington, New Zealand – 41 degrees south latitude
6) Mississippi – 2,320 miles
7) Canada
8) La Paz, Bolivia – 11,942 feet
9) Yucatan
10) Qatar

Quiz 7

1) By area, what is the second largest island in Asia?
2) By area, what is the largest landlocked country?
3) How many countries are there in South America?
4) By area, what is the fourth largest continent?
5) Zanzibar lies off the coast of what country?
6) What is the driest continent?
7) What is the world's widest river?
8) In what location are most of the world's geysers found?
9) What island has the highest maximum elevation?
10) What is the highest mountain in Canada?

Quiz 7 Answers

1) Sumatra, Indonesia – 164,000 square miles
2) Kazakhstan - ninth largest country
3) 12
4) South America
5) Tanzania
6) Antarctica – about eight inches of precipitation annually
7) Amazon – from 7-25 miles wide depending on season
8) Yellowstone National Park, Wyoming
9) New Guinea – 16,024 feet
10) Mt. Logan – 19,551 feet in the Yukon territory

Quiz 8

1) By area, what is the largest body of fresh water in the world?
2) What percent of the Earth's fresh water is in the Antarctic ice sheet?
3) What is the shallowest ocean?

4) What is the driest non-polar desert in the world?
5) What mountain range spans northern Morocco, Algeria, and Tunisia?
6) By area, what is the largest archipelago (chain or group of islands scattered across a body of water)?
7) By area, what is the second largest country in the world?
8) What is the most populous city south of the equator?
9) What is the capital of Qatar?
10) By area, what is the smallest North American country?

Quiz 8 Answers

1) Lake Superior – 31,700 square miles
2) 90% - It is equivalent to about 230 feet of water in the world's oceans.
3) Arctic – average depth of 3,407 feet
4) Atacama – Chile
5) Atlas Mountains
6) Malay Archipelago – 25,000 islands making up Indonesia and the Philippines
7) Canada
8) Sao Paulo, Brazil
9) Doha
10) St. Kitts and Nevis – 101 square miles in the Caribbean

Quiz 9

1) How many landlocked countries are there in the world?
2) What is the second most populous city in Asia?
3) In which country is the Great Victoria Desert?
4) By area, what is the smallest Canadian province?
5) What sea is located between Australia and New Zealand?
6) By area, what is the largest country in Africa?
7) What country would you have to visit to see the ruins of Troy?
8) By area, what is the largest lake that is entirely within Canada?
9) What European country has the lowest population density?
10) What is the deepest lake in North America?

Quiz 9 Answers

1) 44 - Afghanistan, Andorra, Armenia, Austria, Azerbaijan, Burundi,

Burkina Faso, Bhutan, Belarus, Bolivia, Botswana, The Central African Republic, Chad, The Czech Republic, Ethiopia, Hungary, Kazakhstan, Kyrgyzstan, Laos, Lesotho, Liechtenstein, Luxembourg, Malawi, Moldova, Mongolia, Macedonia, Mali, Nepal, Niger, Paraguay, Rwanda, Serbia, San Marino, Switzerland, Slovakia, Swaziland, South Sudan, Tajikistan, Turkmenistan, Uganda, Uzbekistan, Vatican City, Zambia, Zimbabwe

2) Jakarta, Indonesia
3) Australia
4) Prince Edward Island
5) Tasman
6) Algeria
7) Turkey
8) Great Bear Lake – 12,028 square miles
9) Iceland
10) Great Slave Lake in Canada - 2,015 feet deep

Quiz 10

1) What country has the largest number of islands?
2) By area, what is the smallest Central American country?
3) What two South American countries are landlocked?
4) By area, what is the world's largest fresh water island?
5) What is the second longest river in Africa?
6) What country has the most forest land?
7) What country has the most countries or territories bordering it?
8) What is Europe's second longest river?
9) What national capital city has views of the volcano Snaefellsjokull?
10) What country has the world's highest railroad?

Quiz 10 Answers

1) Finland – over 100,000
2) El Salvador
3) Bolivia and Paraguay
4) Manitoulin – over 1,000 square miles in Lake Huron in Ontario, Canada
5) Congo – 2,922 miles
6) Russia
7) China – 14 countries and 2 territories

8) Danube – 1,777 miles
9) Reykjavik, Iceland
10) China – 16,640 feet

Quiz 11

1) By area, what is the largest country entirely in Europe?
2) How many countries border the Black Sea?
3) By area, what is the largest country with English as an official language?
4) There are only two predominantly Christian countries in Asia; the smaller is East Timor; what is the other?
5) What is the most populous city in India?
6) The source of the Amazon river is in what country?
7) What is the coldest national capital city in the world?
8) Timbuktu is in what country?
9) What river rises in Tibet and flows through China, Myanmar, Laos, Thailand, Cambodia, and Vietnam?
10) What country has the highest population density in Europe?

Quiz 11 Answers

1) Ukraine - 223,000 square miles
2) Six - Turkey, Georgia, Russia, Ukraine, Romania, Bulgaria
3) Canada
4) Philippines – fourth largest Christian population in the world and third largest Roman Catholic
5) Mumbai
6) Peru
7) Ulaanbaatar, Mongolia – Winter temperatures of minus 40 degrees Fahrenheit are not unusual.
8) Mali – west Africa
9) Mekong
10) Monaco – over 47,000 per square mile

Quiz 12

1) What desert covers most of southern Mongolia?
2) By volume, what is the largest freshwater lake?
3) What sacred volcano last erupted in 1707?
4) What is the world's warmest sea?

5) In the boot shaped country of Italy, what region comprises the toe?
6) What is the world's oldest surviving sovereign state?
7) What country has three capital cities?
8) What name is given to a ring-shaped coral reef?
9) What is the only Central American country that has English as its official language?
10) What is the name of the deepest known ocean location?

Quiz 12 Answers

1) Gobi
2) Lake Baikal in Russia – It has a maximum depth of 5,387 feet and contains about 20% of the total unfrozen surface freshwater in the world.
3) Mount Fuji
4) Red Sea
5) Calabria
6) San Marino - 301 AD
7) South Africa - Pretoria is the administrative capital; Cape Town is the legislative capital, and Bloemfontein is the judicial capital.
8) Atoll
9) Belize
10) Challenger Deep in the Mariana Trench in the Pacific Ocean – 36,070 feet deep

Quiz 13

1) How many provinces does Canada have?
2) What is the saltiest ocean?
3) What is the only sea without a coastline (no land border)?
4) Mount Kosciuszko is the highest mountain on what continent?
5) What country has the lowest average elevation?
6) What is the longest river in Australia?
7) Which of the Great Lakes doesn't share a border with Canada?
8) What country and its territories cover the most time zones?
9) What percent of the world's population lives in the Northern Hemisphere?
10) What country has the oldest surviving constitution?

Quiz 13 Answers

1) 10 - Alberta, British Columbia, Manitoba, New Brunswick, Newfoundland and Labrador, Nova Scotia, Ontario, Prince Edward Island, Quebec, Saskatchewan
2) Atlantic
3) Sargasso Sea – It is in the North Atlantic Ocean off the coast of the U.S. and is defined by currents.
4) Australia
5) Maldives – 1,200 mostly uninhabited islands in the Indian Ocean; average elevation is 6 feet.
6) Murray River – 1,558 miles
7) Lake Michigan
8) France with 12 time zones – The U.S. and Russia each cover 11 time zones.
9) 88% - About half of the world's population lives north of 27 degrees north latitude.
10) San Marino – 1600

Quiz 14

1) By area, what is the largest country that the equator passes through?
2) What country has the most pyramids?
3) Where is the lowest dry land point in the world?
4) What is the only continent without an active volcano?
5) What country is Transylvania in?
6) The country of San Marino is completely surrounded by what country?
7) What country has the most official languages?
8) What country has the most lakes?
9) How many countries does the equator pass through?
10) What is the only country that falls in all four hemispheres?

Quiz 14 Answers

1) Brazil
2) Sudan – almost twice as many as Egypt
3) Dead Sea – 1,411 feet below sea level
4) Australia
5) Romania

6) Italy
7) Zimbabwe – 16
8) Canada – It has more lakes than the rest of the world combined.
9) 13 - Ecuador, Colombia, Brazil, Sao Tome & Principe, Gabon, Republic of the Congo, Democratic Republic of the Congo, Uganda, Kenya, Somalia, Maldives, Indonesia, Kiribati
10) Kiribati - island nation in the Central Pacific Ocean

Quiz 15

1) What is widely regarded as the oldest continuously inhabited city in the world?
2) By discharge volume, what is the largest river in the world?
3) Europe is separated from Asia by what mountain range?
4) Excluding Greenland, what is the easternmost point of the North American continent?
5) What country has the world's deepest cave?
6) How many time zones does Russia have?
7) What is the largest desert in the world?
8) South Africa completely surrounds what other country?
9) What strait separates Europe and Asia?
10) What is the largest country that uses only one time zone?

Quiz 15 Answers

1) Damascus, Syria – at least 11,000 years
2) Amazon
3) Ural Mountains
4) Cape Spear, Newfoundland, Canada
5) Georgia – Krubera Cave, explored to a depth of 7,208 feet
6) 11
7) Antarctic Polar Desert – 5.5 million square miles
8) Lesotho
9) Bosporus
10) China – Geographically, it has five time zones, but it chooses to use one standard time.

Quiz 16

1) What two countries share the longest land border?
2) What Canadian province or territory is closest to the North Pole?

3) What is the only European national capital not on a river?
4) What color is the most common on national flags?
5) What country has the most active volcanoes?
6) By volume, what is the world's largest active volcano?
7) What is the capital of Australia?
8) What is Europe's largest island?
9) What non-landlocked country has the shortest coastline?
10) By area, what is the largest Japanese island?

Quiz 16 Answers

1) United States and Canada – 5,525 miles
2) Nunavut
3) Madrid, Spain
4) Red
5) Indonesia – 76 active volcanoes
6) Mauna Loa, Hawaii
7) Canberra
8) Great Britain
9) Monaco – 2.4 miles
10) Honshu – 87,182 square miles

Quiz 17

1) What country has the largest Christian population?
2) What country has the largest Muslim population?
3) What is the second longest river in South America?
4) By area, what is the second largest country in South America?
5) By area, what is the largest lake in Africa?
6) What country has the second largest English-speaking population?
7) In what country is the highest point that the equator passes through?
8) What country has the largest Spanish speaking population?
9) What is the second largest landlocked country?
10) What two countries contain Sierra Nevada mountains?

Quiz 17 Answers

1) United States
2) Indonesia

3) Parana – 3,032 miles
4) Argentina – 1,073,518 square miles
5) Victoria – 26,564 square miles
6) India
7) Ecuador – 15,387 feet
8) Mexico
9) Mongolia
10) United States and Spain

Quiz 18

1) The U.S. and China have the first and second largest GDP's; what country is third?
2) How many countries have effectively 100% literacy rates?
3) What country has the most international tourists annually?
4) Based on land area, what is the largest airport in the world?
5) What is the most visited city in the world?
6) What is the largest cocoa producing country?
7) Brazil is the largest coffee producing country; what country is second?
8) By area, how many of the 10 largest countries in the world are in Asia?
9) How many of the 10 most populous countries in the world are in Asia?
10) What is the driest place in the world?

Quiz 18 Answers

1) Japan
2) Five – Andorra, Finland, Liechtenstein, Luxembourg, Norway
3) France
4) King Fahd International, Saudi Arabia - 301 square miles
5) Bangkok, Thailand – followed by London
6) Ivory Coast (Cote d'Ivoire)
7) Vietnam
8) Four – Russia, China, India, Kazakhstan
9) Seven – China, India, Indonesia, Pakistan, Bangladesh, Russia, Japan
10) McMurdo Dry Valleys, Antarctica – row of snow free valleys that haven't seen water in millions of years

Quiz 19

1) What are the only three countries that have Atlantic and Mediterranean coasts?
2) How many countries are completely surrounded by one other country?
3) What is the only continent with land in all four hemispheres?
4) What continent has the most freshwater?
5) What ocean has about 75% of the world's volcanoes?
6) What country has the largest city in the world based on land area?
7) What is the only major city located on two continents?
8) What country has the world's longest freshwater beach?
9) What is the most populous city in Europe?
10) What is the most populous city in Asia?

Quiz 19 Answers

1) France, Spain, Morocco
2) Three – Lesotho (surrounded by South Africa), Vatican City and San Marino (both surrounded by Italy)
3) Africa
4) Antarctica – The ice sheet contains about 90% of world's fresh water.
5) Pacific
6) China – The city of Hulunbuir is 102,000 square miles.
7) Istanbul, Turkey
8) Canada – Wasaga Beach on the shores of Lake Huron is 14 miles long.
9) Moscow, Russia
10) Tokyo, Japan

Quiz 20

1) What is the most populous city in North America?
2) What two countries have the second longest shared land border?
3) What city has the most millionaires in the world?
4) What country consumes the most electricity in the world?
5) What city has the most skyscrapers in the world?
6) What is the sunniest city in the world?
7) What two countries produce a majority of the world's vanilla?

8) What is the most frequently crossed international border in the world?
9) What country is in the eastern Pyrenees between France and Spain?
10) By area, what is the largest country entirely within the Southern Hemisphere?

Quiz 20 Answers

1) Mexico City
2) Russia and Kazakhstan – 4,254 miles
3) Tokyo, Japan
4) China - followed by U.S. and Russia
5) Hong Kong - followed by New York City and Dubai
6) Yuma, Arizona – On average, the sun shines 90% of daylight hours.
7) Madagascar and Indonesia
8) United States and Mexico
9) Andorra
10) Australia – A small portion of Brazil is in the Northern Hemisphere.

Quiz 21

1) What country has the world's longest fence?
2) What three South American countries does the equator pass through?
3) The Anatolian peninsula makes up most of what country?
4) What place on the Earth is closest to the Moon?
5) Of the 25 highest mountain peaks in the world, how many are in the Himalayas?
6) What is the only country in the world without an official capital?
7) What country has the world's tallest vertical cliff?
8) What continent has the most countries?
9) What country has the third most countries bordering it?
10) What is the most populous Canadian province?

Quiz 21 Answers

1) Australia – The dingo fence completed in 1885 is 3,488 miles long.
2) Ecuador, Colombia, Brazil
3) Turkey
4) Mount Chimborazo, Ecuador – It is 20,548 feet elevation but very

close to the equator, so the bulge in the Earth makes it 1.5 miles closer than Mount Everest.

5) 19
6) Nauru – third smallest country in the world in the Central Pacific Ocean with less than 10,000 people
7) Canada – Mount Thor on Baffin Island with a 4,101 feet vertical drop
8) Africa – 54, Europe – 47, Asia – 44
9) Brazil – 10
10) Ontario

Quiz 22

1) Outside of Warsaw, what city has the largest Polish population in the world?
2) Taumatawhakatangihangakoauauotamateaturipukakapikimaunga-horonukupokaiwhenuakitanatahu has what distinction?
3) How many people have been to the deepest part of the ocean?
4) The word Canada comes from an Indian word meaning what?
5) What is the only continent without a major desert?
6) What is the longest river in Canada?
7) What is different about how the flag of the Philippines is flown?
8) Amman, the capital of Jordan, was previously named what?
9) Russia is the most populous country in Europe; what country is second?
10) What country is the largest wine producer in the world?

Quiz 22 Answers

1) New York City
2) Longest place name in the world – a hill in New Zealand
3) Three – Director James Cameron is one of them.
4) Village or settlement
5) Europe
6) Yukon – 1,981 miles
7) It is displayed with the blue side up in times of peace and with the red side up in times of war.
8) Philadelphia – after Philadelphus, the Egyptian king who conquered the area in the third century BC
9) Germany

10) Italy - followed by Spain, France, U.S.

Quiz 23

1) What is the second largest island in North America?
2) The Eiffel Tower was originally intended for what city?
3) What European national capital city is built on 14 islands?
4) At the closest point, Europe and Africa are separated by what distance?
5) Almost half the gold ever mined has come from what single location?
6) What continent has the most French speakers?
7) What is the only country to lie completely above 1,000 meters elevation?
8) What is the windiest continent?
9) What city has the largest taxi fleet in the world?
10) What country has the highest annual average hours worked in the world?

Quiz 23 Answers

1) Baffin – 195,928 square miles
2) Barcelona – Spain rejected the project.
3) Stockholm, Sweden
4) Nine miles – across the Strait of Gibraltar between Spain and Morocco
5) Witwatersrand, South Africa
6) Africa – 120 million French speakers
7) Lesotho
8) Antarctica
9) Mexico City
10) Mexico

Quiz 24

1) What is the most linguistically diverse (highest number of languages spoken) city in the world?
2) Technically, who is the largest landowner in the world?
3) By area, how many of the 10 largest countries in the world are in South America?
4) The United Kingdom and Great Britain are not the same; what is

the difference?
5) Brazil borders all but what two South American countries?
6) What city was the only European capital outside of Europe?
7) What is the most populous democratic country?
8) What country has the largest number of languages spoken?
9) What is the only country in the world named after a woman?
10) What is the smallest population country with at least one Nobel Prize winner?

Quiz 24 Answers

1) New York City – 800 languages
2) Queen Elizabeth II – She technically owns 6.6 billion acres or about 1/6 of the world's land including Canada and Australia.
3) Two – Brazil and Argentina
4) Great Britain includes England, Scotland, and Wales; the United Kingdom includes those countries plus Northern Ireland.
5) Chile and Ecuador
6) Rio de Janeiro, Brazil was capital of Portugal from 1808 to 1822 - Napoleon was invading Portugal at the time, so the Portuguese royal family moved to Rio de Janeiro, and it became the capital.
7) India
8) Papua New Guinea – about 840 languages or one for every 10,000 citizens
9) St. Lucia – It is named after St. Lucy of Syracuse.
10) Faroe Islands – with 50,000 people located halfway between Norway and Iceland

Quiz 25

1) What national capital city has the smallest percent of the country's population?
2) How many debt free countries are there in the world?
3) How many countries in the world require their head of state to be a specific religion?
4) What is the only Asian country the equator passes through?
5) Is the Northern or Southern Hemisphere warmer?
6) How many countries don't maintain an army?
7) What location has the most lightning strikes in the world?
8) By population, what is the world's largest island country?

9) What country has on average the tallest people?
10) What is the world's highest mountain that isn't part of a range?

Quiz 25 Answers

1) Washington, D.C., United States – 0.21% of the U.S. population
2) Five - Macau, British Virgin Islands, Brunei, Liechtenstein, Palau
3) 30
4) Indonesia
5) Northern – 2.7 degrees Fahrenheit warmer due to ocean circulation
6) 22 – including Andorra, Costa Rica, Panama, Grenada, Haiti, Iceland, Liechtenstein
7) Lake Maracaibo, Venezuela - Lightning storms occur for about 10 hours a night, 140 to 160 nights a year, for a total of about 1.2 million lightning discharges per year.
8) Indonesia
9) Netherlands – average 6 feet ½ inches for men and 5 feet 7 inches for women
10) Mount Kilimanjaro, Tanzania – 19,341 feet

Quiz 26

1) What country has on average the shortest people?
2) How many landlocked countries are there in North America?
3) What is the largest city in the Caribbean?
4) What is the largest city in Central America?
5) What is the southernmost city in the world with a population over 1 million?
6) What is the northernmost city in the world with a population over 1 million?
7) By area, what is the smallest country in South America?
8) By area, what is the smallest country in Africa?
9) By area, what is the largest lake in Europe?
10) By area, what is the smallest country in Asia?

Quiz 26 Answers

1) Indonesia – average 5 feet 2 inches for men and 4 feet 10 inches for women
2) Zero
3) Santo Domingo, Dominican Republic

4) Guatemala City, Guatemala
5) Melbourne, Australia – 37.8 degrees south latitude
6) St. Petersburg, Russia – 59.9 degrees north latitude
7) Suriname – 63,252 square miles
8) Seychelles – group of 115 islands covering 177 square miles and lying 932 miles east of mainland Africa
9) Ladoga – 6,834 square miles in Russia
10) Maldives – 115 square mile group of 26 islands in the Indian Ocean

Quiz 27

1) What is the most populous country in Central America?
2) How many countries are in North America?
3) What is the only continent without glaciers?
4) What is the largest island in the world formed solely by volcanic activity?
5) How many landlocked countries are there in Europe?
6) What is the longest freshwater lake in the world?
7) What continent has the most landlocked countries?
8) What is the longest river in North America?
9) What is the highest mountain outside Asia?
10) By area, what is the world's smallest mountain range?

Quiz 27 Answers

1) Guatemala
2) 23 – Antigua and Barbuda, Bahamas, Barbados, Belize, Canada, Costa Rica, Cuba, Dominica, Dominican Republic, El Salvador, Grenada, Guatemala, Haiti, Honduras, Jamaica, Mexico, Nicaragua, Panama, St. Kitts and Nevis, St. Lucia, St. Vincent and the Grenadines, Trinidad and Tobago, United States
3) Australia
4) Iceland – 39,768 square miles
5) 14 - Andorra, Austria, Belarus, Czech Republic, Hungary, Liechtenstein, Luxembourg, Macedonia, Moldova, San Marino, Serbia, Slovakia, Switzerland, Vatican City
6) Tanganyika – 420 miles in Africa
7) Africa – 16
8) Missouri – 2,341 miles
9) Aconcagua – 22,841 feet in Argentina

10) Sutter Buttes in the northern Great Valley of central California - 75 square miles with maximum elevation of 2,122 feet

Quiz 28

1) By area, what is the largest country in the Southern Hemisphere?
2) By volume, what is the second largest freshwater lake in the world?
3) What country is the fourth largest in the Americas (North and South America)?
4) What is the largest island in North America?
5) What two countries share Victoria Falls in Africa?
6) What African country was divided in two in 2011?
7) What country has the highest asphalt road in the world?
8) What is the highest navigable lake in the world?
9) What city of at least 1 million population is furthest away from another city of at least 1 million population?
10) What is the most remote (furthest from the nearest land) island in the world?

Quiz 28 Answers

1) Brazil – A small portion is in the Northern Hemisphere.
2) Tanganyika – maximum depth of 4,820 feet
3) Argentina
4) Greenland – 836,300 square miles
5) Zambia and Zimbabwe
6) Sudan – now Sudan and South Sudan
7) China (Tibet) – 18,258 feet
8) Lake Titicaca – 12,507 feet elevation in Bolivia and Peru
9) Auckland, New Zealand – 1,347 miles away from Sydney, Australia
10) Bouvet Island in the South Atlantic Ocean - 994 miles to Antarctica

Quiz 29

1) By discharge volume, what is the second largest river in the world?
2) The point in the oceans furthest from the nearest land is called what?
3) Germany is closest in size to what U.S. state?
4) Greenland is a territory of what country?
5) By area, what is the largest island nation?
6) What Canadian province borders the most states?

7) What European country is divided into areas called cantons?
8) By area, what is the largest country with Spanish as an official language?
9) What is the largest lake in Antarctica?
10) What country has the second largest Spanish speaking population?

Quiz 29 Answers

1) Congo
2) Point Nemo – It is in the South Pacific Ocean 1,670 miles from the nearest land.
3) Montana – Germany is 137,983 square miles; Montana is 147,040 square miles.
4) Denmark
5) Indonesia – 735,358 square miles
6) Ontario – borders five states - Minnesota, Michigan, Ohio, Pennsylvania, New York
7) Switzerland
8) Argentina
9) Lake Vostok – largest of the subglacial lakes
10) United States

Quiz 30

1) What is the highest waterfall in the world?
2) The world's largest pyramid by volume is in what country?
3) What is the most common symbol on flags of the world?
4) What country is last alphabetically?
5) What country is first alphabetically?
6) What river flows through eight countries and four national capitals?
7) What is the deepest lake in the world?
8) What are Africa's four great rivers?
9) The Somers Islands have what more familiar name?
10) What country contains South America's highest and lowest points?

Quiz 30 Answers

1) Angel Falls, Venezuela – 3,212 feet high
2) Mexico – The Great Pyramid of Cholula has a base of 450 meters each side and a height of 66 meters.

3) Star
4) Zimbabwe
5) Afghanistan
6) Danube
7) Lake Baikal, Russia – 5,387 feet deep
8) Nile, Congo, Zambezi, Niger
9) Bermuda
10) Argentina – 22,841 feet above sea level to 344 feet below

Quiz 31

1) What national capital city is heated by volcanic springs?
2) By area, what is the world's largest island?
3) By area, Vatican City is the world's smallest country; what is the second smallest?
4) What is the world's longest mountain range?
5) What country has the world's second largest Christian population?
6) What is the most populous African country?
7) What is the only country crossed both by the equator and Tropic of Capricorn?
8) What is the largest desert in the Western Hemisphere?
9) By area, what is the largest island in South America?
10) By area, what is the largest Canadian province?

Quiz 31 Answers

1) Reykjavik, Iceland
2) Greenland – 836,300 square miles
3) Monaco – 0.78 square miles
4) Andes – 4,300 miles
5) Brazil
6) Nigeria
7) Brazil
8) Patagonian Desert – 258,688 square miles primarily in Argentina
9) Tierra del Fuego – 18,605 square miles
10) Quebec – 595,400 square miles

Quiz 32

1) What is the second longest river in Asia?

2) What country has the highest per capita electricity consumption?
3) What is the oldest national capital city in the Americas?
4) What is the northernmost Scandinavian country?
5) What major city is on an island in the St. Lawrence River?
6) By area, what is the world's largest sea?
7) What is the only Middle Eastern country without a desert?
8) What is the largest enclosed inland body of water in the world?
9) What river goes over Victoria Falls?
10) What is the most populous city in Africa?

Quiz 32 Answers

1) Yellow – 3,395 miles
2) Iceland – more than four times higher than the U.S.
3) Mexico City – founded in 1521
4) Norway
5) Montreal, Canada
6) Philippine – 2.2 million square miles
7) Lebanon
8) Caspian Sea – It is considered a lake by some, but it has salt water and has 3.5 times more water than all the Great Lakes combined covering 143,244 square miles.
9) Zambezi
10) Lagos, Nigeria

Quiz 33

1) What country has the southernmost point in continental Europe?
2) What national capital city does the River Liffey flow through?
3) By area, what is the second largest continent?
4) What is the only Dutch speaking country in South America?
5) What national capital rises where the Blue Nile and White Nile converge?
6) Of all meteorites ever found, 90% come from what continent?
7) What two cities are at the ends of the Trans-Siberian railroad?
8) What four seas are named for colors?
9) By area, what is the second largest island in the world?
10) What is the smallest population country with two or more Nobel Prize winners?

Quiz 33 Answers

1) Spain
2) Dublin, Ireland
3) Africa
4) Suriname – former Dutch colony
5) Khartoum, Sudan
6) Antarctica
7) Moscow and Vladivostok
8) Red, Black, Yellow, White
9) New Guinea – 303,476 square miles
10) St. Lucia – Caribbean island with 185,000 people and two Nobel Prize winners

Quiz 34

1) By volume, what is the world's largest volcano (active or extinct)?
2) What continent has the highest population density?
3) What is Europe's longest river?
4) What continent has the highest average elevation?
5) By area, what is the smallest of the Great Lakes?
6) What country has the world's highest elevation city?
7) What peninsula do Spain and Portugal share?
8) What is the longest river in the Americas?
9) By area, what is the largest country in Central America?
10) What country's flag has lasted the longest without change?

Quiz 34 Answers

1) Tamu Massif – extinct volcano 1,000 miles east of Japan under the Pacific Ocean
2) Asia
3) Volga – 2,294 miles
4) Antarctica – 8,200 feet average elevation
5) Lake Ontario – 7,320 square miles
6) Peru – La Rinconada is a mining town at 16,700 feet in the Andes and has about 30,000 residents.
7) Iberian
8) Amazon – 4,345 miles
9) Nicaragua – 50,338 square miles

10) Denmark – 1370 or earlier

Quiz 35

1) What country has the largest Portuguese speaking population?
2) What country's flag is incorporated most often in other flags?
3) What African capital city is named for a U.S. president?
4) What is the northernmost country in continental South America?
5) What country has the most tornadoes?
6) By area, what is the largest Scandinavian country?
7) What country has the most earthquakes?
8) How many Canadian provinces border the Great Lakes?
9) What country has the world's southernmost city?
10) What is the official language of Nigeria?

Quiz 35 Answers

1) Brazil
2) Great Britain
3) Monrovia, Liberia
4) Colombia
5) United States
6) Sweden
7) Indonesia – followed by Japan
8) One – Ontario
9) Chile
10) English

Quiz 36

1) Which of the Great Lakes do all the others flow into?
2) What continent has the lowest highest point?
3) How many landlocked countries are there in Asia?
4) What is the world's most populous metropolitan area?
5) What is the second most widely spoken language in the world?
6) The land location furthest from any ocean is in what country?
7) How many Australian states are there?
8) What is the capital of Monaco?
9) Switzerland has four official languages; what are they?
10) What river flows through Rome, Italy?

Quiz 36 Answers

1) Lake Ontario
2) Australia - Mount Kosciuszko at 7,310 feet
3) 12 - Afghanistan, Armenia, Azerbaijan, Bhutan, Laos, Kazakhstan, Kyrgyzstan, Mongolia, Nepal, Tajikistan, Turkmenistan, Uzbekistan
4) Tokyo, Japan
5) Spanish – Mandarin is first; English is third.
6) China – 1,645 miles from the ocean near the Kazakhstan border in extreme northwestern China
7) Six – New South Wales, Queensland, South Australia, Tasmania, Victoria, Western Australia
8) Monaco – It is both a city and a country.
9) German, French, Italian, and Romanish, a romance language spoken predominantly in one canton
10) Tiber